CREDIT
RISK
MANAGEMENT

CREDIT RISK MANAGEMENT

Third Edition

How to Avoid Lending Disasters and **Maximize Earnings**

JoEtta Colquitt

McGraw-Hill

New York   Chicago   San Francisco   Lisbon
London   Madrid   Mexico City   Milan   New Delhi
San Juan   Seoul   Singapore   Sydney   Toronto

1 2 3 4 5 6 7 8 9 10 DOC/DOC 0 9 8 7

ISBN-13: 978-0-07-144660-0
ISBN-10: 0-07-144660-5

Appendix to Chapter 5 was originally published January 28, 1998, as a Carr Futures (now Calyon Financial) research note.

Chapter 7 is a reprint of a Journal of Portfolio Management article. ©1993 by *The Journal of Portfolio Management*, Spring 1993. Reprinted with permission.

Appendixes C and E are excerpted from *JPMorgan Government Bond Outlines*, October 2001. Reprinted with permission of JPMorgan.

Appendixes D, F, and G are excerpted from *JPMorgan Government Bond Outlines*, April 2005. Reprinted with permission of JPMorgan.

To Birch and Mary

CONTENTS

ACKNOWLEDGEMENTS

The following students contributed research to the book under the directorship of Dr. Andrew Economopoulos at Ursinus College in Collegeville, Pennsylvania

Matthew Lebo

Alex Miron

John Sheppard

John Conner

All illustrations were designed and provided by Eiko Ishikawa
Special thanks also to Donald Benners who contributed much to reviewing the materials and providing suggestions along with Joyce Munn, Blaz Gutierrez, Yoske Imai, Barbara Reeder, Serge Sondez, Dr. Anne Gooding, Roger Williams, Bansari Vaidya, Judy Miao and to the many others that I do not have the time or space to name.

CHAPTER 1

Introduction to Credit Risk Management

As the name implies, credit risk management is predicated on the existence of risk and uncertainty to leverage the earnings from lending to a borrower. Credit risk arises whenever a lender is exposed to loss from a borrower, counterparty, or an obligor who fails to honor their debt obligation as they have agreed and contracted. For lenders who extend credit in the form of loans, trading activities, or the capital markets, credit risk is inherent in all their business activities and is an element in virtually every product and service that is provided. Typically, the risk of credit-related losses refers to the type of business transaction that is contracted for and can occur from a variety of credit loss scenarios. The most obvious is the failure to repay interest or principal on a direct or contingent loan obligation. Credit loss can also occur from failing to honor or repay reciprocal financial agreements that still have some economic value, such as a credit derivative contract. Finally, credit loss can occur from a decline in a borrower's credit quality that results in a loss to the value of the debt obligation. These scenarios can be extended further to include additional sources of financial risks when credit risks are integrated into market, operational, as well as throughout the credit provider's enterprise. In fact, compared to 30 years ago, the types of credit loss scenarios found in corporate and business lending today have served to revolutionize how the extension of credit is assessed and managed.

Borrowers demand credit that will be used to reinvest in their businesses and for which they expect to earn a return. At the same time, lenders or financial intermediaries supply credit to earn a return when these companies borrow. This process for extending credit has a multiplier effect on the global money supply, so this is why credit is a powerful driver of our economy. A more varied but also descriptive definition of credit is given by the *Economist Dictionary of Economics*, which states that credit is "the use or possession of goods or services without immediate payment," that "credit enables a producer to bridge the gap between the production and sale of goods," and that "virtually all exchange in manufacturing, industry and services is conducted on credit."[1]

Extending credit would therefore be impractical today, if not impossible, without the events that have been brought on by deregulation, technology, and disintermediation in the financial services industry, all of which have actually changed the psychology of extending business and corporate credit. Beginning with changes that have transpired in the telecommunications industry, credit has evolved from the assessment of a borrower's creditworthiness into a risk evaluation and measurement methodology that lenders and suppliers of credit use to analyze, measure, and manage. Another change has been the dismantling within the commercial banking sector among major credit providers that traditionally had funded corporate and business loans with the liquid deposits of customers. However, the growing number of nonbank competitors that have entered the financial services arena, such as insurance companies, mutual funds, investment finance companies, and the capital markets, have also transformed the fundamental nature of how credit is extended and managed. This has created new sources of credit flows, which has allowed business credit to be extended through the services of brokers, pension and mutual funds, insurance companies, and even by the corporations and suppliers of the goods and services that businesses use. The result has been greater economies of scale, along with lower transaction costs and, to a lesser extent, an increase in the volume of credit market debt. Despite the increased competition and decline of assets faced by banks, the borrowing capacity of the credit markets has nonetheless grown over the years, along with the amount of debt outstanding for business lending, as the amount held by commercial banks has declined in favor of other financial service providers.

Among the most significant lessons learned from the above events is the potential systematic impact on other financial entities when one financial institution holds a significant aggregate exposure for a borrower, obligor, or counterparty. Another lesson learned is that when exposures reach imprudent lending limits because of high credit concentrations, the losses may become too large relative to the institutions' capital and overall risk levels. Finally, we learned that the risk of credit defaults can also occur from exposures based on the concentrations of correlated risk factors that are related to specific risk events such as in the cases of Enron and WorldCom. This supports the contention that credit risk is the biggest source of risk to financial institutions and credit-related suppliers.

This book is therefore designed to look at the total integrated process of credit risk management, beginning with the risk assessment of a single obligor and then moving on to the risk measurement of an entire portfolio. To build on the summary of factors that have led to the current state of credit risk management, Chapter 2 begins by discussing the operational practices and structural processes for implementing and creating a sound credit environment. Because credit risk is managed using a bottom-up approach and begins with the origination of a new transaction, it is important for credit specialists to have a background in the credit selection process. Chapter 3 will therefore discuss the credit selection process that is used to evaluate new business and describe how transaction risk exposure becomes incorporated into portfolio selection risk. Although the origination of credit must ultimately be considered for the effect that it will have on the aggregate portfolio and shareholder's value, the preservation and growth of a portfolio cannot be achieved without first creating value from the loan origination, which culminates in a credit portfolio. Chapter 4 will follow with an overview of the funding strategies of some of the more commonly used financial products in the extension of business credit.

Another function of an integrated credit risk management approach is the analysis of individual borrowers. Chapters 5 and 6 will therefore focus on some of the techniques that are used in fundamental credit analysis. Beginning in Chapter 5, we will outline some fundamental credit analysis applications that can be used to assess transactions through the framework of a risk evaluation guide. Chapter 6 will build upon this with additional approaches to risk in evaluating a borrower's industry and management.

Beginning in Chapter 7, and for the remainder of the book, the focus will be on quantifying and integrating a transaction into the credit portfolio with the applications of credit risk measurement. In addition to defining the role of credit risk measurement, the chapter will also present a basic framework to measure credit risk and discuss some of the standard measurement applications for quantifying the economic loss on a transaction's credit exposure. Chapter 8 will follow with a discussion of the heart of credit risk management today—how the integration of individual transactions will impact the aggregate credit portfolio. Aside from the techniques and tools being used by lenders to manage their credit risk exposure, credit portfolio risk management also encompasses various market tools that are used to help lenders maximize their earnings and profitability. As many of the tools are adapted to the types of infrastructures and technology that a lender has in place, Chapter 9 will discuss the credit rating systems that have come to play a pivotal role in managing credit risk. These tools are further supported by the regulatory prescriptions, which will finally be discussed in Chapter 10.

CHAPTER 2

The Credit Process

2.1 INTRODUCTION

Credit risk arises whenever a lender is exposed to loss from a borrower, obligor, or counterparty who fails to honor their contracted debt obligation, as agreed, in a timely manner. For lenders who extend credit in the form of loans or capital market products, credit risk is inherent in all their business activities and is an element in virtually every product and service that is provided. In general, there are also degrees of differences in the types of risks that credit transactions may hold, all of which need to be specifically understood by the credit organization relative to how they will impact the credit portfolio. Managing the risks that are contained in providing debt services requires a systematic framework to be established throughout the relevant credit areas; this is known as the credit process. This chapter will present an overview of the credit process in the context of how it has evolved in the management of extending business credit. We will then discuss each of the functions having a role in the credit process and how they can impact the delivery of credit services.

The risks associated with delivering credit services can lead to direct or indirect losses if the processes contain internal procedures, systems, or staff members that inadequately service transactions. Similar to the manufacturing and distribution sectors that produce and sell products in the marketplace, there is a parallel in how banking institutions distribute credit services to the business community. Understanding the distribution functions that lenders use to deliver commoditized services requires an overview of the market environment that has evolved in credit risk management.

2.2 A CHANGING LANDSCAPE

Over the past decade, the servicing of monetized assets has been reconfigured to create a more efficient credit process and loan market through the application of new technologies, new financial products, and new market participants. Unlike traditional commercial lending, which at one time was predicated on long-term relationships, today's emphasis is on short-term value-added customer relationships.* This concept of "value-added" has also brought new meaning to commercial lending as customer relationships are defined as either profitable or not profitable. If they are profitable, this must be evidenced by returns that are commensurate with the overall portfolio objectives and for the financial institution's return on capital. A survey taken in 2004 by the Bethesda (Maryland) based Association for Finance Professionals (AFP) seems to support this trend. In the survey, to over 370 corporate finance treasurers from companies earning annual revenues of $1 billion or greater, approximately 57% of the respondents stated that loan issuance for their companies over the previous five years had been linked to investment banking services by commercial lenders. Approximately 63% of respondents claimed that credit had either been denied to their firms or had resulted in the terms and conditions on their loans being shifted when they had failed to grant additional new business to their banks.† The survey also found that "the larger the company, the greater the pressures were on them to attain commercial credit services from the banks." As a consequence, "half of the companies surveyed said they were unable to meet spending requirements without having awarded underwriting or strategic advisory services" to banking institutions. Should these allegations prove to be true, they reflect how the market environment has unfolded in commercial banking by illegally tying commercial credit services to investment banking services. It furthermore implicates how lenders have fared in transitioning from the classical approach to realizing a relationship's profitability under a modern credit approach in order to meet an established hurdle rate of return.

---

*The exception to this, however, continues to be in emerging markets, where lending is based on size, culture, and traditional banking relationships.
†Survey of 370 finance executives unearths widespread bank demands that credit be linked to the purchase of other services; June 11, 2004, Tim Reason, CFO.com

2.3 THE TRADITIONAL CREDIT PROCESS

Under the classical or traditional credit process, the concept of credit risk management had always been to ensure that adequate capital was available for loan funding and that reserves were provisioned according to the borrower's credit assessment. Credit extensions had always used a static approach whereby subsequent to the loan origination, the credit risk of the borrower would remain on the issuing creditor's balance sheet until maturity. Figure 2.1 illustrates the key elements of this approach, which began with the transaction's origination between the account officer and the borrower. Credit requests were prepared and presented for approval to enter into a transaction that more often than not would be underpriced for the risks relative to the proposed facility terms and structure. The credit granting and subsequent monitoring process was oftentimes accompanied by unpredictable financial indicators that had been derived from limited financial

FIGURE 2.1

Traditional Credit Model

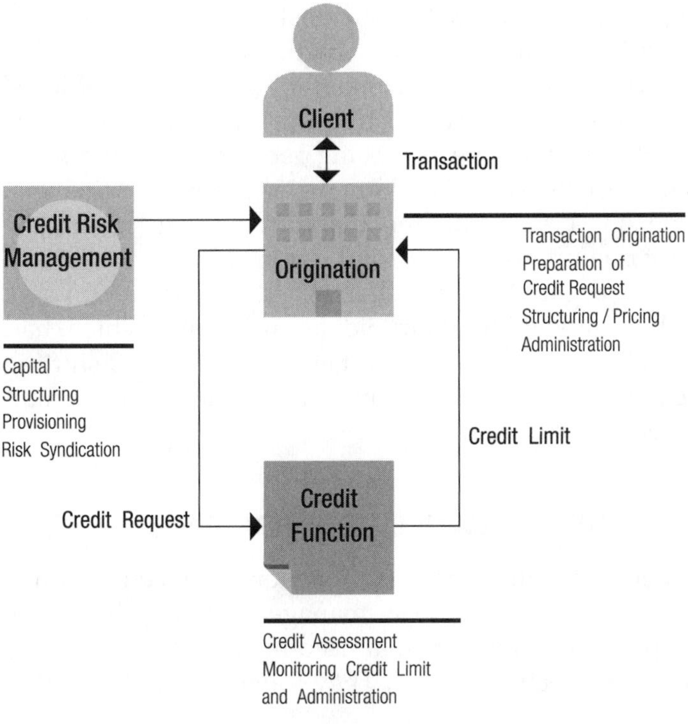

Client

Transaction

Credit Risk Management

Origination

Transaction Origination
Preparation of
Credit Request
Structuring / Pricing
Administration

Capital
Structuring
Provisioning
Risk Syndication

Credit Limit

Credit Request

Credit Function

Credit Assessment
Monitoring Credit Limit
and Administration

analysis and due diligence. A supporting credit department was responsible for independently assessing and monitoring the risks based on financial statements, and the account officer provided credit analysis and, if applicable, collateral appraisals. Loan syndications played an active role in the credit markets at the time however, the emphasis by most lenders was foremost on mitigating credit risks through risk disaggregation rather than managing loan funding for liquidity purposes. In other words pricing was not analyzed to separately identify all of the cost components that lenders incurred for the risks of extending credit, so credit specialists were not able to precisely examine the individual variables that influenced price performance. A common problem under this approach was that the lack of risk-sensitive pricing strategies did not always result in sufficient capital being allocated against rising unexpected losses. This became quite evident as the extension of loans declined from being a leading product for lenders to one of a "loss leader," in anticipation that future ancillary business from borrowers would compensate for the losses on loans. As a result, when defaults did occur, costs were not recovered, which served to further depress credit earnings.

As the credit markets started to change over the years, the rising defaults led to diverging loan costs and firm revenues that spiraled out of control for most banks. An agency conflict started to develop between bank profitability and account officers' performance compensation while funding and administrative costs on defaulted loans were not being recovered. At the same time, the credit markets were also changing as innovative financial products came on stream into the markets, only to reveal the emerging credit quality disparities among borrowers. It was at this point that banks began to examine their traditional credit risk assumptions by challenging their old assumptions, which had been embedded in a static mindset, and eventually started shifting to a dynamic perspective that has now become the modern credit risk management approach.

2.4 THE MODERN CREDIT PROCESS

Banks subsequently began to make comparisons between their historically passive approach to loan management and the more active style of portfolio managers that used most of the same skills and techniques for selecting credits. They found that a distinction between these alternative credit providers and traditional commercial lenders was that portfolio and fund managers did not retain nonperforming assets if those assets failed to provide expected portfolio returns. For banks, however, this required greater emphasis to be placed on portfolio management techniques so that single stand-alone credit requests would be extended to now earn a sufficient economic return so as to maximize the expected credit portfolio returns.

The "modern credit risk approach," as illustrated in Figure 2.2, is considered to be a dynamic application in which all aspects of credit risk are built around an ongoing credit portfolio assessment and measurement process. Credit Portfolio Management techniques

FIGURE 2.2

Modern Credit Approach

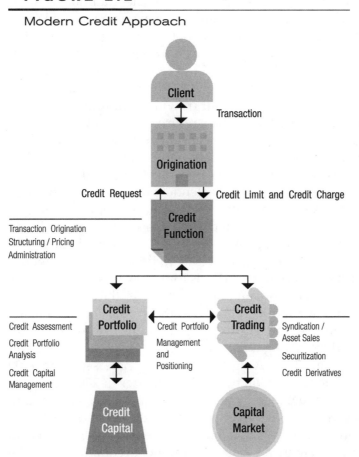

have become an integral part in credit functions for business units throughout banks, beginning with the evaluation of loan originations. Supporting functions, including relationship managers, the credit department, credit administration, and credit portfolio management, all have complementary roles that are driven by several common themes—to reduce the banks' cost of capital and to increase aggregate portfolio performance. In general, transactions are originated by relationship managers in conjunction with each supporting credit function so that when new business is developed it will be based on realizing a hurdle rate of return that is also in line with the banks' portfolio concentration limits. When transactions do not yield the required returns or meet the hurdle rates, the facility is deemed undesirable if the aggregate borrower relationship is found to be unprofitable. Whereas the application of concentration limits under the traditional credit approach had been to reduce the amount of exposure to single borrowers, the practice is now extended to reducing concentration limits to credit events and exposure by borrowers, industries, asset classes, and geographical regions. Credit portfolio analysis is also performed on an aggregate level for borrowers, companies, markets, as well as credit products, all of which are ultimately measured against the desired portfolio's return. As the new vanguards of the credit process, portfolio managers have empowered banks to adopt a defensive risk posture relative to customer relationships. For credit risk exposures that are not value-added or that increasingly outweigh the rewards, lenders will seek to transfer or mitigate them through loan sales, securitizations, or credit derivatives. Transactions are terminated from the lender's portfolio so that they can be quantified, unbundled, and repackaged into newly manufactured credit products for resale to third-party investors.

By repacking corporate credit risk into new pools and classes of debt that are sold to a broad range of investors, the credit markets have created a new product segment in the syndicated, secondary, and capital loan markets. The expansion and growth of the credit derivative markets among U.S. banks over an eight-year period can be seen in Figure 2.3, showing them to have increased from $100 million in 1997 to $1.2 billion by the first quarter in 2004. As a primary hedging product used by financial institutions to mitigate and transfer risks as well as serve to provide credit enhancements, the startling growth of these assets has by no means been limited to the United States. Figure 2.4 illustrates the global composition of the

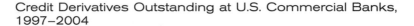

FIGURE 2.3

Credit Derivatives Outstanding at U.S. Commercial Banks, 1997–2004

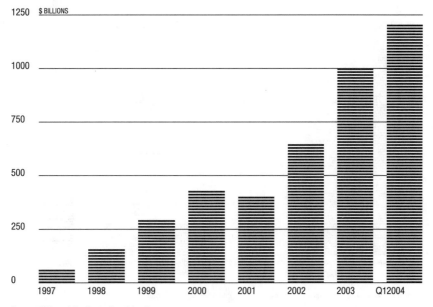

Source: Office of the Controller of the Currency

credit derivative markets in 2004, in which approximately 42% of the market was concentrated in single named credit default swaps, and 27% in multinamed collateralized debt obligations (CDOs). These assets have afforded banks a vehicle with which to shift their roles from originating and holding risk to originating and distributing risk. Another vehicle that has also contributed to the means to liquidate and remove credit exposures off balance sheets has been the growth of the secondary loan market. The growth in secondary loan trading, presented in Figure 2.5 shows a substantial increase between 1991 and the end of 2003 from $5BN to $148BN, respectively. Earnings from these increased sales provide greater liquidity for banks and are used to reinvest in higher returning assets by extending credit to more profitable borrowers.

By adopting the practices of modern credit risk management, the banking industry has also become resilient in managing the deteriorating credit quality among corporate borrowers. Despite having faced two recessionary credit cycles since the 1980s,

FIGURE 2.4

Global Credit Derivatives Market, 2004

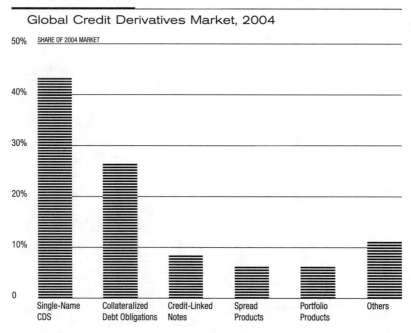

Source: Ernst and Young 2004 estimates; Ernst and Young, 2003

FIGURE 2.5

Secondary Loan Market Value Traded

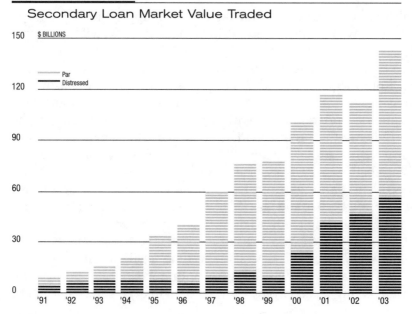

Source: LPC

including 1,414 bank failures between 1989 and 1993 on assets of $554BN, industry volatility begin to stabilize over the years. Although corporate defaults increased between 1999 and 2002, strengthened risk management and measurement practices served to diffuse the impact of these defaults compared to the 1980s. As an example, if we compare bank loan losses during 2001 and 2003 to the industry situation in the late 1980s and early 1990s, the impact of modern credit risk management techniques found the banking sector to be much more resilient. Figures 2.6 and 2.7 and Table 2.1 highlight that global corporate defaults increased by issuers and by debt volume amounts during the economic downturn between 1999 and 2002, at the same time as the returns of the U.S. banking industry in Figure 2.8 exhibit that profitability was at its highest level for the first time in thirty years. Notwithstanding that profitability compared to the rate of loan write-offs more than tripled during this time as banks began to apply portfolio credit risk management techniques. Tighter credit standards were applied, along with more stringent credit terms, in response to credit cycle and recessionary trends well before these patterns reached their nadir.

FIGURE 2.6

Annual Global Corporate Defaults by Issuers

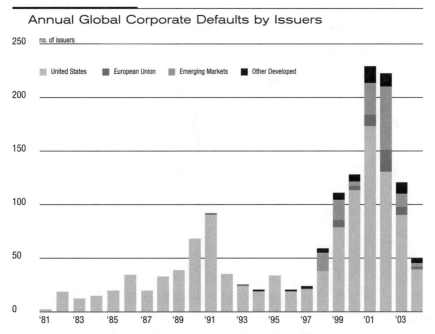

Source: Standard & Poor's Global fixed Income Research; Standard & Poor's CreditPro® 7.0

FIGURE 2.7

Annual Global Corporate Defaults by Amounts

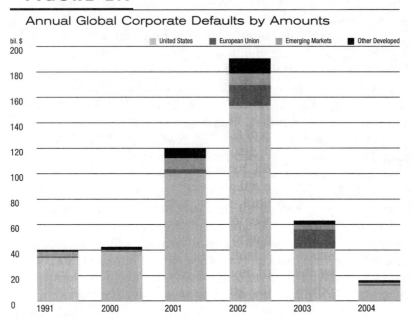

Source: Standard & Poor's Global Fixed Income Research; Standard & Poor's CreditPro® 7.0

FIGURE 2.8

Returns of All FDIC Commercial Banks (1996–2002)

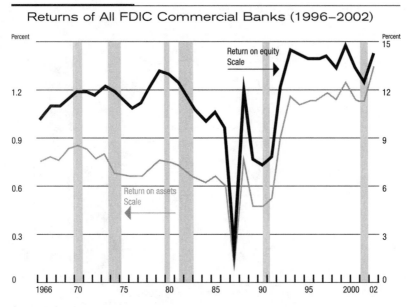

Source: FDIC

TABLE 2-1

Global Corporate Default Summary

Year	Total Defaults*	Investment-Grade Defaults	Speculative Grade Defaults	Defaults Rate (%)	Investment-Grade Default Rate (%)	Speculative Grade Default Rate (%)	Total Dept Defaulting (Bil.$)
1981	2	0	2	0.15	0.00	0.63	0.0
1982	18	2	15	1.20	0.19	4.42	0.9
1983	12	1	10	0.76	0.09	2.94	0.4
1984	13	2	11	0.83	0.17	2.98	0.4
1985	18	0	17	1.04	0.00	4.05	0.3
1986	32	2	30	1.71	0.15	5.66	0.5
1987	19	0	19	0.94	0.00	2.80	1.6
1988	32	0	31	1.48	0.00	4.12	3.3
1989	39	2	31	1.54	0.14	4.18	7.3
1990	68	2	55	2.67	0.14	7.99	21.2
1991	90	3	64	3.23	0.20	11.05	23.6
1992	35	0	30	1.38	0.00	5.88	5.4
1993	25	0	13	0.54	0.00	2.36	5.4
1994	19	1	15	0.60	0.05	2.12	2.3
1995	33	1	28	0.95	0.04	3.38	9.0
1996	20	0	16	0.48	0.00	1.77	2.7
1997	24	3	20	0.63	0.11	1.95	4.9
1998	58	5	49	1.28	0.17	3.62	11.3
1999	109	4	95	2.11	0.13	5.52	37.8
2000	131	5	109	2.31	0.16	5.80	43.0
2001	227	8	177	3.64	0.25	9.21	118.8
2002	236	17	177	3.76	0.52	9.49	190.1
2003	126	3	95	1.84	0.09	4.71	62.5
2004	49	0	36	0.69	0.00	1.82	16.2

*This column includes companies that were no longer rated at the time of default.

Source: Standard & Poor's Global Fixed Income Research; Standard & Poor's CreditPro®7.0.

Referring to Figure 2.9, it can be seen that commercial loan charge-offs represented approximately 45% of commercial loans in 1991, at which time they started to level off until the 2001 credit cycle, when they peaked at their highest level of 50%. Compared to the prior credit cycle in 1991, the volume of distressed debt had fallen from 58% to 35% by 2001, although it rose slightly to 42% by 2003 due to the secondary market trading of 2001 defaults. The decline in write-offs and distressed debt trading between 1991 and 2003 reflects the tighter credit standards imposed by banks prior to the 2003 credit cycle recession.

At the same time, the application of the modern credit approach has resulted in creating additional credit risk as loan transactions now have multiple counterparties and intermediaries. Having so many counterparties involved in related transactions with a diverse range of risk appetites, requires that they are classified, managed, and monitored according to their multiple risk perspectives. This has led to the development and implementation of analytic applications that offer greater precision in the evaluation of credit risk. Credit risk analytics and measurement

FIGURE 2.9

Distressed Loan Trading and Commercial Banks Charge-Offs

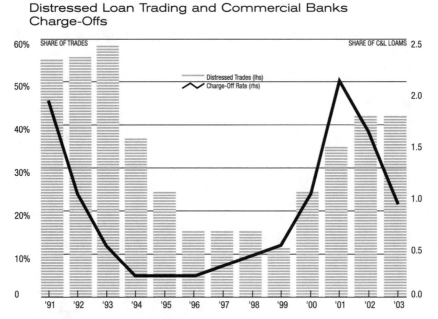

Source: S & P Leveraged Lending 3Q2003 and Federal Reserve

techniques (e.g., including scenario analysis and portfolio optimization) are applied to both single transactions that support the credit assessment of existing and potential borrowers and counterparties as well as in evaluating portfolios to assess customers' profitability and relationships' viability. Although most banks in the early 1990s were initially slow to embrace credit risk measurement tools, at least among the major and regional banks such tools are now incorporated into credit risk infrastructures and management practices. An example of a lender that transitioned from the traditional to the modern approach of credit risk management is highlighted in the case study on Citibank (Case Study 1), which emphasizes how one leading commercial lender came to understand the impact of portfolio credit risk in the early 1990s.

CASE STUDY 1 CITIBANK

Citibank is a practical and realistic example of a commercial lender that some have said was forced into a role of leadership under the market stresses that have led to modern credit risk management techniques. Like most of the banking industry during the late 1980s and early 1990s, the high concentration of leveraged buyout and commercial real estate loan defaults that besieged Citibank provoked former CEO and Chairman John Reed to take an active role in reassessing the bank's credit risk management practices. During an interview with *U.S. Banker* in 1989, Reed stated that "he was becoming concerned, somewhat belatedly, that Citi was getting "unduly transaction oriented."[1] Reed also stated at the time that "the business was not performing the way people said it was. I didn't sense that they properly understood what was happening or could work it." The problems were exacerbated after bank auditors and loan review personnel missed warning signs that almost brought Citibank to insolvency. In the book by Philip Zweig on "Citibank and the Rise and Fall of American Financial Supremacy," he summarizes Citibank's credit problems by stating:

> Citi's problems were heavily concentrated: domestic real estate, Australia, Brazil, and highly leveraged transactions. The biggest chunk of the leveraged deals—16 percent—were in media and entertainment. By 1991, Citibank had made more than $13 billion in commercial real estate loans, more than a third in the western United States. Nearly 43 percent of them were now nonperforming. Citibank had lent up to 80 percent or more of the value of the properties, putting Citibank's

investment underwater when values plunged 40 percent or more." "By the mid-1990s, cross border, real estate, and LBO's had cost Citicorp upward of $9 billion in write-offs alone, enough, in theory at least, to have bought Chase Manhattan, with Wells Fargo thrown in for good measure (based on year-end 1992 valuations). Reed concluded that the problem with the loan portfolio was not the structure of individual deals but the portfolio concentrations. "We never have had a focus on portfolio management," Reed said. Now they were plagued by self-doubt and uncertainty about the survival of their institution. First and foremost, Reed had to repair the damage to the bank's risk-management systems, including its credit culture and methods for monitoring loans. As the portfolio grew, Citibank had not felt it needed a system for monitoring loans and establishing exposure limits by industry and location. Now, humbly, it set up a system to do just that. Reed was determined to give credit policy officers a more "independent" check-and-balance role than they had enjoyed in the past, and to focus on market risk as well as credit risk.[2]

The increased complexity of risks that had evolved under increasing regulatory restraints, made Reed feel the "lack of a real-time portfolio information system had become obvious."[3] In response to this, Citibank began to restructure the corporate lending and credit functions to incorporate a credit portfolio management strategy. Citibank began to emphasize the development of credit risk measurement techniques for loans similar to an options valuation model that would support mark-to-market analysis and portfolio credit risk for the bank's entire portfolio. Although the focus was primarily on large corporate and middle market facilities, it eventually led to the development of the Citibank Loan Index (CLI). The index was designed to function like an equity or bond portfolio through which loans are bought and sold based on performance objectives. It contained over 1,000 credits for 600 public companies totaling $400BN, and was used to monitor and control obligor risk and bank profitability. Loans that did not meet performance objectives were either sold off or transferred according to index objectives. Although the CLI was discontinued in 1996 for more advanced risk applications, it represented the initial stages of Citibank's efforts to develop measurement tools that would monitor and control its credit risk exposure. Overall, success of the banking sector's modern credit risk management practices, and in particular Citibank's resurgence, was revealed in the following statement by the *Economist Magazine*, which stated that *"America's banks revealed record profits for 2003, $120 billion in all. The biggest of them, Citigroup, clocked up $17.9 billion, the most ever made by a single bank."*[4]

Although some have argued that the increase in debt among corporate and business borrowers globally serves to also explain why Citigroup earned record profits in 2003, it is nonetheless a fact that cannot be disputed that commercial banks, on aggregate, realized improved industry performance. These achievements, however, have been aided by leveraging transactional information with credit risk analytics to provide a higher level of financial transparency for lenders in credit risk management.

2.5 RISK ASSESSMENT VERSUS RISK MEASUREMENT

At this point, it is important that the distinction between credit risk assessment and credit risk measurement is clarified. A rule of thumb that can be used to distinguish these applications is to understand what the three fundamental goals are that each seeks to determine. The credit assessment process is a holdover from traditional credit risk management, which is grounded in fundamental credit analysis to identify and control risks by determining the borrower's probability of repaying the debt. Through credit analysis, an assessment is made of the borrower's income, balance sheet, and cash flow statements, along with character, capacity, and capital adequacy, all of which are dependent upon data that are provided by the obligor. The second goal of credit assessment is to identify a borrower's primary source of debt repayment that will be available to repay an extended credit obligation. Similarly, the third goal of credit assessment is to evaluate the probability that a secondary repayment source will be available in the event that the primary source becomes unavailable.

Whereas credit assessment relies on the borrower's provided information, credit risk measurement, on the other hand, relies on the lender's analytics and risk measurement tools rather than the borrower's. Credit risk measurement also has three goals, the first of which is to **limit the credit risk exposure** that the lenders accept when extending the debt. By determining the probability of a loss and the loss exposure amount over a period of time, the debt facility can be better structured and managed. A second goal of credit risk measurement is to ensure that **adequate compensation is earned** for the risk undertaken. It is concerned with the revenues and profit margins earned on the credit products and services that lenders provide. Credit risk measurement tools and techniques are used to ensure that the credit risks on loans are appropriately priced and that portfolio returns yield the targeted established financial values. Finally, the third goal of credit risk measurement is to **mitigate the credit risk exposure** by structuring transactions to protect against loss as well as into asset classes that can be marketed to third-party investors. Credit risk measurement models will quantify transaction exposures and attempt to reduce the risk of credit loss by deriving the asset classes to sell units of risk based on risk analytics. When transaction yields do not equal the lender's desired rate of portfolio returns, then the credit may be transferred, neutralized, or sold off. Although we will discuss the respective credit risk techniques and tools throughout this book, it is important to point out here that the basis for determining the credit process is grounded in the functions that are performed within the credit organization. Aside from being responsible for the credit policies and procedures related to all new and existing transactions, the credit organization also ensures that appropriate controls exist throughout the credit process.

2.6 THE DRIVERS OF THE CREDIT ORGANIZATION

Although every banking or lending organization has a custom-designed credit process, the fundamental framework is essentially similar. At the center is the ability to earn profits while also ensuring that an organization has adequate regulatory capital for economic losses and shareholders' requirements. This requires a hierarchical structure throughout the credit organization tailored to the credit process, although it can vary in procedures, size, and functions, as well as be designed along geographic, product, industry, or international divisions. A small bank, for example, might only have a minimum number of relationship managers to perform different aspects of the credit process, while a larger bank may have more support staff and credit specializations. A hypothetical example of the credit organization in a large bank is exhibited in Figure 2.10, operating under the management of senior vice presidents that oversee various divisions. When credit responsibilities are divided across geographical regions or product lines, as well as borrowers and industries, international lenders or those with niche market positions advocate the benefits of specialization. In

FIGURE 2.10

Example of the Credit Organization in a Large Bank

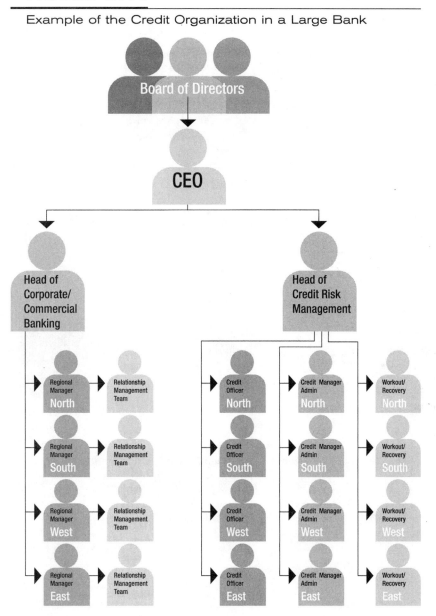

contrast, lending organizations that seek to have greater focus on product development for structuring, mitigating, and transferring risk emphasize client groups and product lines such as in Figure 2.11.

FIGURE 2.11

Example of Credit Organization Focusing on Product Development

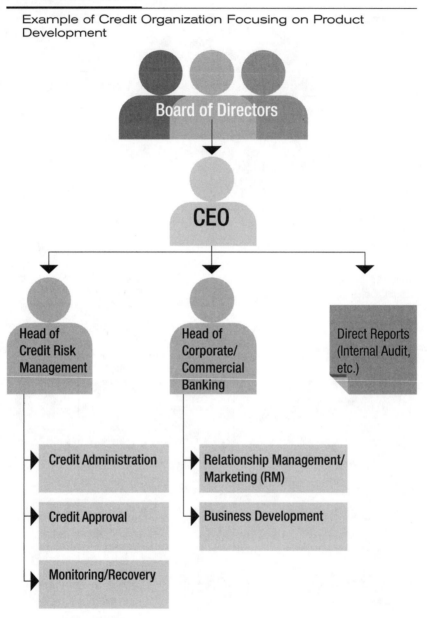

Whatever functional approach is established within the credit organization, the credit process will typically begin with the origination of new business and revolve around the supporting credit functions that are highlighted in Figure 2.12. Marketing or

Relationship Management is usually conducted by the business development or loan department and is the original and sometimes primary contact with borrowers. Because Relationship Managers (RM) are also charged with having full knowledge about the borrower's business and industry, they will usually propose to the credit department or approving authorities the supporting reasons to extend new credit transactions in the credit application. The credit application therefore becomes a primary document to drive the credit process in that it serves as a basis to derive historical borrower information that will subsequently be used in credit risk measurement. Information relevant to borrower characteristics, exposure amounts, and facility types will be gathered and collected from credit applications to measure future potential losses from credit exposures. Credit risk approval is then based on the credit assessment and risk measurement applications after assigned risk ratings are given to support the credit analysis and quantify a borrower's probability of default to exposure loss. Credit rating systems have been a significant development in modern credit applications and, depending on the type of system that is used, the credit process can be integrated to appropriate information systems technology so that credit functions can inclusively perform a variety of tasks. As we will discuss in Chapter 9, dual-tier rating systems such as those used by larger organizations to risk rate both borrowers and facilities can provide accounting information and monitor credit limits as well as perform quantifying calculations on credit risk exposures. Approved transactions also require that the credit organization have a credit process in place that oversees loan documentation prior and subsequent to the disbursement of funds.

Once all of the required documentation is obtained and the funds are disbursed, an established system will need to be in place for the ongoing servicing and monitoring of facilities. Credit Administration is therefore a vital function in the credit process that requires the lender to monitor transactions through customer reviews on annual or more frequent terms. This will allow the lender to understand the borrower's financial and operating conditions, as well as to better identify problem credits. Credit Administration will also support portfolio objectives by monitoring and controlling collateral in order to ensure that the appropriate liens remain current and are perfected on security along with any required covenants. Monitoring the total exposure limits for

FIGURE 2.12

Functional Approach to the Credit Process

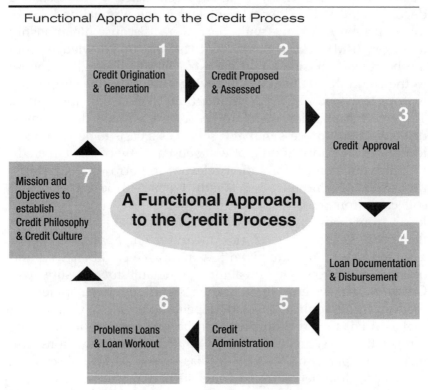

the maximum transaction amounts is also essential to prevent the risk of credit loss, particularly for lenders that engage in capital market activities. By assessing the concentration and credit exposure limits on a daily basis, lenders can remain abreast of how credit assets are performing throughout the term of the facilities. Because lenders cannot avoid having some losses, even if only a minimal amount, a workout unit or group to manage borrower transactions that do default is also a required credit process and functions to recover funds from defaulted credit obligations.

A distinguishing factor that is illustrated in Figure 2.13 relative to modern credit risk is that the entire credit process revolves around credit portfolio management to ensure that appropriate pricing and portfolio returns are attained on credit extensions. As an active part of the credit organization that has taken on an increasingly visible role, credit portfolio management is charged with reducing the cost of capital while also increasing portfolio performance. For example, Figure 2.14 depicts how

FIGURE 2.13

Building the Credit Processing Functions Around the
Credit Postfolio

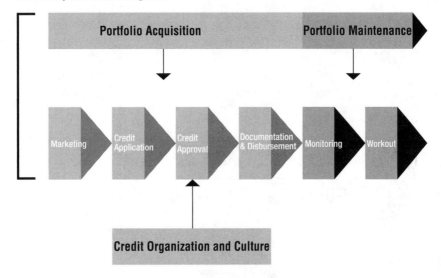

the extension of a credit facility to a firm that is below investment
grade, but accompanied by high yields, may contain a credit
default swap to mitigate future loss exposure. Credit portfolio
management is also a subcomponent of the credit monitoring
function that heavily relies on advanced information system
applications to measure daily analytic credit risk activities on
the overall credit portfolio composition and asset quality. Various
applications and approaches are used to address particular
questions relevant to credit risk on individual transactions and
portfolios. Techniques such as Value-at-Risk (VaR) along with other
scenario conditions are applied to stress-testing circumstances
under various conditions to determine how credit portfolio
transactions can impact capital allocations and earnings profitability. However, the management of the credit process by each of the
above credit functions is driven by the supporting credit
departments and functions that establish the credit foundation. An
overview of each of these supporting functions is important to
build a credit process.

FIGURE 2.14

Managing the Credit Risk Transaction

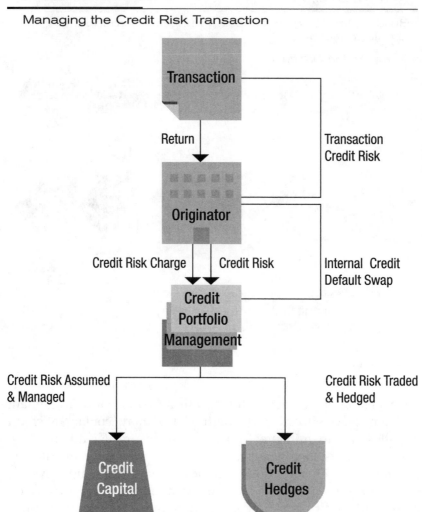

2.7 SUPPORTING CREDIT DEPARTMENTS AND FUNCTIONS

Bank Credit Departments have traditionally been considered the "gatekeepers" for managing credit risk by serving as the decision-making and approval functions for credit extension. Although they continue to operate in an independent capacity, the specific role of their functions has been reconfigured to assume credit portfolio management responsibilities. Many banks have now expanded credit portfolio management into existing credit departments as an active support to business and credit divisions, while others have established their functions into becoming centralized departments. Depending on the organization, credit departments will work with marketing in specific line-business or industry groups to structure transactions as they are originated. Proponents of this approach feel that having everyone involved in the loan approval process will contribute to a more efficient understanding of the credit at both the transaction and the borrower level. In other organizations there may be highly centralized credit departments that operate to retain strong barriers and controls on the credit-granting functions. As risks have become more integrated and regulatory concerns have advocated for designated management to be separate from the marketing and credit functions, some organizations have felt that this was most effective to manage overall credit portfolio risks. If, for example, questions need to be answered by the credit department before loans can be approved, those organizations that prefer to maintain strict segregation from business units will prefer not to meet with clients, but rather separately interact with relationship managers. The argument against this structure is that it slows down the credit processing time by excluding credit department personnel along with the account officer from meeting with the customer.

Lenders that have supporting credit portfolio groups separate from the credit department emphasize that the basic objectives are to reduce event and concentration risks, to improve portfolio value and liquidity, and to support business growth. Credit organizations that have centralized these groups are typically operated by institutions that have a strong Board of Directors who believes in the utility of this function as a separate business unit. In addition to implementing the bank's credit risk strategy, individual department credit portfolio groups also oversee other business units as individual profit centers for specific asset classes. Having a centralized credit portfolio management function has resulted in this group evolving from a monitoring and reporting function into a more active role that participates in loan originations along with deciding on hedging techniques and engaging in secondary market sales as well as asset acquisitions. Among some lenders, it has brought an active support role to business departments. Credit portfolio managers, for example, among certain major European lenders, now act as the preliminary approvers on individual stand-alone transactions as well as provide suggestions for structuring the credit requests. At the same time, in other banks, they are restricted to solely managing credit portfolios, where the focus is on whether to transfer or sell facilities that are not yielding the required returns.

A more common approach used by small- and medium-sized lenders is a decentralized process that extends lending limits and authority based on strict standards and guidelines. After questions are answered relevant to the facility structure and credit analysis, credit requests can either be approved by authorized credit officers or forwarded to a Loan Committee. More often practiced in the United States, lending decisions based on limits and authority have been controversial in Europe and other regions of the world. In the United States, the trend has been to centralize credit decisions and approvals by using a limited number of highly trained and specialized credit professionals that focus on regional markets. Proponents believe that this approach is more cost effective than having many industry specialists involved in lending decisions, because approval is concentrated among fewer individuals. Alternatively, critics argue that the approach results in a lack of the specialty skills needed in particular sectors, as well as reducing the time spent understanding the obligor and its business.

Although the use of loan committees has become less of a trend at many of the larger banks, some of the regional and smaller banks have continued to use Loan Committees to finalize their credit decisions. Other institutions, on the other hand, have chosen to delegate approval to a Chief Credit Officer, based on lending limits or according to their credit policies and procedures. In general, Loan Committees are represented by the most senior members of a bank's credit organization and are viewed as a means to remove any bias or criticism that comes from extending approval limits and authority to a single credit officer. The benefits of a loan committee vary from taking on greater credit portfolio management applications to structuring transactions, given that the individual members have valuable professional experience and have seen many "faux pas." Portfolio functions that are performed by loan committees include decisions on balance sheet implications such as whether or not to accept a particular asset into the port-folio. Loan committees are also known to resolve disputes that may occur with lending officers, such as whether or not to downgrade or upgrade facilities as well as to transfer or sell assets. As lenders become engaged in transferring assets for portfolio objectives, this has become an area of dissension for borrowers as well as for account officers who feel that it can jeopardize their credit account relationships. Herein is a criticism of Loan Committees in that they are not as close to a transaction nor are they necessarily required on certain types of lending such as large syndicated loans. At the same time, Loan Committees can also be limited by the bureaucracy that they attract, as well as for being known to be too conservative on matters such as opposition to a particular borrower rather than on the benefit of accepting a particular transaction.

2.8 CREDIT ADMINISTRATION

Credit Administration is a bank internal loan monitoring function for overseeing the credit quality of transactions. In many banks, the role of loan review and credit administration can be either a single or dual function. A single credit administration function can engage in analyzing the loans on an annual basis to assess whether a facility's existing risk rating should remain the same, be upgraded or down-graded. If the role has a dual capacity function to review loans and administer credit facilities, administration can also include control-ling loans to ensure that borrowers are complying with the respec-tive terms and conditions. This monitoring role can also be charged with ensuring that all security documentation is in compliance with the terms of approval and is enforceable. For new and existing facil-ities this includes having in place the proper assignment of assets to pledge collateral along with appropriate insurance coverage. In other words, the borrower is unable to withdraw funds before all of the loan documents are signed or, in the case of existing transactions, before any new draw downs. Given the relationships between loan business and the client, the credit culture has not always enforced these standards.

Because of the independent nature of Loan Review, there can be political challenges in the role of monitoring credits through the loan review process. The loan review function at many banks continues to lack the independence that is needed because their ability to affect risk ratings can ultimately affect the capital alloca-tions required for loan loss reserves. Among the common themes that emerge among banking professionals is the separation of duties that should exist between and among credit approval officers, loan review, and audit. It is important to note here the distinctions between the last two groups. Although loan review is a monitoring function, audit is an internal control function. No matter what type of credit organization is in place, the audit function should always be separate from other credit functions, to maintain an appropriate system of checks and balances. However, a limitation of audit is their limited knowledge of individual credit "names." One reason for this is that audit functions deal more in loan documentation. Although the audit function conducts independent inspections to ensure compliance with lending guidelines, operating procedures, and bank policies, the departmental emphasis is more focused on questions such as: Is the guarantee on file? Is the security agreement in place? Have current financials been received? Audit personnel will usually lack the credit training and first-hand experience to determine if the required documentation is appropriate given the loan structure. This has contributed to the reason why the loan review function was established, although its independence has not always been successful. In addition, the lack of credit training makes it difficult for internal auditors to report on declining credit quality when the focus is on documentation. Technological innovations in credit review software methodologies, including two-dimensional risk rating systems, are starting to respond to this matter.*

The credit process is also driven by the hierarchical structure of the credit organization, which is customized to reflect the credit philosophy and lending strategy. The credit risk philosophy and credit culture is, in fact, the basis for determining the credit process that the organization practices. In the next section we will examine how credit philosophies and credit risk strategies are ultimately tied to credit portfolio returns and shareholders' values.

2.9 WHAT IS THE ORGANIZATION'S CREDIT PHILOSOPHY

An institution's Credit Philosophy and Credit Culture represent the mission, objectives, and lending strategies to legitimatize the value

---

*A two-dimensional risk rating system is part of the advances in credit risk management that enable the risk rating of both the obligor and facility. It is discussed in greater detail in Chapters 6 and 9.

placed on credit quality and safe sound lending practices.[†] Each institution's philosophy and culture reflect the processes, customs, and protocols regarding how credit might be extended. As a result, the cultural attitudes and beliefs that brand how lenders are defined become established. Traditionally, and prior to deregulation, banks were known to be conservative in their lending practices as well as advocating high-quality credit standards. However, the pressures to survive in a competitive environment during the 1980s and early 1990s led to conflicting goals, in which loans were extended that were not compatible with many institutions' credit philosophies. As the objective in defining a credit philosophy and culture is to reflect what role the lender wants to play in the market, a "top-down" approach must be used and implemented throughout the organization. This means that credit practices and processes must begin with The Board of Directors' and CEO's input and be communicated throughout the organization by a strong senior management. The use of the top-down approach in this manner makes the credit philosophy become both a formal and informal part of the institution. Formally, the credit philosophy should be documented in written policies detailing the corporate priorities to which the credit process and procedures will be applied relative to the credit risk strategy and credit portfolio management. Because they are the primary tool for communicating throughout the organization, the credit policy and procedures should be derived from consensus in order to integrate a disciplined bank-wide credit approach. Informally, the credit policy not only defines the credit process, but is also the foundation for establishing an institution's credit culture.

To better illustrate the credit process framework, refer to the top-down approach in Figure 2.15, beginning with the Credit Philosophy and Credit Culture. An effective credit philosophy must be disciplined with a definitive credit policy that articulates the lender's business strategy as it relates to the desired business composition and loan markets. It should specify the maximum annual growth rates for loans and weighted credit quality goals for bonds, as well as the targeted returns that are to be measured

---

†There are differing viewpoints among some lenders as to how they define high credit quality. Some lenders may view a weak credit to be strong and structure the transaction with collateral that may prove to be worthless as time goes on. Alternatively, a lender may feel that covenants protect it without considering that the borrower may find ways to circumvent those covenants, such as by attaining supplier credit.

FIGURE 2.15

The Framework for the Credit Process

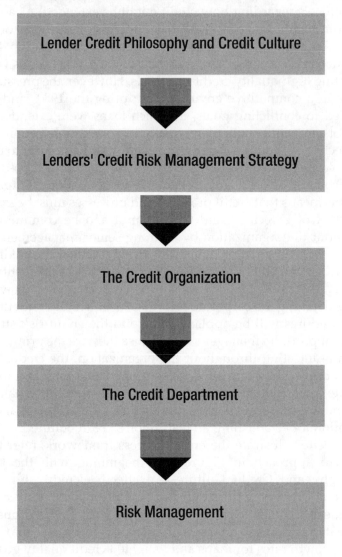

against inclusive of any asset price changes and interest spread income. Acceptable exposure levels should be quantified for the loan mix of the portfolio according to the liquidity and term structures of the different debt types.

Ideally, the credit philosophy should define the desired portfolio composition as one that emphasizes diversity across customer, industry, product, and even geographical lines in order to mitigate risk exposure should a particular sector hit a decline. The desired portfolio growth and targeted earnings should also be clearly articulated and dynamically revised as market conditions dictate. As an example, suppose a commercial bank wants to expand into energy lending with the goal of attaining a leading market position as a major energy financer over the next few years. The top-down approach will require this strategy to be implemented within the umbrella of a revised credit philosophy and will require identification as to how this strategy will affect the portfolio composition. The specific energy sectors and companies that will be targeted for new business should be identified along with the credit standards applicable for the respective industry. The credit policy should specify how the organization anticipates it will achieve a diversified energy portfolio, including quantifying the lending limits acceptable for each energy industry business sector (i.e., 30% for fully integrated and diversified oil companies, 25% for natural gas companies, 20% for independent power producers (IPPs), 15% for utilities, and 10% for project finance). The breakdown should also specify the aggregate exposure amounts by geographical regions that are to be targeted and that are to be incorporated as a percent of the portfolio. This is especially important for small niche market lenders that lack the resources of larger banks.

The credit standards used in evaluating loan requests should also be detailed for each type of loan extended (i.e., revolving lines, working capital, term loans, and so on), along with underwriting guidelines for each loan that is approved. Lending authority and approval limits also need to be specified according to the level of personnel experience, which serves to delegate responsibilities as well as controls for the lender. This is especially important when the lender is small and lacks the resources of a large bank, because it clearly allows for the implementation of sufficient checks and balances to promote the segregation of duties. Having the business development officer serve as the credit officer as well as market, analyze, propose, structure, and approve loan facilities can create chaos within the credit function, and potentially lead to ethical concerns and even fraud. Notwithstanding that, having a credit committee with minimal knowledge about the details of approved transactions opens management to criticism about excess layers of personnel that need to be eliminated. Superfluous layers of decision making in both personnel and levels of approval may also serve to protect credit personnel from responsibility.

When everyone in the credit organization that is connected to extending business credit fully understands the details of the credit process, the lender can promote its credit philosophy and be able to attain the desired portfolio return. Recognizing the effectiveness of a lender's credit philosophy is based on whether it maintains stable earnings and portfolio credit quality over various credit cycles. If performance indicators show a loan portfolio of quality assets that has profitably grown from the targeted market areas outlined in the credit policy, this indicates a successful credit philosophy and effective credit risk management. Alternatively, if the loan portfolio exhibits volatile earnings and profitability, which are inconsistent with the credit risk exposure, than there is a lack of discipline and weak credit culture throughout the credit organization. Most likely, credit policy communications may not have been clear about the processes and procedures that should have been mandated. Nor are uniform standards being applied throughout the credit organization, starting at loan originations and continuing throughout the duration of the credit facilities. It could very well be that credit is also being dictated by account officers who are motivated by bonuses to originate loans, regardless of the credit quality.

2.10 FORMING THE CREDIT CULTURE

If the credit philosophy is not consistently integrated and reinforced into the credit culture, the credit process will become dysfunctional. A lending organization's credit culture represents the attitudes, perceptions, behaviors, styles, and beliefs that are conducted and practiced throughout the credit organization as a result of management attitudes towards credit risk. The credit culture can sometimes be challenged if the lender's mission and objectives are in conflict with the formalized credit policies and procedures. For example, if the lender's mission and objectives are stated as being a conservative lender to high-quality investment-grade borrowers, this objective would be inconsistent if 50% of loan portfolio obligors were below investment grade. Inconsistencies such as these will affect how management attempts to lead the organization, as well as the role it seeks to play in the market. If market conditions change to the point that a lender decides to finance below investment-grade borrowers, then the credit philosophy must also be revised along with the appropriate risk guidelines relative to those borrowers. These revisions and guidelines should not necessarily be dictated by increased market competition or weak profit margins, but rather by having the capacity and skills to profitably service these types of credits. Similarly, if the lender's credit policy states that loans for speculative purposes will not be granted, the approval to extend such a loan should not be granted for the sake of current earnings. It leads to a flawed credit policy and culture that will also affect the perceptions in the market. Also, it will eventually expose lenders to greater risk, regulatory scrutiny, as well as capital reserve requirements. If, for example, the relationship manager calls on a borrower and indicates conflicting terms and conditions relative to the credit or underwriting standards that are subsequently extended, the borrower's perceptions about the lender can become confused and unfavorable. Provisions should therefore be made for when and why exceptions or amendments to the lender's credit policy will be applied.

John McKinley and John Barrickman also define credit culture in their book *Strategic Credit Risk Management* to be "the embodiment of the bank's approach to underwriting, managing and monitoring credit risk." They go on to further state that the "credit culture is the glue that binds the credit process and forms the foundation for credit discipline." As illustrated in Figure 2.16, there are four common types of credit cultures that can prevail in a lending environment. Each characteristic type is defined by its primary focus, which serves to motivate or drive the credit environment. Distinguishing these cultures can also be highlighted by how success is measured as well as particular hidden or underlying characteristics.

2.11 CREDIT RISK STRATEGY

A credit risk strategy is derived from the credit philosophy by defining the institution's risk appetite and determining how risks are managed throughout an organization's credit culture. It is therefore the basis for how credit risk is monitored, controlled, and responded to. Although risks are inherently a cost of doing business, the successful lender is one that can effectively anticipate such risks and apply mitigating strategies to protect the organization from been harmed by them. The credit risk strategy should be clearly understood by everyone in the credit organization in order to pursue new business opportunities. For example, business units

FIGURE 2.16

Types of Credit Culture

Characteristics of the Four Credit Cultures

Characteristics	Values Driven	Immediate Performance Driven	Production Driven	Unfocused (alias Current Priority Driven)
Top Priority	Long Term Persistent Performance	Current earnings, stock price	Market share, loan growth and loan volume	Tends to change frequently
Driving Force	Corporate Values and Market Consistency	Annual profit plan	Commitment to the largest	Changes as priorities change; management is reactive
Credit Environment	Strong credit organization with few policy exceptions and excellent communication	Generally strong emphasis on credit quality when economy is strong and not much difference from a values driven culture, however, in periods of weak loan demand, there is a tendency to enter or increase into risky lines of business	Well managed, market-driven banks have strong systems, controls and good credit leadership; but as leaders are pressured to produce, line and credit will be in conflict over priorities, in very aggressive banks credit approvers find themselves increasingly limited in their influence on loan decisions as they are directed to "find a way to do the deal".	Line units may have their own views of credit quality, credit risk management tries to respond to frequent changes in direction.
Hidden Policy	Not a factor - consistent with written policy.	Conflicts with written policy during soft loan market periods as lenders become confused over management priorities	Lenders understand that their job is to do the job regardless of the written policy.	Lenders are confused by inconsistency and shifting priorites
Success Factor	Balance between credit quality and revenue generator, avoids tendency to control lending function	Credit risk management must be strong enough to resist lender pressure to enter riskier markets in downcycles	Credit risk management must control the loan approval process, keep individual loan authorities low and resist production pressures.	Credit quality can be maintained if credit risk management policies, systems and leadership are strong.

should know the proportion of total loan business outstanding and the limits on a specific industry or borrower before accepting new business. If management has determined that no more than 5% of its loan portfolio should be to the auto industry, under what conditions, if any, are new loans to be made that will increase auto industry exposure to 6%? What type of limits should the lender place on industry sectors and product lines, for example?

An effective credit risk strategy should be implemented by the various functions of the entire credit organization after it has received board approval, together with senior management, as part of the credit process and policies. This is a key risk control measure to ensure that the credit process is segregated according to credit function responsibilities. The segregation of duties has become a best practice application to reduce mistakes, fraud, and criminal activity, as well as to provide internal controls to sound credit risk assessment. The credit risk management strategy will also vary for different lenders based on their size and lending objectives; for example, a regional bank will have a different strategy than a large multinational bank. To illustrate how the business composition of the credit portfolio is driven by the type of credit risk management strategy, let us refer back to our original example of Citibank. Based on excerpts from its 2004 annual report, Citibank describes a credit process that "relies on corporate wide standards" that, are "grounded in a series of fundamental policies." They further explain that their credit strategy is to apply consistent credit standards on all borrowing transactions across each business unit for loan originations, assessment, and measurement. Citibank's annual report gives, as an example, the processes it uses to monitor credit risk by having "a consistent risk rating system across product lines and business segments to avoid subjective judgment by loan officers." Another example of how the bank controls credit risk is that "borrowing limits for each obligor is based on individual risk ratings and the loan maturity length." Credit risk is also controlled with "established approved lending authority and limits by requiring two credit officers to approve each transaction." The bank further responds to credit risk through the composition of its portfolio and by "ensuring that adequate capital is allocated for each of its loan facilities." According to Citibank's annual report, their credit risk management process and strategy makes risks both visible and measurable. Table 2.2, indicates that Citibank's portfolio composition is primarily related to businesses in North America and the credit risk exposure is mitigated by having a geographical scope that is globally diversified. Another indicator that supports a diversified portfolio is summarized in Table 2.3, which illustrates that the bank is not heavily concentrated in any one industry, as the most significant concentration of credit risk was to the U.S. government and its agencies in 2004. Citibank also appears to be a moderately conservative lender, as outlined in Table 2.4, with 83% of portfolio borrowers rated investment grade BBB or higher.

Although Citibank's annual report indicates a desire to have a values-driven culture in the role they want to play in the markets, the news events that unfolded during 2004 seem to have reflected an unfocused credit culture. For example, the breakdown of the

TABLE 2-2

Citibank's Portfolio Mix

	Dec 31, 2004	Dec 31, 2003
North America	42%	41%
EMEA	29%	30%
Japan	3%	3%
ASIA	15%	14%
Latin America	4%	5%
Mexico	7%	7%
Total	100%	100%

Portfolio mix: The corporate credit portfolio is geographically diverse by region. The table shows direct outstandings and unfunded commitments by region.

Source: Citibank 2004 Annual Report.

TABLE 2-3

Portfolio Credit Risk by Industry Sector

	Direct Outstandings and Unfunded Commitments	
	2004	2003
Government and central banks	10%	14%
Other financial institutions	8%	9%
Banks	7%	6%
Investment banks	6%	5%
Utilities	5%	5%
Insurance	4%	5%
Agricultural and food preparation	4%	4%
Telephone and cable	4%	4%
Petroleum	4%	3%
Industrial machinery and equipment	3%	3%
Autos	2%	3%
Freight transportation	2%	2%
Global information technology	2%	2%
Chemicals	2%	2%
Retail	2%	2%
Metals	2%	2%
Other industries	33%	29%
Total	100%	100%

Source: Citibank 2004 Annual Report, New York.

TABLE 2-4

Rated Facilities as Percent of Portfolio

	Direct Outstandings and Unfunded Commitments	
	2004	2003
AAA/AA/A	54%	54%
BBB	29%	27%
BB/B	15%	16%
CCC or below	1%	2%
Unrated	1%	1%
	100%	100%

Source: Citibank 2004 Annual Report.

Euro Treasuries market in August 2004 by members of its trading personnel, along with the dismissal of senior executives in its Asian operations for unethical practices, reflects diverse subcultures across the bank's global business units.* The response by Charles Prince, the bank's CEO, did, however, appear to support management's commitment to a disciplined credit environment. During a conference of senior executives, Mr Prince "publicly stressed the need for ethical behavior and the importance of compliance," showing "how far up the corporate agenda" these events had reached."[5] The fact however, that senior management addressed these issues indicates that top management is striving to display leadership on ethical matters. Over the long run, this should serve to filter down as part of the organization's credit philosophy and become embedded in the credit strategy and culture. At the same time, Citibank's size and global market position also exhibits elements of a production-driven credit culture, despite its diversification across industries, credit quality, geographical reach, and products. For example, in Citibank's European bond trading incident, a memo was obtained and reported that the goal was to

*Citigroup was forced to suspend operations in Japan and apologize to the Japanese government. In addition, in 2004, the bank suspended two of its senior investment banking staff in China relating to the presentation of false information for an IPO to the bank and its regulators.

capture the market as a dominant player. Although the personnel responsible for this incident were reported by the bank to have been either discharged or reprimanded, this type of behavior is indicative of a driving force to be the largest.

To better understand the framework for implementing a credit risk strategy, refer to Figure 2.17, which depicts the primary credit risk components in lending to include transaction and portfolio risk. Transaction risk is the credit risk exposure from extending a single loan asset and is incorporated into the loan portfolio as part of the cumulative portfolio risk. Transaction risk is evaluated and measured by using a risk evaluation framework that encompasses the risk assessment and risk measurement processes. It is based on specific analytical identifiers that will be discussed in Chapters 5 and 6. Identifying a loan's transaction risk is a key component in defining the credit risk strategy because it will support the lender's underwriting guidelines.

Transaction risk is also a result of the type of risk selection and facility funding that the lender undertakes. When a lender decides to book a transaction, the transaction risk exposure should be accompanied by the requisite skills sought by particular borrowers, especially those that have certain niche financing needs. An example would be an independent oil and gas company that desires a syndicated loan from a medium-sized community bank.

FIGURE 2.17

Primary Credit Risk Components

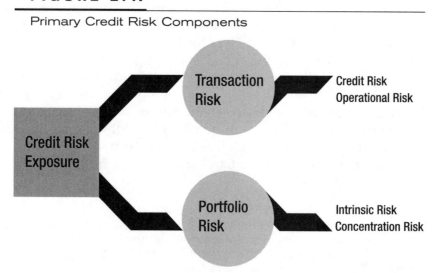

As community banks would not normally specialize in providing syndicated wholesale loans and most likely will lack the expertise to analyze a oil and gas financing request, such a transaction would not be an appropriate undertaking. If the community bank's desire were to undertake new business that included syndicated lending, it should also consider whether it is a realistic business strategy. Lenders can also become exposed to transaction risk by relying on the due diligence from the agent of a syndicated loan and by lacking the specialized in-house knowledge for complex credit products. Transaction risk can also arise from exposure to particular companies and industries, which exposes the lender to intrinsic risk. The question must be addressed how a large concentration of loans will affect the lender's portfolio if, for example, it has significant exposure to highly capital-intensive manufacturers dependent on escalating oil prices that result in increases in the volatility of their earnings. This type of intrinsic risk requires that the lender understand how a significant number of loans to one or several companies will affect the credit portfolio.

Loan transactions that are underwritten or serviced with the support of operational systems and infrastructure are exposed to operational risk, which is also an inherent part of transaction risk. Operational risk exposure can be quite significant and occurs when there is a failure by or of people, computer systems, processing, or other adverse external events. Much emphasis is now being placed on measuring the costs of operational risk that may occur from errors committed by inexperienced management or poor corporate governance standards such as lax controls, fraud, and faulty or misused technology. Greater demands are being placed on banks to provide a level of operational certainty, particularly by institutional investors who view such operational failures as that of Nick Leeson in 1999 with the collapse of Barings Bank, to expose the lender to reputational risk. The risk of damage to a financial institution's reputation has been known to result in costly litigation. The $6.25BN settlement charge, for example, by Citibank in 2003 for corporate and stock market scandals affected the bank's reputation.[6] Citibank, however, is not the sole lender affected by a damaged reputation. Some of the other banks include the Bank of America and JPMorganChase, which also financed bankrupt companies such as Enron, and experienced damage to their reputations. Although most of the lenders have reached a settlement in the Enron case, they have nonetheless expressed concern about unfair treatment regarding the legal liability exposure, because the extension of credit to Enron, for example, in their view, was based on the company's reputation itself.

A more recent area related to operational and reputation risks is the concern for security and fraud, particularly since the 2001 terrorists attacks on the World Trade Center in the United States, which have led to an increase in investment by lenders for security, technology systems, and data protection. Emphasis has also been on new initiatives to involve the financial services sector in the pursuit and capture of possible terrorists. Among the legislation that has been enacted is the USA Patriot Act, which specifically focuses on international money laundering and antiterrorism.* Regulatory requirements for data protection such as Anti-Money Laundering (AML) are now mandating that financial institutions have the requisite infrastructure and quantification tools to ensure that assets will not be mishandled due to operational failures.

The culmination of transaction risk that guides a lender's credit risk strategy is assessed and measured by its portfolio risk. Portfolio credit risk strategy is dictated by the intrinsic risk that a lender may be exposed to from a specific borrower or industry. Lenders that had significant exposure to the telecommunications industry in 2002, such as Worldcom, had intrinsic portfolio risk. As a result, their credit risk strategy subsequently required them to reduce their telecom sector exposure and increase loan loss reserves. At the same time, the credit risk strategy for lenders that had intrinsic exposure to General Motors and the cyclical automobile industry in 2005 prompted those lenders to either reduce sector exposure to those industry participants, including related firms with revenues dependent on the industry, or mitigate the risk by transferring these loans. Corresponding to intrinsic risks are concentration risks, which are the proportion of loans across asset classes and credit products (real estate, project finance, leveraged transactions, derivatives, and emerging markets). Concentration risks are also an indicator of a bank's credit risk strategy as it defines the sector limits and degree of portfolio diversification. Credit staff will usually monitor concentration risk exposures on a daily, weekly, and monthly basis, as a part of their portfolio analytical techniques.

---

*The USA Patriot Act stands for Uniting and Strengthening America Act by Providing Appropriate Tools Required to Intercept and Obstruct Terrorism.

2.12 HOW A WEAK CREDIT PROCESS CAN IMPACT THE ORGANIZATION

Despite the many reasons for banks having failed, rarely has it been without the actions, or lack thereof, of management. A common threat for many bank failures has been a lack of prudent lending practices, which have resulted from weak underwriting standards in response to competitive pressures and earnings decline. Failures have also occurred from having excessive concentration exposure levels and the application of inadequate credit processes. Whatever the many reasons for an organization's failure, the consequences reveal the ways in which senior management responded to the market challenges, by directing the institution's priorities, people, and credit processes. A review of how this can transpire is found in the classic case of Long Term Capital Management (LTCM; Case Study 2). This case serves as a primary example of how a financial entity's leadership can impact the effective functioning of the credit process.

CASE STUDY 2 LONG TERM CAPITAL MANAGEMENT (LTCM)

LTCM, under the leadership of John Meriwether, the founder, and contributing partners that included David Mullins, a former regulator, along with Robert Merton and Myron Scholes, both Nobel Peace Prize Winners, faced enormous default and credit risks by virtue of failing to appropriately manage the hedge fund's credit risk exposure. The professional credibility of the managing partners was shaken in August 1998, after LTCM came close to collapse when the market moved against an aggregate $1.3 trillion derivative position that was backed by only $4BN in hedge-fund equity assets. In a speech before the U.S. House of Representatives banking and financial services subcommittee in March 1999, the former President of the Federal Reserve Bank of New York, William J. McDonough, attributed the fiasco of LTCM to the following: "A lack of key risk management practices on three factors— "insufficient information on counterparties, exposure measurement and stress testing."*

*Statement by William J. McDonough, President, Federal Reserve Bank of New York, before the Subcommittee on Capital Markets, Securities and Government Sponsored Enterprises (GSEs) of the Committee on Banking and Financial Services, U.S. House of Representatives, March 3, 1999.

Mr McDonough went on to explain that the lack of financial information on respective counterparties resulted from the lender's inability to engage in thorough credit analysis for the types of risks to which LTCM was exposed, particularly regarding their leveraged trading positions with credit extensions to their banking counterparties. At the same time LTCM was also found to be highly leveraged, with $1 trillion in off-balance sheet derivative contracts and liabilities that were not reflected in the $125BN in balance sheet assets and $4BN capital base. Credit exposure resulted from counterparty trading positions with LTCM held by some of the largest multinational banks in the world, who had no idea about the true financial and leverage position of the firm. Being exempted from the regulatory standards that are required by most financial institutions, LTCM had not been at all transparent about the disclosure of its financial condition to bank financial counterparties. Major banks such as Credit Suisse First Boston, Bear Stearns, Merrill Lynch, UBS, and Sumitomo Bank, among others, had no mechanism in place to assess the activities of LTCM, and they loss a combined $2.2BN of aggregate exposure; nor were they aware of its leverage position and other counterparty exposures.[7]

Nor did LTCM have sufficient collateral relative to the credit exposure that it held in the different types of trading activities that it was operating. Had the credit assessment on LTCM performed by these banks been more transparent, they would have learned that the collateral held was insufficient for the leverage and counterparty exposure, as well as that their values had declined over several weeks. In addition there was the failure to perform stress testing to anticipate or evaluate the effects that could transpire from "worse-case" scenarios, particularly as it related to the respective market conditions on their Russian counterparties. Had LTCM been more knowledgeable about its concentration exposure to highly leveraged institutions, most likely different trading strategies and credit decisions would have been made relative to market and credit risks that were embedded in the trading books. "According to LTCM managers their stress tests had involved looking at the 12 biggest deals with each of their top 20 counterparties."[7] Consequently, this only produced a worst-case loss of around $3BN against the mark-to-market losses, that were estimated "just on those 240-or-so deals that might reach $5BN. And that was ignoring all other trades, some of them in highly speculative and illiquid instruments."[7] Aside from the foregoing shortcomings, the hedge fund's management had also failed to develop and implement detailed credit policies and procedures, which could have aided in either preventing or mitigating their losses.

2.13 INTEGRATED RISKS HAVE LED TO INDEPENDENT RISK MONITORS

As made evident by the near fatal collapse of Long Term Capital Management, because credit risk can reach across sovereign borders, it is also integrated into the global economy. The integration of these risks, particularly with market and operational risks is why central banks have modified capital allocation requirements to be more aligned with reality. Although the management of these risks is usually the responsibility of independent organizational functions, they have nonetheless become significant enough that lenders now organize all of their risks under the aegis of a Chief Risk Officer. This has led to the concept of Corporate and Enterprise Risk Management functions among all types of business and financial institutions. It was during the early 1990s that the banking and lending industry began to redesign their credit risk functions to include a Corporate Risk Management division that oversees the integrated risks for the entire institution. In 2001 and 2002 the industry was faced with the highest corporate default rate since the Great Depression, at which time the modern credit organization became widely accepted and the concept of group risk became central to the credit process. In addition there were expanding challenges in commercial lending that also created an increase in the volume of risks, resulting in shareholders and regulators demanding for greater accountability in responsibilities and reporting standards.

A Corporate Risk Management function is responsible for developing, communicating, and implementing the operational processes to manage an organization's risks on a global basis. In many banks, Corporate Risk Management has become a global function by region and product financing type, and overseeing the integration of the credit process has become part of the organization-wide support services for risk information standards and best practices. A factor contributing to this development has been the elevation and accountability up to the Board of Directors for the broad range of risks and potential losses that are faced by institutions. In the 2004 Global Risk Management Survey by Deloitte Touche Tohmatsu, "59% of senior financial services executives reported that overall responsibility for risk management was either managed by the board or a board-risk management committee."[8] Compared to the 2003 survey, this represented a 25% increase in board accountability for risk management. Another finding of the survey was that "81% of executives said that their firm had a Chief Risk Officer (CRO) with 75% of the CROs reporting to the CEO or the board of directors."[9] Chief Risk Officers have become equivalent to Chief Credit Officers and in some cases are more senior, and operate as the central source for enterprise risk strategies, methods, and tools that support risk management. James Lam, who is widely credited as the author of the Chief Risk Officer (CRO) concept, summarizes the role of the CRO in the following extract:

> It used to be that the CRO reported to the CFO or COO," he observes, "whereas now they more often report to the CEO. The new class of CROs is more senior and their compensation levels are higher. It wasn't long ago that the first CRO broke the seven-figure mark; now people several levels below the CRO are being offered that kind of money." Lam points out, however, that the CRO role is splitting into two distinct positions. "There are two basic models emerging. In one, the CRO is a genuine partner in business management. They play a critical role in terms of growth strategy, product strategy, M & A and so on. That job is about really integrating risk into business activities—building it into pricing, capital allocation and so on." This path is similar to that followed by the traditional market risk management function, in which firms that had developed superior market risk skills applied them to launch highly profitable businesses such as derivatives, trading and hedge funds. The other role, Lam says, is a 'chief compliance officer' who shoulders the responsibility for corporate-level reporting, operational risk and regulatory compliance. New regulations such as Sarbanes-Oxley, Basel II and a plethora of other governance and regulatory standards have raised the workload to the point that a new senior position is becoming necessary. Some of these individuals will come from audit, compliance and finance; others may be operational risk specialists.[10]

The Risk Management Guide presented in Figure 2.18, highlights the functions overseen by the CRO and provides a framework for corporate and enterprise risk management. As a separate organizational function, the office engages in risk analytics, capital and risk allocations among business units, and is also responsible for overall corporate risk policies and procedures. Business decisions such as evaluating how profitable individual business units are relative to their risks, including compensation based on personnel contributions to the profits and shareholders' value relative to the amount of overall bank capital that is consumed. Lenders now integrate their global business activities by establishing independent monitoring functions across all of their business segments, often with the approval of a Senior Risk Officer. Business units typically have clearly documented policies and procedures that detail their business strategies and risk management functions, through which accountability for risks and returns are the responsibility of the respective units. The result of integrating risks under a senior risk officer has been found to provide a basis to better manage integrated risk measurement and

FIGURE 2.18

Risk Management Guide

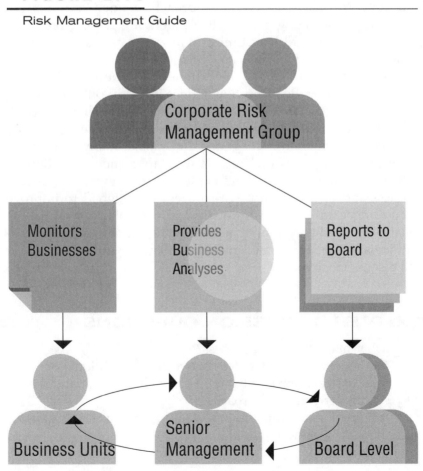

more accurately approximate and minimize regulatory capital requirements. In doing so, credit providers are better able to define and support the lending objectives, which we will discuss in Chapter 3.

2.14 CONCLUSION

The credit process is composed of the systematic operational processes and procedures that lenders require to establish sound credit granting practices. Because credit risk is inherent throughout the entire process, the nature and sources of risks have to be identified and measured to prevent losses. Many applications and techniques that are used in the credit process are derived from advances that have been made in managing credit risk under the traditional or classical credit approach. Under the modern approach of managing credit risk, lenders are relying on credit portfolio management to optimize returns and capital allocations. Although organizations will tailor their credit processes to their individual operations, the effectiveness of these practices is contingent on how the institution defines its credit philosophy and credit risk strategy. These structures will also dictate how the credit culture services and provides the extension of business credit. As risks have become more integrated and global, many institutions are incorporating a Corporate Risk Management function to oversee and manage the combination of risk exposures across business and product lines. This process is designed to improve monitoring and credit administration controls as well as to enhance the credit granting practices. Without doing this, the credit process will be weak and impact the lending objectives, as we will discuss in Chapter 3.

CHAPTER DISCUSSION QUESTIONS

1. What is the credit process?
2. Describe the differences between the traditional or classical approach to credit risk management and the modern credit approach.
3. What is the difference between credit risk assessment and credit risk measurement?

4. Distinguish the differences between the types of credit cultures that can exist in the commercial lending environment?

5. What is the purpose of concentration limits and why are they used?

6. What is the difference between the credit philosophy and the credit risk strategy?

7. How are credit organizations structured to function?

8. Describe Citibank's Credit Risk Management applications and practices?

9. Discuss the role of Credit Portfolio Management.

10. What role does the Chief Risk Officer play in the credit process and how does it differ from that of the Chief Credit Officer?

11. What is the impact of a weak credit process?

12. What elements of LTCM's credit process attributed to its collapse?

13. Distinguish between the account officer, credit specialists, and portfolio manager? What roles do each of these credit professionals play in the organization and how do they contribute to the portfolio selection process and optimizing shareholders' value.

BIBLIOGRAPHY

Allen, Sheila, "'Chief Risk Officer' No Solution." *American Banker*, 170, 24, Feb. 4, 2005, p. 11. Ante Up For Chief Risk Officers; Carol Lippert Gray, Feb. 11, 2005. www.news.careerzone.americanbanker.com

Barr Taylor, Ann and McWhorter, R.P., "Understanding and Strengthening Bank Credit Culture," The Journal of Commercial Lending, April 1992, pp. 6–11.

Beans, Kathleen M., "Effective Risk Management Is Sought by Regulators, Bondholders, and Shareholders," *The RMA Journal*, September 2001, pp. 54–56.

Blake III, Melville E., "Rethinking the Corporate Credit Process," *The Bankers Magazine*, 175, 1, Jan.–Feb. 1992, p. 28.

Citibank, *2004 Citibank Annual Report*, 2004.

Credit Research Foundation, *Analysis and Evaluation of Credit Management Functions*, Credit Research Foundation, 1953, p. 297.

Dorfman, Paul M. "A Credit Officer's Response to Revenue Pressures," *Journal of Commercial Lending*, 77, 2, Oct. 1994, p. 13(5).

Grafstrom, John, "Seven Characteristics of an Effective Credit Risk Management System and How to Test for Them," *The Journal of Lending and Credit Risk Management*, December 1996, pp. 55–60.

McKinley, John, and Barrickman John, *Strategic Credit Risk Management*, Philadelphia: Robert Morris Associates, 1994.

McKinley, John, How to Analyze Your Bank's Credit Culture, Philadelphia: Robert Morris Associates, 1990.

Morsman, Jr, Edgar M., "Defining the Credit Culture," in *Credit Culture*, Philadelphia: Robert Morris Associates, 1994, pp. 17–21.

Mueller, Henry P., "Risk Management and the Credit Culture—A Necessary Interaction," in *Credit Risk Management*, Philadelphia: Robert Morris Associates, 1995, p. 77.

Oleksiw, Irene "Legacy of the 1980s: Changes in Credit Risk Management," *The RMA Journal*, Feb. 2003, pp. 74–78.

Shirreff, David, "Lessons From The Collapse of Hedge Fund," Long-Term Capital Management. IFCI Risk Institute www.ifri.ch. pp. 136–152.

Strischek, Dev "Credit Culture: Types of Credit Cultures," *The RMA Journal*, 85, 4, Dec. 2002, p. 35.

Subcommittee on Financial Institutions Supervision, Regulation and Insurance, "Banking Industry in Turmoil," A report on the condition of the U.S. banking industry and the Bank Insurance Fund: Report of the Subcommittee on Financial Institutions Supervision, Regulation and Insurance of the Committee on Banking, Finance and Urban Affairs, U.S. G.P.O, 1990.

CHAPTER 3

Analyzing the Transaction: What are the Lending Objectives

3.1 INTRODUCTION

In this chapter we will discuss how transaction risks are incorporated into the credit portfolio during the credit selection process for new and existing transactions. We will start with an overview to how credit decisions that are linked to the lending objectives can increase shareholders' value by following certain guidelines during the preliminary loan screening process. The credit selection process is a fundamental topic to build upon for Chapter 4, where we will review some of the more common funding strategies that are used in the extension of business credit. Althouth the credit process is constructed from the top down, the origination of credit is managed with a bottom-up approach, which credit specialists must understand in selecting transaction exposures. After the credit philosophy and strategy has been explicitly defined by the Board of Directors and CEO, it should be communicated down throughout the organization as a guideline for all relevant parties to follow in credit originations. Relationship managers, in conjunction with related parties, should clearly understand the lending objectives of individual and portfolio transactions as well as for the type of business that should be sought.

3.2 THE IMPORTANCE OF CREDIT SELECTION TO INCREASING SHAREHOLDERS' VALUES

Perhaps the most significant challenge in credit risk management has traditionally been and continues to be to find a balance between credit quality and portfolio growth. This is a critical objective for lenders in order to sustain long-term profitability and to increase shareholders' value, all of which is grounded in the credit suppliers' lending objectives. Meeting these goals means that credit policies should be aligned with an organization's credit philosophy and strategy in order for the credit selection process to be consistent with credit quality. Although the originations of new credit must ultimately be considered for the effect that it will have on the aggregate portfolio, the preservation and growth of a portfolio cannot be achieved without first originating new loans that create value. A preliminary credit assessment serves to address how corporate and commercial lending objectives should ultimately capture improved portfolio returns that have a dedicated focus on credit quality. Meeting these objectives under modern credit risk requires that lenders realize intelligent growth by monitoring the profitability of bank relationships and cross-selling higher return financial products. This will also contribute to a more effective credit process in that credit risks are lowered or mitigated to increase the required returns for shareholders. Transactions that create value and yield adequate returns together with appropriate hedging strategies are the keys to extending business credit and maximizing earnings.

3.3 WHAT ARE THE LENDING OBJECTIVES

Among the lessons learned under modern credit risk management has been that emphasis on the volume of transactions to increase portfolio growth does not always coincide with a defined credit risk management strategy. Whereas classical credit placed greater emphasis on the transactional side of the business, modern credit has come to place greater accountability on account officers and how respective business units contribute to credit portfolio quality. Credit decisions should therefore be consistent with a credit process that supports portfolio risk selection and prescribe to the underwriting guidelines of the core lending objectives as well as the lenders' maximum limit system. Credit personnel must there-fore be aware of the effect that new transactions will have on the credit portfolio when originating corporate and commercial loan business. This is why, at most banks around the world, a dual approach is now being practiced in the loan origination process. Although account officers originate the business and credit specialists evaluate the risks separately, both parties, however, should agree on the terms and conditions for approval. Because transaction originations are the initial stage of the portfolio selection and monitoring process, credit decisions and extensions must be analyzed with the appropriate credit assessment and borrower due diligence. This begins with the account officer's understanding of the transaction, while also ensuring that the borrower recognizes the risks that they are assuming.

3.4 PRELIMINARY CREDIT SELECTION PROCESS FOR ANALYZING TRANSACTIONS

Credit risks that are inherent in new loan transactions initially have to be assessed before they are measured. The credit risk assessment process is derived from the financial and other borrower provided data to identify the specific risks within a new transaction. This is a core lending requirement that is usually undertaken during the preliminary credit assessment on new and existing facilities. It encompasses the execution of basic due diligence on borrowers or counterparties to evaluate their ability to repay the debt and not default on a credit agreement. Typically, there are six phases to this preliminary credit selection process that credit specialists will undertake when evaluating transactions. A general framework for this process is highlighted in Figure 3.1, which can be used by relationship managers and credit personnel to evaluate new and existing credit requests.

The first phase of the process is the assessment of a borrower's general creditworthiness. Although no single method of analysis or review will work for all of the many types of credit transactions that require borrowing needs, the essential components to examine the borrower's creditworthiness should encompass financial and nonfinancial analysis that implicitly and explicitly can assess the risks of a firm. Aside from looking at both internal and external factors, a variety of tools are used to evaluate the borrower's debt service capability; this will be discussed in Chapters 5 and 6.

3.5 FOLLOWING THE MONEY TO DETERMINE THE REPAYMENT ABILITY

The repayment ability should be established in the second phase of the credit assessment to determine from where the debt sources of

FIGURE 3.1

Evaluating A New Loan Proposal

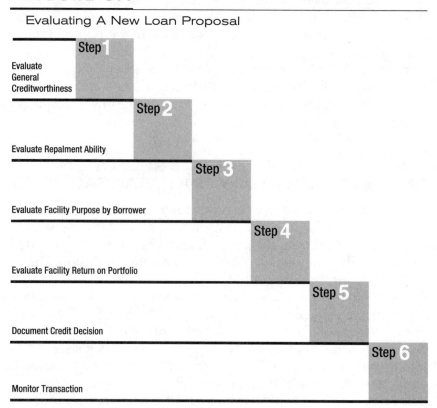

payment will be derived. To avoid having a structurally subordinated or a weaker repayment position in relation to other lenders should a default event occur, the credit specialist must fully examine the corporate ownership structure of the borrower. In general, lenders only want to extend credit to the most profitable entity of a corporate or commercial borrower. This is because lenders can become structurally subordinated to the debt claims of more senior creditors that must be repaid before the subordinate debt. However, as our example in Figure 3.2 illustrates, a loan originated to Pacific Oxygen Holdings on behalf of its operating subsidiaries for their usage can result in the lenders to the holding or parent company being structurally subordinated to the lenders of Pacific Tubing, Pacific Financial Services, and Pacific Leasing. Should bankruptcy or default occur at any subsidiary level, creditors to Pacific Holdings will only have a junior claim on the assets of the operating companies and it will be limited to the residual value of

FIGURE 3.2

What is the Company Structure?

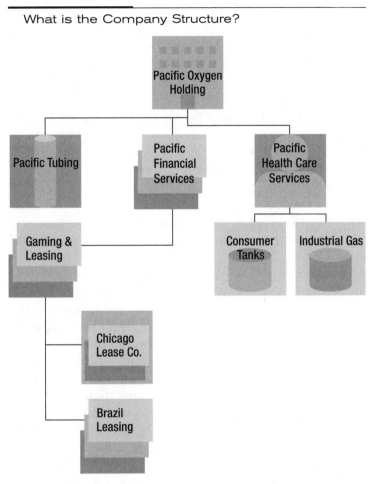

the subsidiaries assets that remains after all other direct liabilities are settled. Structural subordination can also exist when credit is extended to an unprofitable or related group entity that is dependent on the dividends or cash transfers from affiliate companies as the source of repayment. As an example, a loan extended to Pacific Financial to be repaid from the dividends of Industrial Gas can lead to structural subordination in the event of bankruptcy by the gas subsidiary. For this reason, when a parent or any of its subsidiary companies within the same group apply for separate loans, the lender must follow the money throughout the group to where the corporate assets and cash flows reside. Although the lender may naturally assume and accept from the borrower that repayment will be derived from the firm's operating cash flows or the sale of assets, nonetheless the actual source of debt repayment must still be determined and confirmed by the credit provider. Credit specialists must therefore identify whether the debt repayment in question will be derived from the borrower's operating cash flows, asset sales, and investments, or whether it will be from the lenders, stockholders, as well as other sources.

Consider the fact that most automotive companies have finance divisions and that a proposed loan request is made to extend credit to General Motors Acceptance Corporation (GMAC), the finance division of General Motors Corporation (GM). To further illustrate this with elements of realism, let's also presume that the credit request was presented prior to the company's financial woes, which ultimately led to its noninvestment downgrade in 2005. A preliminary approval is given to extend the facility to GM rather than to GMAC because the credit department concludes that the parent company, GM, owns all of GMAC's equity stock. Although in theory this strategy may sound logical, the question then becomes how well protected is the lender for repayment in the event of default? If the finance division and therefore the parent company starts to have real financial difficulty and becomes forced into bankruptcy, how well protected will a lender be under these conditions? Despite the fact that at this point GM has not yet declared bankruptcy, the estimated $850MM first quarter loss that was reported in February 2005, in conjunction with an existing $2BN cash flow deficit, was followed by higher interest spreads on the cost of debt, and fueled investors to start selling off the company's bonds. Note that at the time, the finance division was GM's most profitable operating entity and the one on which GM had come to rely for it's profits and dividends in order to contribute to its deteriorating financial situation. Under this scenario, the parent company's ownership of subsidiary stock is suddenly not worth as much to the bank as the actual cash flows of the finance division. By having extended the loan to the parent company, the lender has now become structurally subordinated at the same time that the value of its stock has declined. The point to emphasize here, however, is that the preliminary credit selection must follow the money within a corporate group entity to where the borrowed funds will ultimately be disbursed. The lender should determine from which entity are the cash flows to be derived and whether the borrower is a holding company, an operating company, or a

TABLE 3 - 1

Priority of Debt Rankings

Debt secured with higher quality operating asset collateral
Debt secured with lesser quality operating asset collateral
Senior debt of the operating company
Senior liabilities (rank pari passu with senior debt)
Subordinated debt
Junior subordinated debt
All other operating company liabilities
Senior debt of the holding company
Subordinated debt of the holding company

subsidiary company, so that potential mitigating factors can be emphasized in the loan structure.

In general, structural subordination for subordinated and unsecured creditors is the result of how a credit facility is structured. A summary of debt priority rankings, as highlighted in Table 3.1, details that in the event of a default, the senior debt is always repaid first on the interest, maturity, and amortization of the borrowing entity. The lender to the borrowing entity that is structurally considered to be the subsidiary operating company based on its geographic location and other legal considerations will have the priority of claims, which gives it superior access to the assets and cash flows for repayment. The senior debt must be repaid in full prior to repayment of the subordinated debt, thereby making the term of the senior debt ahead of all other claims. In practice there is usually an intercreditor agreement that is used in advance of a default situation to clearly establish priorities of payment in a default situation along with the mechanisms and procedures. Despite structural mechanisms such as cross-default clauses or cross-acceleration provisions, whereby default on one debt can affect all other forms of debt, senior secured lenders are afforded significant negotiating power in the loan documentation by virtue of the importance that they provide borrowers with liquidity under distressed scenarios. Bondholders, for example, are often significantly impaired in liquidation scenarios compared to lenders, because debt restructurings ultimately tend to rely more heavily on lenders than on bondholders. This is attributed to the fact that access to bond markets is lower for credit defaults over the near term. Among syndicated loans, many of the major providers of finance to a borrower or issuer will often have exposure to each layer of financing, beginning at the senior level and continuing through to equity holders. Although equity holders usually have the most disadvantaged position in a liquidation situation, they can also have one of the strongest positions in restructurings. If the lender happens to have both a debt and equity position, they can use the workout process to their advantage, because the hope will be for them to inject additional funds into a bankrupt company. Prior to taking credit risk in a transaction, lenders should consider who the equity providers are in the preliminary credit selection and whether or not they have deep pockets in the event of default. Consideration may also be given as to what are the objectives of the equity investors and whether or not they have a different agenda from that of the lender. If the only interest is to take the money and run, which is often typical for senior secured lenders, how will the structure of the facility in the event of default impact the lenders' risk of credit loss and credit portfolio returns. Although restructurings require the agreement of all parties, they are usually a preferred liquidation route for all parties other than the senior secured lender because it usually results in more cash being injected into a firm.

Another issue related to structural subordination and debt monitoring that must also be determined is the quality of assets at each of a corporate borrower's operating divisions or, in the example that we have been using, the corporate assets of GM. What controls, if any, will the lender have on the source of repayment inclusive of security and collateral needs to be known in order to mitigate the credit risk exposure. The lenders' ranking in terms of the security and collateral must also be verified to identify its priority to repayment compared to other creditor claims. Although these risks can be mitigated depending on how the facility is structured, a benchmark that lenders have used in evaluating security and collateral is to give a higher credit rating and better loan pricing to a weak subsidiary that is owned by a strong parent, rather than to rate and price the credit as if it were an independent entity. Alternatively, a strong subsidiary that is owned by a weak parent is rated no higher than the parent, who could raid a subsidiary's corporate assets and cash flows if it was faced with financial trouble. In fact, prior to GM's noninvestment downgrade in May 2005, there was much speculation among many within the banking and financial community that the proposal by GM to sell off portions of GMAC was very much an example of this. After announcing its estimated first quarter losses in February 2005, General Motors subsequently announced that it would be undertaking significant restructuring efforts.[1] Several factors prevailed that led management to make this decision. One, the reported losses excluded additional charges that the company had incurred from its declining market share, as a result of high labor, production, healthcare, and pension costs that far exceeded its nonunion Japanese competitors.* Added to this was the revised ratings outlook on the company from stable to negative, with Standard & Poor saying that "it might lower GM's rating to junk status," while Fitch downgraded the company from BBB to BBB−.[2] Subsequently, the proposal by GM to sell off portions of GMAC as part of its restructuring efforts sparked laughter among a number of creditors and investors, because, in their opinion, the value of the subsidiary was no higher than the parent itself. A chief critic of this proposal was the CNBC television talk show host Jim Cramer, who basically described the proposal as a joke in his daily "Wall Street, Main Street—Mad Money" television program. Cramer, however, was not alone in his view, as he was supported by callers who phoned into the show to agree with this opinion. Shortly thereafter, GM sought to obtain a split rating for GMAC separate from its own in order to mitigate the risk exposure that it faced on its long-term funding strategies. Although GM may have the last laugh if the proposed $1.3BN purchase of 60% of GMAC's mortgage operations becomes finalized, the point to again emphasize is how relevant are security and collateral issues if the credit is now extended to GM or any failing corporate entity.† Nonetheless this example with GM illustrates that the extension of credit to the automotive or a related corporate sector can have greater credit risk exposure, which may not improve in the near future.

---

*In the first quarter of 2005, GM made a $2BN settlement with FIAT SpA, the Italian industrial group, for a dispute related to an options contract purchased by GM to acquire an interest in the company. The company also had write-offs from the restructuring of its European operations as a result of loss of market share and sales decline.

†A proposal by private equity investors was put forth by a consortium consisting of Kohlberg Kravis Roberts, Goldman Sachs Capital, and Five Mile Capital. The deal will allow GMAC to expand after being limited by access to capital due to GM's credit rating.

3.5.1 Can the Lender Monitor and Control Repayment

Lenders must also assess their ability to monitor and control the credit as well as exert influence over the credit relationship given that the complexity of security and collateral issues can eventually lead to difficulties. Credit quality for each corporate division must be fully assessed by lenders to determine whether a parent–subsidiary relationship is too complex to monitor. The decision by GE Capital (the financing arm and subsidiary of General Electric Corporation), in March 2005, to terminate its $2BN credit facility to GM after news broke that the automaker was subject to being downgraded, did not reflect confidence about their ability to monitor and control the facility that had been extended. Reports by GE Capital were that its decision was attributed to a clause in the loan agreement that allowed it to cancel the debt in the event of a credit downgrade. Still others questioned why the borrowing relationship for a major industrial firm was not considered in lieu of the facility termination, and thought that it said much about GM's declining credit quality and the market perceptions that followed. Although the cancelled facility that GM had used to provide financing for suppliers was subsequently replaced by GMAC as the new debt provider, it nonetheless placed increased costs and liquidity pressures on GMAC at the time the parent sought to sell it off in portions.

3.5.2 Control of Collateral and Security

Similar to the situation for monitoring and controling a credit facility, it is also important to note where, if applicable, the collateral and security may reside. For example, if the loan is to be collateralized by security that resides offshore in another country where the lender may have no jurisdiction or legal claims, the lending strategy and initial assessment must therefore consider how to best protect and minimize credit exposure. Suppose, for example, that Comerica, a regional U.S. bank headquartered in Detroit, Michigan, has a credit facility with GMAC, which is secured by a lien on the subsidiary operating cash flows, but that the loan is also used by GM for subsidiary operations in China. In this case, because the borrower is in the same jurisdiction as the lender, the country risk exposure would be minimal. The credit specialist should certainly assess how China's political, legal, and economic issues relative to GM's foreign direct investment in the country will affect repayment of the particular credit facility. However, relevancy of these issues now becomes slightly mitigated by the fact that the borrower and credit facility is extended onshore, as well as by how the facility may be structured. Under this condition, the credit risk may be limited to the amount of the debt facility and secured by the cash flows of the subsidiary as the primary source of repayment. Alternatively, if the credit facility is extended to GM China as the borrower, the lender would then have country risk exposure to the loan because both the borrower and debt provider would now reside in different legal jurisdictions. If the facility is collateralized by the offshore borrower's operating cash flows or, in our example, with GM China, the assets would then be considered to be a secondary repayment source. Although primary sources of repayment can consist of both onshore and offshore corporate cash flows, lenders usually prefer onshore cash flows as the primary repayment sources, because there is greater control of security when assets reside onshore. In addition, secondary sources of repayment are also usually derived from the borrowers' balance sheet as well as from corporate and personal assets. This could increase credit risk exposure on a loan facility in which GM China was the borrower, if a host country placed restrictions on the amount of funds that GM was able to repatriate out of China and back into the U.S. home country.

A strategy that the credit personnel might consider in the control of collateral and security is to require GMAC as the borrower to guarantee the facility for GM. Although guarantees have ultimately been known in many instances to be a source of "cold comfort," in general, if the borrowing relationship is profitable and the credit is extended for relationship purposes, the credit specialist could determine this to be a more appropriate structure because the assets of the business are at the subsidiary level. The main point, however, in originating and assessing the transaction is to ensure that a credit extension will not become exposed to a loss for the lender.

The above principle should similarly be considered when a single investor or family controls a group of companies, relative to where the funds will ultimately be disbursed. Controlling shareholders have been known to move cash and assets among various related companies at the banks expense. Adelphia Communications Corporation in 2002 was such an example, when the founder John Rigas and his sons were accused of using $3.1BN of bank debts that were disguised as off-balance sheet corporate loans for personal family purposes. Another well-known case for raiding cash and corporate assets is currently pending against the former CEO and founder of Hollinger International (the Canadian publishing entity), Conrad Black. In 2003, Black, along with several other company shareholders, was accused of systematically looting the firm of over $400MM in payments in unjustified management fees and personal expenses.

3.6 WHAT IS THE PURPOSE OF THE FUNDS

The third stage in the credit process is to examine the exact purpose for which the borrower will use the funds. Simply because a borrower requests funding does not imply automatic approval. This becomes even more prevalent for small- and medium-sized firms where credit is often more limited than it is for large corporations. Although the majority of loans, on average, are usually for additions to current assets and working capital requirements, the specific purpose of the funds may actually be for emergency payroll or to pay overdue suppliers. However, to accept without evidence that the loan will be used for working capital purposes exposes the lender to significant credit risk, particularly if the facility proceeds are otherwise used to support operating losses. Also, the funds may be used for fraud or some other illegal purpose. Trade scams such as those that were linked to ABN Amro in December 2005, where shell companies were used as conduits to smuggle illegally generated cash, can also open banks to serious compliance violations.*

The purpose and type of facility a borrower requests also may not be the most appropriate credit product to service the obligor's needs. Medium and small companies may not always be aware of the borrowing risks behind certain credit requests and can therefore benefit from the guidance of relationship managers in these matters. Although large corporations are staffed with personnel knowledgeable in the varying loan products, smaller firms may not always know about the appropriate debt products available for their funding needs. A critical question that any account officer should ask when a loan request is made is "For what purpose will the facility be used?" Having a clear understanding of the purpose will also contribute to evaluating the company's repayment ability.

---

*ABN Amro is a top European Bank based from the Netherlands, which has been accused of criminal violations by the U.S. government for allegedly transferring billions of dollars into the United States for shell companies, with little scrutiny of who was moving the funds and for what purposes.

3.7 IS THE PRICE OF THE FACILITY ADEQUATE FOR PORTFOLIO RETURNS

Given the nature of the industry in which financial intermediaries now operate, the extension of credit in corporate banking, particularly loans, has become a low-margin business that requires lenders to define how loan assets will benefit the overall portfolio. Consequently, the price of credit facilities must be considered in the fourth phase of the preliminary approval and credit risk assessment. Under classical credit risk, the lack of pricing transparency for the cost of maintaining unprofitable bank relationships contributed to the decline in bank profitability. In addition, rudimentary mechanisms were used in pricing that made it difficult to measure profitability and price facilities that otherwise should have been declined. The growth of the primary syndicated and secondary trading markets, however, brought to the attention of banks the need for credit pricing strategies that could accurately measure performance and profitability of new transactions on the portfolio. This was also aided by the entry of nonbank financial investors, which forced the corporate and commercial banking sector to move away from interest margin pricing towards the practice of transaction pricing. Besides providing a consistent measurement to reflect the risks undertaken on a risk-adjusted basis, transaction pricing also became essential to increase overall bank earnings in order to improve the investment by shareholders.

As modern credit risk management techniques continue to be integrated into financial institutions worldwide, lenders now apply pricing based on risk-adjusted performance measures such as RAROC (risk adjusted return on capital). Additional tools that are also being used include the application of default models in individual risk ratings. Although the topic of pricing will be further discussed in Chapter 9, the point is that, with loan margins having averaged over the prior five years at most around 25 basis points above the lender's cost of funds, adequate returns on capital for margin pricing could not have been earned. Because credit continues to be the greatest risk for financial institutions, the primary reason that loans are still extended is for relationship purposes. Thus, a distinction of modern credit risk is that relationships have to be profitable as well as viable and therefore priced accordingly. Many account officers have found it difficult to separate themselves from the borrowing relationships while also practicing transactional pricing appropriately. This is why, in some banks, credit portfolio managers also participate in loan originations in order to ensure that transactions earn risk-adjusted returns and do not erode portfolio growth. Because portfolio transaction pricing is also based on a credit culture that recognizes the advantage in this practice, the credit culture should clearly understand pricing to be inclusive of the credit mission and strategy. New transactions must therefore be evaluated for their profitability relative to the income of the borrowing relationship as well as to allocate the minimum capital requirements.

3.8 THE CREDIT APPLICATION AND REQUEST

The fifth phase in the preliminary approval process is to document for review and use by the credit organization a proposed credit request that can be referred to as part of the approval decision. As we discussed in Chapter 2, depending on the organization's loan approval structure, credit personnel may be authorized to approve transactions based on seniority within limits, amount, and collateral value. Alternatively, the credit request can be submitted and recommended to higher management authority, or presented to a Loan Committee to decide on whether the credit should be approved, declined, or approved on specified conditions. Although the particular format for documenting and recommending proposed credit requests may differ among financial institutions, it generally should include a summary of the facility characteristics along with all of the risks and mitigating factors relevant to the transaction and portfolio credit exposure.

Decisions to approve a facility transaction should also be accompanied by any supporting data (e.g., projection and stress testing, business plan provided by the borrower, and so on), along with the terms and conditions for extending the loan. The clarity and detail in a credit memorandum is also essential for loan monitoring and regulatory reviews. Furthermore, account officers should be aware of the consequences and legalities in minimizing risks. Lender liability has become quite prevalent, with higher credit risk exposure for what some investors perceive to be a failure by financial intermediaries to undertake the appropriate due diligence and credit assessment on approving transactions. JPMorgan for example, was forced to agree to repay $2BN to settle a Worldcom investor lawsuit after investors claimed it did not perform a thorough due diligence before underwriting the stock and bond issuance on behalf of the U.S. telecommunications firm. The bank chose to settle the case after a December 2004 ruling by the judge stating that the "underwriters would need to show that they had conducted a 'reasonable investigation' before under-writing the securities."[3] This settlement by JPMorgansChase was preceded by Citibank's $2.65BN settlement in May 2004, after CEO Chuck Prince stated that the potential liabilities without settling could have been a $54BN payout.[4]

3.9 MONITORING AND SERVICING THE TRANSACTION

Finally, if the facility is approved, the credit must be subsequently administered by ongoing monitoring of the borrower's performance and industry trends. Credit facilities should always be reviewed on an annual basis to include site visits, interviews, and verification of covenant compliances. Many banks find that, if the borrower is highly rated and is meeting its loan obligations, then annual loan monitoring should be sufficient. However, as has been seen with Enron and Worldcom, for example, this may not always be the best practice for detecting any changing credit qualities. Banks that do have ongoing and continuing monitoring processes in place such as quarterly covenant compliance checks, industry competitor reviews, and that follow newspaper and trade journal updates, are in the best position to monitor their portfolios.

3.10 CONCLUSION

The preliminary credit selection process is the initial qualitative practice that credit organizations should undertake prior to proposing new or existing transactions. It exhibits that the credit organization understands the lending objectives and knows that they are essential to increase shareholders' value along with overall lending profitability. Although we have used the current situation with the U.S. automaker General Motors as an example to the concerns that credit specialists must consider, the preliminary credit selection process must begin by making an initial assessment of the borrower's general creditworthiness. It should be noted, however, that because this process is known to be, more often than not, purely a matter of judgment, the degrees of bias that it may contain have been the basis for credit risk measurement practices, which will be discussed in Chapter 7. Next is the concern for the ability to repay the debt and how the lender can protect itself from structural subordination. The ability to monitor and control debt repayment must also be addressed, especially as it relates to collateral and security matters. The purpose and use of the funds must also be evaluated to ensure that the lender will not be contributing to operating losses or other fraudulent means. Pricing the facility on a risk-adjusted basis is important for credit quality and overall portfolio growth. The findings of the preliminary credit assessment should therefore be placed in a proposed credit request and application, for which the credit organization will use in risk measurement and other tasks. Among these tasks will be monitoring and servicing the transaction throughout the life of the facility, which will be dependent on the funding strategy that is structured. This will be the topic of Chapter 4.

CHAPTER DISCUSSION QUESTIONS

1. What are the six steps in a typical loan approval process?
2. When extending credit, what are the objectives of the loan officer, credit specialist, and credit organization?
3. Why is it important to document the credit proposal in a credit memorandum?
4. You are engaged in a credit assessment and preliminary loan approval process. The assessment is for a long-established consumer products company that cooperates in a mature market, producing detergents and soaps globally, and wants to diversify its product line. The credit request is to purchase equipment to expand into herbal health products, which is a new sector in which the company has not previously been involved. The product is intended to be manufactured in Mexico, and will include new and previously untested technology. The client is looking for 100% financing and wants the borrower to be a newly established special purpose vehicle that will be secured by the new entity's assets and cash flows. The facility will also be unsupported by the parent company and

extended on a stand-alone basis. Would you approve or decline the preliminary loan approval? If so, for what reason?

5. A Korean construction firm and subsidiary is operating in the United States on behalf of its Korean parent which is rated BBB− by both Moodys and S & P rating agencies. The subsidiary approaches the lender regarding financing for entry into the NAFTA (North American Free Trade Agreement) construction market. The firm approaches the lender for a project finance facility to build a chemical plant in Mexico that will be government-owned and -operated. The firm has no experience in constructing a chemical plant, although it does have several long-term chemical purchase agreements with global pharmaceutical suppliers. According to the purchase contract, the primary source of revenue is expected to be derived from a new research chemical that the entity will produce and be used in a new cancer drug. The borrower has the support of its Korean parent, along with the Mexican government, who will also be funding 25% of the project costs, including providing the land and labor for the project. Although the construction entity has experience in several major road construction projects in the United States, it does not have experience in constructing and operating chemical plants and this will be the first time it is undertaking such a project. Based on the above, what have you already determined in your preliminary loan approval and credit assessment process and why?

6. Pacific Holdings is a diversified conglomerate that has rapidly expanded over the past five years. In 2004, the company reported earnings of $2BN, with net income of $850MM and a market capitalization of $4.5BN. Pacific has various subsidiaries that operate in a range of sectors including health services, leasing, and tubing, among others. The holding company needs a $2BN revolving credit line, which will be used to provide working capital for its various operating subsidiaries. Pacific has pledged the equity stock in each of the operating subsidiaries from which it states that repayment will also be derived from the dividends that

are upstreamed to the holding firm. Prior relationship with the borrower has been good, but limited to only hedging products for swaps and foreign exchange. Although the corporate structure of the holding company has always been obscure, you notice in your credit assessment that Pacific Holdings derives all of its revenues from the operating divisions. Would you extend or decline the preliminary loan approval?

7. An apparel manufacturer want to borrower $25MM for the purpose of financing fabric, with only the personal guarantee of the owner as collateral. What would be the probable primary and secondary sources of repayment and the potential credit risks to approve this credit request?

8. Suppose you are the credit officer reviewing a credit proposal for a noncollateralized $10MM overdraft facility that is stated will be used to formalize an outstanding overdraft. What is our preliminary assessment of the facility and what, if any, additional information would you like to have?

BIBLIOGRAPHY

Berger, and Harris S. Gearin, William F., Due diligence: two important words for all those who wear the white hats, *RMA Journal*, 87, 2, Oct. 2004, p. 39, article A123561384.

Caouette, John B., Altman, Edward I. and Narayanan, Paul, *Managing Credit Risk, The Next Great Financial Challenge*, Canada. John Wiley & Sons, Inc. 1998.

Dahiya, S., Puri, M. and A. Saunders, "Bank Borrowers and Loan Sales: New Evidence on the Uniqueness of Bank Loans," *Journal of Business*, 76, 4, 2003.

James, C. and Smith, D, "Are Banks Still Special? New Evidence in the Corporate Capital-Raising Process," *Journal of Applied Corporate Finance*, 13, 2000, p. 52–63.

Simpson, Glenn R., "How Top Dutch Bank Plunged Into World of Shadowy Money; ABN Amro Conveyed Billions To U.S. Shell Companies Amid Slow Fed Response," *Wall Street Journal*, December 30, 2005, p. 1.

Toub, Styder, "GM Seeks Separate Rating for GMAC," Stephen Taub, May 12, 2005, CFO.com.

Company Funding Strategies

4.1 INTRODUCTION

Preliminary loan approval and credit risk assessment of new transactions, which was discussed in Chapter 3, must also be evaluated for the particular type of credit product to be extended to support the borrower's funding needs. In this chapter we will discuss some of the common funding strategies that companies use to finance their current operations and support future growth. Our focus will be to emphasize some of the more common types of credit facilities that credit specialists should be familiar with, along with a brief description on the analytical techniques that are used to evaluate related transaction credit requests. Under classical credit risk management, financial service firms often segmented credit specialists into categories for loans, equity, and fixed-income analysts. The rationale was that the market required uniquely contrasting specialized assessment skills for each of these credit sectors. However, the advanced applications that have been developed under modern credit risk management have led to credit specialists having to assess a broad range of debt transactions that are structured to encompass all aspects of corporate finance. As deregulation has eroded the protection that had traditionally been afforded commercial banks and other financial entities, credit specialists should have a general familiarity with the products that have converged into the loan and trading books. This chapter will provide an introductory understanding of the funding strategies and analytical techniques used in their assessment, as well as serve as a foundation to build upon for Chapters 5 and 6.

Although a company's credit demands will typically be a function of its primary funding needs, the types of credit products available to service these needs are normally classified according to their short-, medium-, and long-term maturity structures. To meet the funding strategies for commercial and corporate business, lenders have a range of credit products that they provide to service cash flow, asset conversion, or refinancing needs. In the next section, we will begin our discussion of these strategies by highlighting how companies use short-term funding products for asset conversion needs.

4.2 SHORT-TERM FUNDING PRODUCTS

Among the common types of products that are used to meet a company's asset conversion needs are trade finance lines of credit, asset-based lines of credit, demand, and revolving lines of credit. These short-term debt products are typically used to finance seasonal inventory and temporary working capital needs for up to eighteen months or less. **Asset Conversion Loan Products** are used to finance the production of inventories into finished goods that will eventually be sold. These facilities are also referred to as commercial credit lines to support the acquisition of inventory. To maintain adequate inventories while also incurring ongoing operational expenses oftentimes can result in a firm mistiming cash flows. Companies will use asset conversion loans to support such cash-flow deficiencies in order to maintain operations until the goods are produced, then sold, and ultimately receive payment in the form of cash. In addition to financing inventory increases, seasonal business cycles must also be financed, by which the nature of a firm's operations can lead to having a concentration of sales during certain times of the year. This is most often the case, for example, with retailers, who tend to report their fiscal year ending in March rather than in December, as sales tend to be higher during holiday seasons than at any other times of the year.

An example of how manufacturing and merchandising firms finance their business cycles is illustrated in Figure 4.1. The company orders raw materials to produce a final product, which leads to the creation of an account payable. If the borrower is a manufacturer, it can take time before the product is finally converted into the finished good, although during the interim of the production process, the materials are considered to be work-in-progress.

FIGURE 4.1

Financing the Business Cycle

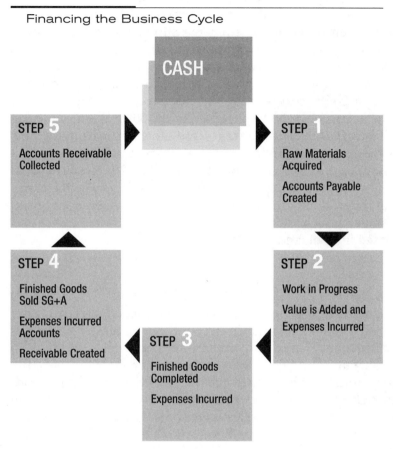

Source: LPC

The value that is being added to the product at this point does not preclude the company from continuing to incur the costs of labor, overhead, and other expenses. However, once production for the final product is completed, all of the expenses related to that item become incorporated into the cost of the finished goods. Because the finished goods are usually sold on account, the manufacturer will most likely incur an accounts receivable. It is only when the account receivable is collected in the form of cash that the manufacturer's business cycle is completed. The manufacturer therefore needs to ensure that it has sufficient cash flows to meet its out-of-pocket costs between the time it pays for the raw materials and the time that it receives the cash payment. Suppose a swim suit manufacturer were to place an order to buy fabric that will be used to produce the upcoming summer season swim suit line. The company receives the fabric from the supplier and has 30 days from the receipt of the order to pay for the goods. The invoice is paid according to the terms of the contract in 30 days. At this point, the company is out of cash. It takes 50 days to complete production and another 20 days to ship the finished product to the customer and issue an invoice, which is not paid until 100 days after ordering the raw materials. Excluding wages and other costs, from the time it pays for the fabric to the time payment is received, the manufacturer is out of pocket for cost of goods sold for 70 days. The most common types of funding requirements that will service the firm's ongoing operations during this period are asset conversion loans, among which are included trade or commercial finance and asset-based lines of credit.

4.2.1   Trade Finance Lines of Credit

Trade Credit is probably the most common short-term asset conversion product to finance account receivables. Firms need commercial bank loans and other traditional debt products to ensure that sufficient financial resources are available to meet daily working capital needs. Commercial lenders extend trade finance lines of credit by establishing credit limits that the firm can draw down on and repay at a prearranged date. If a borrower with a $2,000,000 trade finance credit line, for example, draws down $500,000 for three months, there will still be $1,500,000 available of the unused loan commitment that can be drawn upon until the full $2,000,000 is fully drawn. Borrowers purchase inventory or supplier goods with interim financing for a predetermined number of days until it is repaid (30, 60, 90, and in certain cases 120 days). The credit funds extended to purchase goods from suppliers represent cash to borrowers that does not have to be repaid before a stated due date. Multinational banks such as Hong Kong Shanghai Bank (HSBC) offer a comprehensive range of trade finance credit facilities as part of their niche product brand, which are tailored to respective geographic regions and local borrowing needs. Niche market lenders such as these cater to businesses that use trade credit for export or import financing as well as export credits. Trade credit is also provided by various industry manufacturers as a specialized lending and supplier service. Automotive companies, such as General Motors Corporations, for example, offer trade credit to the dealers that distribute and sell car products through their finance subsidiaries, as we discussed in Chapter 3 for the case of GMAC.

4.2.2 Commercial Credit Lines (L/Cs)

Letters of Credit (L/Cs), which are also referred to as commercial credit lines, are one of the oldest forms of trade finance to guarantee payment to a beneficiary on behalf of borrowers for goods or services. "The L/C beneficiary is normally a third party or another bank customer for a stated period of time and contingent upon certain conditions being met."[1] For example, consider that a letter of credit is issued on behalf of a lending customer to an overseas exporter. When the goods are received by the importer and the terms of the sale are complete, the exporter is paid the amount that is due and the bank now has credit exposure to the importer. Although L/Cs are more often used to finance international trade transactions, they are not limited to this and are also used for domestic financing needs. For example, a **standby letter of credit** is a contingent future obligation of the issuing bank to a designated beneficiary if the customer fails to perform as required under the terms of a contract. Many nonbank corporate suppliers who extend trade credit will often require that companies open standby letters of credit that can be called on in the event of default by the bank's customer. Unlike a commercial L/C, which backs the customer's normal operating acquisition of inventory, standby L/Cs usually back transactions, which if drawn upon are typically considered to be a secondary repayment source. In extending this facility, the bank is typically helping the borrower obtain favorable financing terms from suppliers, and will be obligated to repay the supplier if the borrowing customer defaults.

4.2.3 Bankers Acceptances (BAs)

Bankers Acceptances (BAs) are short-term investment vehicles or time drafts that nonfinancial firms draw upon and banks guarantee. A BA is often used by commercial businesses that are also involved in international trade transactions. Sellers of the goods will draw a trade draft on the buyer for the amount of the transaction. Typically, an importer will present the BA to the bank for acceptance; the bank will subsequently discount it by giving the importer less than the face value. The importer will then use the proceeds to pay the supplier or exporter for the goods and the bank will either hold the BA or resell it in the secondary market. Buyers and sellers can also draw drafts on their behalf or arrange pre-export financing for firm contracts. The BA is normally due within 180 sight or 180 days from the "bill of lading" date. The bill of lading is a term used by shipment companies that indicates when the merchandise is placed on board the ship. Once the buyer accepts the BA by agreeing to pay the terms at maturity, the facility then becomes a trade acceptance. When the draft is submitted to a bank that is willing to accept the credit exposure on the buyer's name, the bank accepts the draft and, for a fee, will then become the "Banker Acceptance" of the facility. At maturity, the bank will pay the draft and be reimbursed by the drawee or buyer. At this point, because the draft is an unqualified obligation of the accepting bank, it can be discounted in the market to provide liquidity for the seller at the discounted rate based on the quality of the lender's name and reputation.

Highly rated drafts are often sold in the money markets for open market purchases. Companies rated noninvestment grade or speculative and unable to access the commercial paper market also use BAs in the money markets for short-term funding purposes. In addition, when little is known about a foreign trade partner, for a fee, a BA can serve to guarantee payment by the bank. Because they do not have to be held to maturity, BAs are often sold at discounts over their face values, which contributes to an active secondary market.

4.2.4 Credit Assessment

The analysis and assessment process for asset conversion or trade finance facilities typically should focus on evaluating the financial projections to ensure that they demonstrate there are sufficient cash flows to support the expansions in inventory, sales, and receivables. Lenders want to determine that peak funding needs coincide with the time the company uses the funds as well as the extent that inventory is relied upon to support the extension of credit. Seasonal short-term working capital transactions should also focus on cash flow projections along with the firm's working capital cycle.

4.3 ASSET-BASED LINES (ABL) OF CREDIT

Asset-Based Lines of Credit has undergone significant changes over the past two decades as a result of securitization. Historically, under classical credit, ABL was a form of structured finance for large corporate borrowers, but has since come to be widely used by small and middle market borrowers under modern credit. Companies in an array of industries and at varying stages of their lifecycles now use asset-based loans for a multitude of reasons, as detailed in Table 4.1

When asset-based lines of credit are extended, they in effect enable borrowers to monetize their balance sheet assets in order to expedite the cash collections of their account receivables. Consequently, asset-based loans have become a predominant credit product that is offered by both bank and nonbank financial service companies. According to the Commercial Finance Association, ABL more than tripled from $117BN in 1994 to over $362BN by 2004. The growth in this credit product is attributed to the advantages that it offers compared to the traditional cash flow funding strategies. Unlike cash flow loans that usually have restrictive covenants placed in their lending agreements and are based on the borrower's operating performance, ABL primarily emphasizes the borrower's balance sheet assets and also serves to provide greater funding liquidity to the borrowing firm.

Typically, an ABL is extended as a revolving line of credit that is based on a borrowing based formula, which normally is derived from multiplying a factor by a specific value of accounts receivables

TABLE 4-1

Typical Uses of Asset-Based Finance

Enhanced Growth	Fuel Expansion	Leverage Capital markets	Solidity Performance
Capital expenditure needs	M & A	Refinance recapitalization	Turnaround
	Leverage buyout	Stock repurchase	Debtor-in-possession
Working capital needs	Geographical product expansion	Dividends	Exit financing
High organic growth			

Source: Bank of America, April 2006.

and inventory. An example would be a customer who advances against a portion (less than 90 days) of their accounts receivable up to a maximum of 85% and up to a maximum of 50% of the raw materials or finished goods that make up their inventory. Lenders tend not to advance against work in process, as the goods are harder to liquidate in the event of a customer's default, although this can vary by company as well as by the respective borrower's industry. The users of ABL are diverse in industry sectors and often include manufacturers, wholesalers, and retailers. Firms that use these credit lines include businesses experiencing rapid growth and require financing that is too large to extend under traditional lines of credit. The companies may also be small, start-up firms that are thinly capitalized but have high-quality assets, as well as companies in cyclical industries. Asset-based lines to small-and medium-sized firms such as the latter are often associated with moderate- to high-risk profile borrowers. These borrowers, however, could also have a high sales volume that limits their growth due to insufficient working capital and cash reserves. Although many of these firms are highly leveraged with erratic or marginal profitability, depending on a given volume of sales and business operations, the borrowers can realize sustaining growth with an appropriate asset-based line of credit. The accounts receivables and inventories financed by these lines are generally collateralized by the borrower's merchandise along with other company assets. Given that these facilities are considered to have a complex financing structure that requires the securitization of the company's assets, they tend to have a higher degree of transaction risk, which requires appropriate internal controls of the collateral by the lender.

The ABL can also be structured as a multi-featured facility to include a secured term loan, for example, on the firm's fixed assets such as machinery, equipment, or real estate, as well as intangible assets such as intellectual property or trade names. Another structural feature that has become increasingly common in the use of these products is what is known as a second lien loan, which also serves to provide enhanced liquidity for borrowers. A second lien loan on an ABL extends credit on the 10 to 20% excess collateral value that has already been calculated on the original borrowing base at a discount. Due to the demand by hedge funds and institutional investors, second lien loans have become a preferred funding strategy, with an increase in volume from $0.57BN in 2002 to $16.3BN in 2005.[2]

4.3.1   Credit Analysis and Assessment

Asset-based lenders therefore need to be skilled in effectively structuring and underwriting as well as ensuring that liens are properly perfected on a borrower's internal operations. Along with analyzing the working capital cycle time that is required to convert assets into cash, the credit analysis should also focus on the quality and liquidity position of a company's assets. Given that ABLs are a common funding strategy among niche industry firms such as medical equipment companies, for example, the credit assessment may furthermore require specialized industry or leasing skills. In addition, the projections should specify that sufficient assets are available under the maximum drawdown of the line as the source of the primary repayment. The projections should also demonstrate evidence that the borrower has sufficient working capital available for all obligations, including the ability to meet interest costs.

4.4   CASH FLOW SHORTFALLS

Another short-term funding strategy that is used in lieu of an asset conversion facility is to support shortfalls in working capital, which is known as a cash flow shortfall facility. A common facility is the **demand loan**, or line of credit that remains outstanding until repayment is demanded. As there is no specific maturity date attached to it, the facility can be recalled at any time by the lender. Demand Lines of Credit can vary by lender and are structured to either prohibit reborrowing once a draw down has occurred or allow multiple drawings under a clean-up and/or draws payable provisions. **Clean-up provisions** require that a borrower fully repay any outstanding balances at some time during the year and maintain a zero balance for a specified time period (usually 30 days). Many of these facilities contain a **Draws Payable** provision clause on each draw down that is to be paid within a certain time period.

4.4.1   Revolving Lines of Credit

Revolving Lines of Credit are more often used by larger firms that borrow a specified amount for a stated period of time, which usually ranges from one to five years. Borrowers can draw down on the loan at any time during the loan period, as well as repay the debt during the life of the facility. A distinction should be made between lines of credit and commitments, as lines of credit are not the same as loan commitments. **Commitments** are legal obligations that lenders have allocated and set aside for a particular borrowing customer's need according to agreed terms of the transaction. **Lines of credit**, however, can be revoked without the borrower's consent, and are often secured by collateral. Because they have a revolving continuing availability feature, revolving lines of credit are usually intended and used for working capital purposes.

4.4.2 Credit Assessment

The credit analysis for revolving credit lines must be assessed for cash flow availability, which emphasizes a borrower's operating capabilities to ensure that it balances with inventories and accounts receivables. To support the loan structure and underwriting standards as well as mitigate the credit risk, the analysis should demonstrate that loan repayments are matched with the borrower's expected cash flows.

4.5 MEDIUM-TERM FUNDING PRODUCTS

Short-term funding products are also used for medium-term financing purposes, but are structured for longer terms of maturity. A common medium-term funding product is a **Term Loan**, which is often extended to finance capital expansions and acquisitions as well as to purchase fixed assets. Term loans are binding agreements between the borrower and the financial institution by which committed funds are disbursed to the borrower for a period of time and are not expected to be repaid before maturity, unless the borrower does not perform as required. Term loans also have flexible repayment schedules that can be tailored to fit the borrower's needs with a **bullet** (full repayment of principal and interest at maturity), **balloon** (remaining facility principal is repaid in a final lump sum), or **periodic repayment** (repayment at regular intervals). The interest rate charged is usually set at a spread over some reference rate such as LIBOR or the Treasury bill rate. In contrast to revolvers, borrowers are not able to redraw on term loans once repayment has been made. However, there are revolving/term loan facilities that are often used in acquisition financing that combine both a revolver and a term loan instrument. Initially, this type of facility is used as a revolving loan that can be borrowed and repaid as needed during a specified period of time. At the end of the specified period, the outstanding facility balance will subsequently become converted into an amortizing term loan.

4.5.1 Credit Assessment

The credit assessment should consider the primary repayment source and whether it will be available to service the facility. The borrower's operations should also be analyzed to ensure earnings sustainability during the tenor of the transaction and even beyond. Stress tests should further be applied to consider what would happen should events of default prohibit repayment.

4.6 BRIDGE LOANS

Bridge Loans are an interim funding credit product that can be used by borrowing firms to bridge the waiting time between receiving permanent financing. For example, many developers will seek out bridge loans to start a construction project rather than wait until the process is further developed to seek permanent financing. These facilities are also used for interim financing during the preparation and completion of initial public offerings (IPOs) or bond offerings. Bridge loans are typically extended on a floating rate basis until they are replaced by permanent or long-term funding, which is usually at a fixed-rate cost.

4.6.1 Credit Assessment

The preliminary credit assessment for bridge loan transactions requires that the lender is first satisfied that the event will occur when anticipated and, second, that the borrower can repay the debt should the event not transpire. Thus if a company is seeking a bridge loan until an equity or bond offering is completed, the lender must evaluate the reliability that this will happen. Consideration must also be given to whether the proceeds received will be sufficient to repay the outstanding amount of the loan. Typically, when bridge loans are used, lenders will take a security interest in the project or offering by having repayment made directly from the proceeds of the permanent financing. If the facility entails a revolving credit, the borrower's operations should be analyzed to ensure that the company has long-term earnings sustainability for repayment. Although the lender will most likely find that the company has higher than normal debt levels, it will still want to determine that the cost of financing is manageable.

4.7 LONG-TERM FUNDING PRODUCTS

When the use of short- or medium-term credit products are impractical for companies' long-term objectives and growth strategies, then long-term funding strategies will be applied to meet the particular financing needs. Long-term credit products are usually more expensive because of the higher risk exposure that accompanies uncertain future market conditions and for which lenders must be compensated. Because these funds are committed in lieu of being used by the lender for other short- or medium-term facilities, the lender is compensated with a higher interest charge for the cost of credit to extend the facility term as well as by fees (e.g., facility fee, upfront fee, and so on) for making the commitment. A common funding strategy for companies that have long-term borrowing needs is the basic vanilla **Term Loan**. This facility is often customized to accommodate large capital improvement projects such as machinery and new equipment purchases, making capital acquisitions, as well as serving as a working capital source for business restructuring. Although the standard term loan life ranges between 7 and 10 years, they can also be structured for dual purposes that consist of both a term and revolving loan facility.* Although structured to initially begin as a revolving loan facility, the company will borrow and repay as needed for a specified period of time until the revolving portion ends, at which time the outstanding balance becomes an amortizing term loan. Revolving/term loans are often used in syndicated loan facilities and other large-volume bank financing such as project finance.

4.7.1 Credit Assessment

The credit assessment on extending long-term loans should consist of evaluating the cash flows for debt repayment, according to the long-term borrowing needs of the company. Unlike short-term facilities in which lenders identify the liquidation of current assets

---

*Clarification should be made that some lenders classify long-term loans to be up to seven years and preferably no more than five years. Loans that are extended for up to 10 years are usually for project finance funding needs.

as the primary source of repayment, long-term committed facilities are dependent on repayment from continuing positive future cash flows. Critical analysis is therefore required in the credit assumptions of the firm's historical and projected cash flows as well as in reliably matching the debt repayment schedules against the projected cash flows. Projections should also reflect the long-term earnings potential and industry fundamentals for the company. Sensitivity analyses are further applied to evaluate a borrower's performance under unfavorable events and to determine how such events will affect margins and debt repayment schedules.

4.8 STRUCTURED FINANCE

A primary development in the modern practices of credit risk management has been the innovation in new structured finance credit products. Although originally introduced to the market in the 1970s with the government issuance of mortgage backed securities (MBSs), structured finance has since become a financing source for companies with unique or complex funding needs for which conventional loan products may not appropriately service. These debt products are used by all types of corporations who seek to deconsolidate certain balance sheet assets to improve their financial position. Similar to the growth of asset-based loans, which we discussed earlier, structured finance transactions have expanded debt accessibility for companies that previously were not attractive candidates to the funding markets. For example, middle market companies who require less than the funding amount of a syndication loan and could also not afford the high cost of debt, can now access these markets with securitized structured finance products. Through structured finance transactions such as asset securitization, companies have accessibility to what is now an acceptable source of working capital rather than what was once considered a financing vehicle for poor credit quality borrowers and smaller companies. Asset securitization is a form of transferring credit risk by separating the credit risk of the originator from that of the underlying assets. This has also been a long-standing process in the lending industry as receivables in nonfinancial sectors would be financed by selling them off to gain immediate liquidity. Over the past thirty years however, the applications for which securitizations have been used has expanded to be frequently used to transfer and neutralize credit risks for portfolio optimization and regulatory capital purposes, which will be discussed later in the chapter.

4.8.1   Credit Assessment

The credit assessment focuses on identifying company assets such as receivables that are separated from their respective cash flows, against which a firm can borrow. For example, if an aircraft manufacturer has sold on account planes to commercial and private aviation buyers, an asset securitization could be structured to identify and finance quality aircraft receivables to lend against. The lender will loan the manufacturer funds against the receivables to enable the company to attain payment earlier rather than wait to receive future periodic payments as the receivables mature. A lien would be taken on the receivables against other creditors for security in the event of bankruptcy or default. As structured finance is tailored to the borrowers' needs, it includes a wide array of financial debt instruments that credit specialists should be familiar with. Among the most common types of structured credits for commercial and corporate borrowers are syndicated loans, leverage loans, and project finance. In addition, there is a range of credit derivative products that are also used on both single-asset facilities and credit portfolios; that has come to promote greater uniformity in the banking and trading books. In the following is an overview of some of the more common structured credit products that commercial and corporate banking provides and with which credit specialists should be familiar. Although our discussion is not exhaustive with regard to the many types of existing and developing structured credit instruments, it should serve as a conceptual framework upon which to build in understanding the converging credit markets.

4.9   SYNDICATED LOANS

Syndicated loans is a classical credit approach for transferring risk that dates back to the early 1970s, when banks originally begin to use this funding strategy to finance large corporations and sovereign governments. The sellers that participated in the syndication were able to transfer or sell portions of the assets and increase their liquidity funding sources in the syndications market as well as reduce their exposure and capital requirements. A syndicated loan consists of one or several lenders agreeing to provide funds to a borrower under the same credit facility according to specified terms and conditions. These loans are usually put together by an arranging bank(s) that negotiates the respective terms with the borrower and subsequently produces information memorandums that are marketed and distributed to other prospective lending participants. The lenders that commit to the syndicate will purchase a portion of the total loan amount and hold it to maturity or until the facility is sold in the secondary loan market. Suppose, hypothetically, that a firm wants to borrow a $1BN revolving term loan for general working capital purposes from JPMorganChase. Although JPMorganChase is certainly large enough in size and has the resources to fund a $1BN debt instrument, it chooses instead to minimize its funding and capital requirements by asking other banks to share in the facility. The rationale behind this is that the return it will earn on the $1BN does not outweigh the credit exposure it will incur to a single customer nor the required capital that it must allocate to the transaction. Instead, the bank would prefer to provide the funding for the customer and act as the syndicated arranger. Arranging a syndicate loan can be a lucrative role for the bank, not only because of the fees that it will earn, but also for the visibility and prestige that it holds in reputation. However, despite servicing this market for the fees that they generate, arrangers rarely retain a significant portion of these facilities, if any at all, due to the high concentration risk that it can hold to a borrower or industry. This is an advantage to funding syndicated loans because larger sums of money can be raised through this process than any one lender would want to provide, although the more complex the syndicate structure becomes, the higher the fees that will be earned. For the syndicate members that do participate in the $1BN facility, they will usually each commit specific loan portions that on average may range from $1MM to $100MM. Borrowers are obligated to repay each syndicate member with an undivided repayment schedule of the total amount loaned.

Lenders participating in syndicated loans can have different roles requiring various funding obligations and responsibilities. In addition to the role of the arranging bank, funding roles can also include a co-agent, a lead manager, a manager and participant, with the prestige of the roles decreasing from the arranger down to the participant. Thus the fees and total income that will be earned by each participant will be dependent on the role that they hold. The arranging bank will also earn additional service fees for preparing and marketing the Information Memorandum in addition to raising the funds, but a managing bank will only earn fees on the funds that they have committed.

Syndicated credit facilities are usually structured into several credit tiers or tranches, in which portions of each tranche may have different risks, yields, and maturities. Tranche structures can be comprised of varying funding strategies or credit products that may also include a term loan, revolver, letter of credit, and acquisition or equipment line. A revolving syndicated credit, for example, could be structured to have options that may include a **swing line** (for overnight borrowing), a **competitive bid option** (bids submitted by lenders for funding), a **term-out** (allows borrowed funds to convert to a term loan), as well as an **evergreen clause** (facility that can be renewed for additional years). As many of these facilities are often used for large cross-border project financing transactions, additional features can also be added such as providing a multicurrency portion to the tranche. This is often used by multinational corporations that commit to syndicated loans and requires, for example, a term loan and multicurrency line as commercial paper backup for European funding obligations. Such a facility may be structured to consist of an A tranche that has an amortizing term loan with principle and interest payments during the life of the facility and a 364-day revolving multicurrency B tranche that provides a swing line to replace domestic for euro commercial paper.

The syndicated loan market is composed of primary and secondary functions. The primary syndicated loan market is a combination of bank market loan participants holding amortizing term and revolving loan facility tranches as well as institutional loan tranches. Since the early 1970s and 1980s, when syndicated loans were introduced as a funding vehicle for sovereign and large corporate borrowers, the primary and secondary markets have come to serve as a "gateway" for increased participation by non-bank lenders into the corporate loan market. Figures 4.2 and 4.3 illustrates the growth of syndicated loan issuance since 1987 through the first quarter of 2004 as an example of how this funding strategy has evolved from a private, corporate banking credit relationship into a securities market for both primary and secondary loans. Much of this growth is attributed to nonbank investors such as hedge funds and other money managers that have come to dominate the market since 1999. Prior to this period, bank investors were the major participants in the syndicated loan market until the trend began to change when rising defaults coincided with a credit cycle downturn that forced commercial banks to withdraw and tighten their credit underwriting standards. If we take a closer

FIGURE 4.2

Syndicated Loan Issuance, 1987–2004

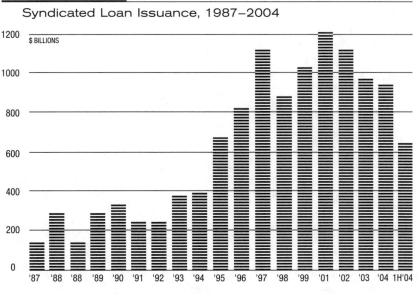

Source: LPC.

look at the market in Figures 4.4 and 4.5, it can be seen that the decline in bank investors has been offset by nonbank institutional investors, which have held over 50% of the syndicated loan market since 2000. Growth in the secondary market has also been phenomenal and consists of brokers engaged in bank trading by matching buyers and sellers on loans that are sold in the market for resale. Secondary loan trading has been a means for financial institutions to readjust their portfolios to nonbank institutional investors seeking higher yields from leverage loans and distressed debt in lieu of high defaults. Distressed debt trading has become an active part of the secondary loan market as investors in this market acquire assets of bankrupt companies that are subsequently restructured into profitable entities. By selling off portions of large syndicated corporate loans into the secondary market, banks have been able to diversify their credit risk exposure from particular borrowers and industries as well as reduce their risk concentration levels. This has attributed to a 1,700% growth rate in secondary market trading from a volume of $8BN in 1991 to $145BN by 2003, which works out as a compound annual growth rate of 27% per year.[3] Consequently the volume of distressed debt by 2001 had become an active part of the secondary loan market, increasing to $117BN.[4]

FIGURE 4.3

Secondary Loan Market Value Traded, 1991–2003

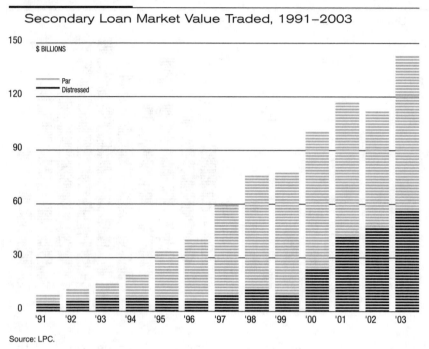

Source: LPC.

Syndicated loans can also be **fully underwritten** (arrangers guarantee the entire amount to the borrower), on a **best-efforts basis** (arrangers commit to underwrite a portion of the loan with the remainder sold according to market demand) or as a **club** (limited to no more than $150MM by a small number of relationship banks). If a syndicated loan is a club facility, it is usually underwritten with a few elite relationship bank lenders or it can be on a **bilateral** basis with many bank participants. Figure 4.6 identifies the types of syndicated loans that are most commonly used in the market and Figure 4.7 summarizes the primary purposes of their usage. The primary uses, in addition to acquisition financings and debt repayment, are for leveraged and project finance, which will be discussed later, as well as for liquidity funding of commercial paper.

Among the advances that have also taken place to contribute to the growth of the syndicated loan markets was the introduction of assigned credit ratings by Standard and Poor in 1996. This was in response to the demands by institutional and nonbank investors seeking greater accuracy and reliability in measuring debt assets.

FIGURE 4.4

The Decline of Pro Rata Investors in the Primary Market, 1997–2004

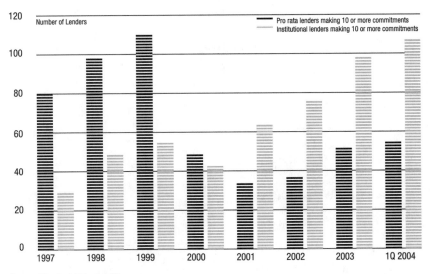

Source: Standard & Poor's LCDy.

FIGURE 4.5

The Growth of Donbarks in the Primary Market, 1994–2004

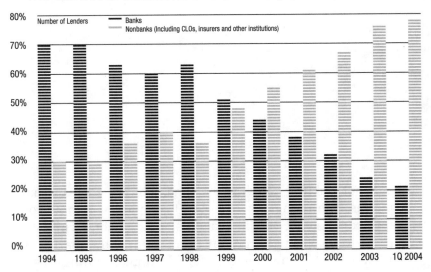

Source: Standard & Poor's LCdy.

FIGURE 4.6

Types of Syndicated Loans

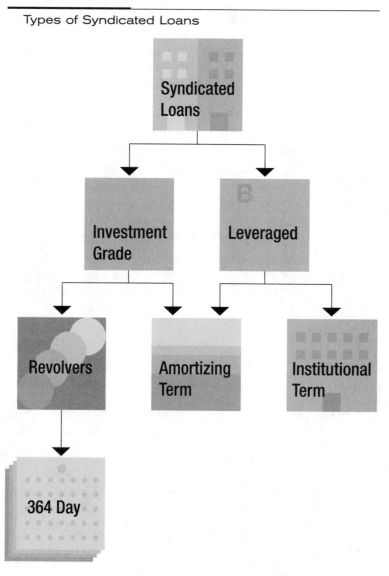

Although not publicly rated at the time, syndicated loans have since increased in ratings for over 1,300 companies, to now comprise approximately $935BN in total outstanding debt. As investors have come to increasingly rely on these ratings, the market has grown globally to now include 267 European ratings as of July 2004, which had an aggregate estimated equivalent value of

FIGURE 4.7

Syndicated Issuance by Purpose, 1990–2003

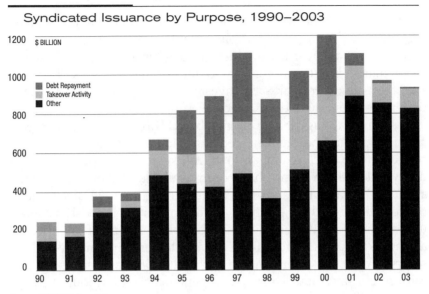

Source: LPC 2004 Annual.

$265BN.[5] The other advancement in this market has been the
flexible pricing mechanism known as market flex pricing, which
reflects a facility's true credit quality, and which was introduced
by JPMorganChase in 1997. The mechanism was needed because
syndicated investors were unprotected against changing market
conditions between the interim time after committing to the syndication and the time the loan went to the market. Because pricing
would be prenegotiated and fixed with the borrower, participants
had to accept the documented pricing terms, which contained
no provisions for adjustments if the market or borrower's credit
quality changed. This would often expose investors to higher
credit risk when market conditions deteriorated or if a borrower
was downgraded by the time the loan finally went on the market.
Consequently, profit margins of regional or smaller banks seeking
to enter the corporate loan market were affected and potential
institutional investors became reluctant to participate. By incorporating market flex pricing into the loan agreements, investors and
participants had better protection against uncertainty with compensating margins on under priced loans in exchange for variable
interest rate margins.

4.9.1 Credit Assessment

Participation in the syndications markets should be undertaken according to the targeted portfolio returns and the optimum use of economic capital over the medium to long term. Because the syndication market is also a mechanism to transfer the credit risk of specific loan assets to other banks and investors, participants should always undertake their own due diligence rather than fully rely on the assessment of the agent or arranging bank. This is particularly important for foreign and smaller credit providers that have used these products as a vehicle to enter into the market for large corporate loans that would otherwise not have been available to them. In general, agent and arranging banks will initially offer their syndicated loan participations to their premiere correspondent relationship banks, unless the borrower indicates otherwise. As most syndicated arrangers are primarily dominated by the larger banks, many of these sellers of credit risk were known in the late 1980s and early 1990s to call on less savvy but eager participants as an afterthought in the effort to sell off weaker credits to what was perceived to be the "first takers." Given that the arrangers of syndicated loans usually have respectable, well-known reputations, participants would accept their presentation of the facility in the Information Memorandums at face value as the official credit assessment. Minimal concern was given as to how the transaction fit into the organization's credit philosophy and strategy, as well as the impact on the portfolio throughout the duration of the facility. Because these lenders were high in liquidity but low on assets, neither were they always astute regarding the most prudent facilities, and oftentimes lacked the credit skills necessary to understand the borrower's operations. In other words they did not always apply appropriate techniques in credit assessment. Given the large amount of capital that may be funded under these facilities, however, every effort should be made for the lender to be confident in their own assessment of the borrower's creditworthiness prior to committing to participate in a syndicated transaction. This is also why every attempt is made to structure repayments that accommodate the borrower's needs so that they are afforded the optimum terms to make full and timely repayment and avoid undue stress on their funding obligations. At the same time, the covenant terms and conditions on syndications also tend to be stricter than for other debt transactions, thereby making each participant a senior creditor having equal claims against the borrower and priority over junior creditors.

4.10 LEVERAGED FINANCE

Leverage loans have played a significant role in the syndicated market and particularly as a funding strategy for below investment-grade high-yield borrowers. Companies seeking leverage loans generally have high borrowing needs and find bank debt to be one of the best financing sources. Many of these firms are typically engaged in leveraged buyouts (LBOs) that are financed by private equity investors or by former senior managers that enter into a management buyout (MBOs) to acquire their firms by using huge sums of debt as leveraged borrowers. Figure 4.8 illustrates how a leverage finance structure for the acquisition of an entire company or division is primarily financed by using up to 70–80% in debt with the remaining 20–30% in equity funding. Leveraged loans are usually issued as floating rate notes by middle- to large-sized companies with different tranche features, similar to syndicated and structured finance transactions. Typically, the different tranches are bundled and sold to respective banks and institutional investors according to their distinguishing risk appetites. The more risky tranches are sold for higher interest margins and usually to institutional investors with maturities that can range from 3 to 10 years and with delayed amortizations. The equity portion of the acquisition is injected into a shell company that is created by the buyer (LBO or Equity Sponsor) to form a new entity that becomes the borrower for the debt. Simultaneously, the buyer will acquire

FIGURE 4.8

Key Concepts in an LBO

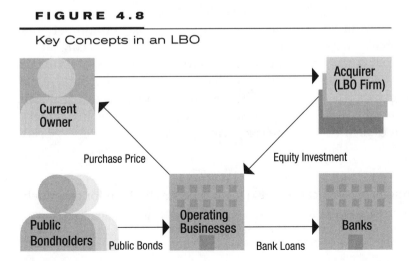

the operations of the purchased company and, after several years of profitable performance, will eventually offer an IPO to sell all or portions of the firm. Emerging or start-up firms and companies considered to be rising stars that have yet to gain a reputation or level of operational performance for investment grade are also leveraged finance borrowers.* Many of these firms have high debt levels and operate in cyclical and capital-intensive industries, and have also produced established branded products. These borrowers may be mature companies in low-growth industries that tend to generate large cash inflows as well as distressed or bankrupt firms.

The growth in corporate banking for LBOs and distressed debt restructuring has continued to rise since the end of the 1990s, after having rendered huge losses for lenders in the late 1980s. Between 1990 and 2003, leveraged loans, on average, represented approximately 29% of the primary loan market and had captured 35% of the secondary loan market.[6] Since 2003, the United States and Europe have specifically had a tremendous upsurge in highly leveraged acquisitions and refinancing transactions. Leveraged loans represented approximately 45% of the primary syndicated loan market in 2003, as illustrated in Figure 4.9. In fact, these loans as an asset class have started to overtake the investment-grade debt market. Between July 2004 and March 2005, "more than $100BN of high-yield debt was sold to institutional investors primarily because of the higher paying yields that they earned."[7] Common tranche holders in leverage loan syndications are nonbank institutional loan investors, which began to capture the market after a decline in foreign bank participation from 40% in 1993 to less than 20% by 2001.[†] The concentrated numbers of lenders that control this market have established a strong distribution network to syndicate these transactions to market investors. According to Loan Pricing Corporation, "over 30% of all leveraged loan deals done in 2002 were syndicated by 3 banks and more than 50% by the top seven banks."[8] These debt products now include cash-rich hedge-fund investors and only require a minimum investment amount of $1MM. Nonetheless because of the higher degree of risk

---

*Rising stars are growing companies that have the potential and are predicted to be investment grade at some time in the future.

†The exit by foreign banks also coincided with the 1998–1999. Asian currency crisis that resulted in a departure by Japanese banks, which were subsequently replaced by hedge funds and other nonbank investing participants.

FIGURE 4.9

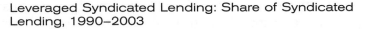

Leveraged Syndicated Lending: Share of Syndicated
Lending, 1990–2003

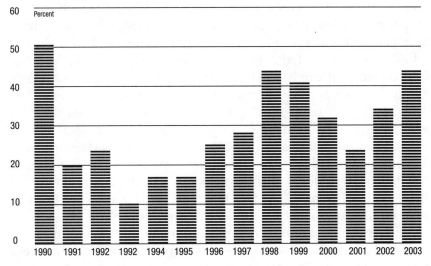

Source: LPC 2004 Annual.

that they usually carry, the invested amounts are also encouraged
to be large enough to obtain optimal returns.* A primary factor that
also contributed to the growth of the leveraged loan market and
efficiency has been proprietary market indexes, which serve as performance benchmark indicators that have been promoted by the
nonbank investors who seek to quantify their risk-adjusted
returns.[†] This information has come to serve as an indicator for
determining the market's receptivity to a particular instrument, as
well as for pricing transparency.

4.10.1 Credit Assessment

Leveraged loans should be assessed with an emphasis on fundamental credit analysis and a focus on the borrower's earnings
potential beyond the medium-term duration of the facility.

---

*Brain Ranson, Most fund managers and nonbank financial investors that purchased
leverage loans approximate a minimum portfolio size of $75MM.
[†]Among some of the common market indexes are Standard & Poor's Leveraged
Commentary Data (S & P LCD), Loan Pricing Corporation (LPC), Credit Suisse First
Boston (CSFB), and Bank of America.

Although leveraged financing is an important funding strategy for mergers and acquisitions, refinancing, equity buyouts, and business or product line expansions, these facility structures are also more complex than plain vanilla syndicated loans, which is why they will have higher risk but offer more favorable pricing returns. This is because leveraged borrowers have a diminished ability to adjust to unanticipated events and changes in market conditions. Consequently, it can have significant implications for the lender's credit risk exposure along with challenges to managing this risk. The credit assessment should therefore demonstrate that the firm will have steady predictable operating cash flows and limited working capital requirements. Stress tests should also be applied to consider what will happen should a buyout not succeed if an IPO has fewer subscribers than anticipated. As debt repayment for these types of transactions is often dependent upon asset sales or new equity injections, the projected cash flows and stress tests should detail the worst-case scenarios, including having to divest any of the assets over time. The assessment should also address how the borrower's capital structures will be impacted by credit ratings and spreads. Consideration should be given to the different financial instruments that may be used to structure a leveraged loan facility.

Higher risk transactions such as leveraged loans also require ongoing frequent monitoring relative to the overall credit exposure and limits to this sector. Often, these facilities rely heavily on enterprise value as a secondary repayment source that requires ongoing asset valuation and review of collateral. The credit process should therefore have strong internal controls relative to the effects that a leveraged transaction will have on the portfolio.

4.11 PROJECT FINANCE

As the name suggests, project finance is intended to finance specific large-scale, capital-intensive projects such as the construction of a chemical plant or public infrastructure projects (e.g., hospitals, roads, and so on). It has become widely used for high-profile corporate ventures, including the construction of Euro Disneyland in Paris, France, among others. A project finance facility requires a high level of financial engineering, because it must be structured so that the risk and reward allocations are acceptable to the entire group of project parties involved. Consequently, the intricacies of the facilities can be complex to arrange and administer due to the number of different contractual parties involved. As the construction of major building projects such as an oil and gas refinery involves the contribution of so many participants, project finance transactions are structured with risk-sharing matrices based on a complex set of contracts. Because of the number of parties that can be involved, each of the project supporters will naturally have different perceptions and risk appetites. This can affect the roles played by each project participant, which in turn can lead to individual risk and return issues. Underwriting and closing these transactions can take between 6 and 12 months to complete, compared with corporate loans, which can be assessed, approved, and extended within one month.

The basis for underwriting a project finance transaction is to support the creation of a special purpose vehicle (SPV) or company that will operate as an economically viable stand-alone entity for a specific purpose. Figure 4.10 details the basic elements of a project finance. A project finance entity's operations must function like any market provider. Despite the distinctive patterns

FIGURE 4.10

Basic Elements of a Project Financing

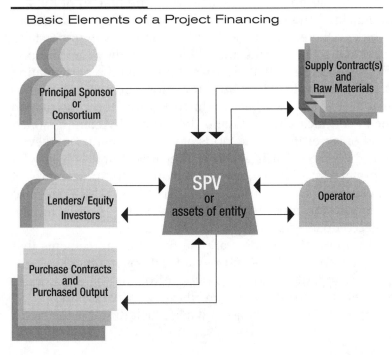

in particular project sectors that determine the project finance structures and roles, raw materials must still be acquired and subsequently processed by the SPV to deliver an output that will be sold. All parties that are involved with the operation of the SPV will have designed roles that must be filled, including the lender, project sponsor, contractor, purchaser, supplier, and operator. Depending on the project, however, there may be some variation among the key roles, although at a minimum the required parties must include a lender, a purchaser, and a sponsor. Nonetheless, the role of sponsor in certain types of project finance transactions is generally combined with multiple tasks, and in other sector projects there can be distinctive patterns that determine the structure and roles. In the power sector, for example, the sponsor can have multiple tasks and, in some form, be both the operator and maintenance contractor, because the complexities of operating a power station requires assurance that daily operations are conducted by a specialized operator and highly trained staff.

4.11.1   Credit Assessment

The credit analysis and assessment will require that all of the key risks be managed and controlled according to the use of their contracts. The key therefore for the credit specialists is to understand the contractual arrangements and identify how they impact upon the various project risks that are shared between the participating parties. For example, financing for most power projects is constructed on a turnkey basis, which requires the construction operator to contractually build and deliver a fully commissioned power station according to the terms of the agreement. Any deviation from the agreement is a risk to the project and is also why lenders prefer well-experienced contractors in the power project sector. Long-term energy purchase agreements, which are also used in this sector, must be evaluated to ensure supply for the power is accompanied by the power demand.

Most important to lenders are the financing agreements that outline basic responsibilities and risk allocations in other supporting documentation that provide strict controls on the activities of the borrower. In addition there are the basic financial reporting requirements on all of the project owners, including for the credit standing of the key project parties. As an example, syndicated loans, which are often used in project financing, will require ongoing reporting to monitor any difficulties in the project operations, on a regular monthly and quarterly basis. This includes meeting key financial ratios and various reserve account requirements that are established to ensure sufficient long-term maintenance funds. The ability of lenders and other providers of funds to have control rights over the project during the duration of the facility must also be evaluated.

Unlike corporate loans, where analysis of repayment is based on the general creditworthiness of the borrower, the facility repayment for project finance is primarily dependent on the cash flows that will be generated by the SPV. This is why the expected cash flows to be generated from the project are usually secured by the lender along with the project assets that are financed. As well as the variety of terms and conditions for which the facility will be evaluated, it will also need to be demonstrated that future project cash flows will be sufficient to service the debt.

Unlike the corporate credit ratings that determine pricing for corporate loans, project finance loans are priced to reflect the project rating. Given that a project finance transaction will have no operating history at the time it is initiated, the creditworthiness of the project is therefore dependent on profitability of the venture and the ability of the contracted parties to service their obligations. Among the major questions that the credit specialist must verify, for example, is whether the service provider of the raw materials can satisfy the required quantities to operate a project. It should also be determined whether the project has a secure source of revenues to repay the debt. Are the capital and operating costs controllable? If they are not, then the risks will be too uncertain and the lender will usually not want the credit exposure? If the project involves the use of a particular technology, it must also be verified that it works as a proven technology, even if the technology is new. This is simply because the credit organization must be assured that once the project becomes operational, it will function as a viable economic and profitable entity. Most importantly, in addition to cash flow projections demonstrating sufficient debt repayment, the project should also exhibit a secondary repayment source that can be realized from any asset disposals.

4.12 CONVERGENCE IN LOAN AND TRADING PRODUCTS

Companies may also choose the capital markets for financing long-term debt obligations. In fact, under modern credit risk management, the capital and trading markets have come to represent the majority of corporate and commercial funding sources. The credit products that we have been discussing thus far in this chapter have components of credit risk that are now being bundled and repackaged to create new credit instruments. This development of new credit products over the years has led to a range of financing choices that now give both buyers and lenders greater "options" in extending business credit. Credit derivative products have advanced market funding strategies with the application of new product structures while also providing a new economic function within the credit markets. By segmenting and bundling the underlying credit risk of a group of debt instruments and then categorizing them into different asset classes, many of which are traded, it has served to shape convergence of the loan and trading books. What has contributed to this process is a preference for transparency that the market is perceived to provide, as well as the distribution of debt instruments that are now available for the risk appetite of investors. This has contributed to credit derivatives becoming another option for lenders to manage their credit risk exposure. Similar to the users of credit derivatives, (which will be discussed later in this chapter), option users are in essence managing their risk exposure by transferring it or having insurance against the risk of financial loss. Another contributing factor to the market transformation of these products is the implementation of standardized documentation that has led to tighter pricing for derivatives and end-users. According to Robert Pickel, CEO and Executive Officer for ISDA, "Standardized documentation both encourages liquidity and assures legal certainty for the parties involved."[9] The result has been an increase in credit market participants so that the credit selection and preliminary approval process now encompasses a multiple of transaction counterparties. Analysts who were previously confined to counterparty transactions or fixed income credit analysis are now involved in individual loan transactions. This requires for them to undertake credit assessments on newly manufactured credit exposures in order to participate in any market purchases, which often includes a variety of bundled credit risk products all under one transaction. The converging credit risks between loan and trading product will be discussed in the next section.

4.12.1 Bonds

Bonds vary by type and can include corporate bonds, government, or sovereign bonds issuances. These fixed-income obligations can fall into many market sectors and can have convertible features that are linked to equities. Because of the large variety and types of bonds that exist in the market, our emphasis is to give an overview of the mechanics and credit risks that are inherent in the extension of bonds as a funding strategy. Bonds are contractual debt obligations to repay a stated sum consisting of the **principal** amount or face value, along with periodic interest payments known as the **coupon**, which is expressed as a percentage. Although the minimum maturity time for a corporate bond is usually five years, the longer the repayment terms, the higher will be the yield to maturity. The **yield to maturity** is the coupon rate of return that bondholders receive and reflects the risk of the obligor. Bonds can also be structured as either fixed or floating instruments, although fixed-rate bonds are the largest class of bonds that are issued. Bonds can be either investment grade (rated BBB or Baa or higher) or non-investment grade. If they are investment grade, they are considered to be a higher quality. Non-investment-grade bonds will carry a lower credit rating (lower than BBB or Baa) and are often referred to as junk bonds to reflect the higher credit risk. The majority of corporate bonds that are issued to the public are rated by the major rating agencies (Standard and Poor's, Moodys' Investor Services, and Fitch Rating Agencies) to reflect the credit risk of the issuer or borrower's general creditworthiness and debt repayment ability.

When companies decide to seek credit through the issuance of a **bond** offering, the credit risk and structure must be assessed before the facility is underwritten in exchange for any cash proceeds. An important aspect in understanding the credit risk assessment for bonds is to know that the credit fundamentals that affect bond prices will be impacted by fluctuating price changes, and lenders and investors can either benefit or lose. Lenders become exposed to interest rate risk if the coupon is fixed and the price fluctuates from changing interest rates. The key relationship for credit specialists to consider is that when interest rates rise, a bond's fixed price will decline. Conversely, when interest rates decline, the value of the bond will rise. The interest on floating-rate bonds, in contrast, is adjusted based on changes in a reference rate that is also known as the benchmark interest rate. The typical pricing benchmark that is used is the three-month Treasury bill, and LIBOR rates, which are regularly applied to floating-rate bonds that have quarterly or semi-annual base rate changes. Credit specialists will typically use the yield curve to evaluate the direction that interest rates are moving towards as an indicator for how bond prices will be impacted by the market environment. Yield curves reflect the relationship between interest rates and different bond maturities. The shape of the curves serves to provide a benchmark against which the yields of all other bonds for different maturities and with similar credit ratings are compared. The normal shape of the treasury yield curve is upward or positively sloped, as shown in Figure 4.11, which reflects the market rates of interest for the most liquid bonds that are used to construct the curve. These are the most recently issued bonds that sell at the highest prices for the lowest yield, meaning that the yield will increase with maturity. If the yield curve is flat, as shown in Figure 4.12, the returns and yields are expected to be equal for both short- and long-term bonds. In other words, the term structure of interest rates or the credit spread differences between securities of different maturities

FIGURE 4.11

U.S. Treasury Yield Curve

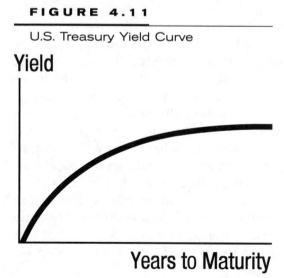

Yield

Years to Maturity

FIGURE 4.12

Flat Yield Curve

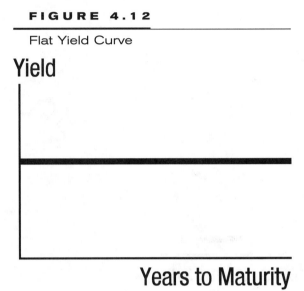

Yield

Years to Maturity

on a given day are the same or not very wide, and uncertainty prevails regarding the future. This was evident in 2006, when the yield curve had become inverted for the first time since December 2000. After the inversion, the yield curve remained flat on U.S. securities, so that a yield on 10-year Treasury notes, for example, was quoted at 4.37%, but the yield on two-year notes was only slightly lower at 4.35%. An inverted yield curve that is negatively sloped in a downward motion, such as in Figure 4.13, is an indicator that returns on bonds will most likely decrease with maturity because yields on short-term bonds are higher than those on long-term bonds. Inverted yield curves have typically been an indicator that the credit cycle may be directed towards a decline. Finally, if the yield curve in Figure 4.14 is humped, short-term and long-term yields are equal, but interest rates vary on medium-term yields.

Bonds may also be structured with optional provisions, which can affect their value. Among the typical bond structures are callable bonds, which allow the issuer to call, or repay, the bond earlier than its maturity date. If the bond has a call option and interest rates decline to a low enough level, the issuer will recall the bond to issue a lower coupon instrument in order to refinance the issue with cheaper debt. Bondholders will then cease to receive the interest payments, although they will receive the outstanding principal on the recalled bond. Because high inflation rates can erode the real

FIGURE 4.13

Inverted Yield Curve

Yield

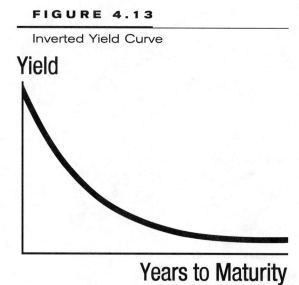

Years to Maturity

value of the income received from bonds, inflation can jeopardize any fixed-income streams that bonds provide.

There are some classes of bonds (e.g., mortgage-backed) that are subject to prepayment risk. Similar to call risk, prepayment risk is the risk that the issuer of a security will repay principal prior to the bond's maturity date, thereby changing the expected payment

FIGURE 4.14

Hump-Back Yield Curve

Yield

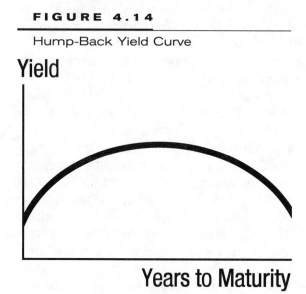

Years to Maturity

schedule. Bond investors are also faced with reinvestment risk—the threat that if interest rates fall, the interest payments and principal that investors receive will have to be reinvested at lower rates. The importance of this is that the yield-to-maturity calculation assumes that all payments received are reinvested at the exact same rate as the original bond's coupon rate. However, as this is rarely the case, lenders, brokers, and portfolio managers seek to account for reinvestment risk by calculating a bond's duration to recover the true cost of a bond with the present value of all future coupon and principal payments. The duration of a bond is the number of years from the purchase date that is required to recover the true cost of a bond and is used to compare bonds with different issue and maturity dates, coupon rates, and yields to maturity. It is a tool that helps creditors and investors gauge the price fluctuations as a result of interest-rate risk exposure. In simple terms, the duration of a bond will determine how the bond's price is affected by the change in interest rates and can be derived from the expression

$$\text{Duration} = \frac{(1)(\text{PVCF}_1) + (2)(\text{PVCF}_2) + \ldots + (n)(\text{PVCF}_n)}{(k)\,(\text{Price})}$$

where n = the number of payments to maturity,

$\quad k$ = the number of coupon payments per year, and

PVCF = the present value of the cash flow for the period.

If interest rates, for example, rise by one percentage point, from 6% to 7%, the price of a bond with a duration of five years will move down by 5%, while a bond with a duration of 10 years will move down by about 10%. Specifically, the bond's duration, coupon, and yield to maturity, as well as the extent of the change in interest rates, are all significant variables that ultimately determine how much a bond's price moves. In other words, all components of a bond are duration variables. Finally, bonds carry the risk of default, where the issuer will be unable to make future income and principal payments. This is the assessment of the obligor's creditworthiness and credit quality as reflected by its credit rating or internal assessment, and it is also an indicator of the probability of default. The greater the credit risk in a bond, the lower its credit rating will be and the higher the required return must be in exchange for investors acceptance of more risk. In addition to assessing the credit fundamentals of a bond issuer, bonds must also undergo valuation techniques related to price, as well as technical applications relative to the market. The credit assessment should focus on the relative valuation of the bond based upon the years to maturity, the payment structure according to the market yield and coupon for similar bonds, and external factors related to economic market conditions.

4.13 A GROWING MARKET FOR CREDIT OPTIONS AND DERIVATIVES

Credit products have converged over the years to integrate with debt and equity funding strategies, resulting in a range of financing choices that now give both borrowers and lenders a greater number of "options" in extending business credit. This has particularly been apparent in credit derivatives and credit option products. Credit options are similar to having insurance against the risk of financial loss. Any unfavorable losses due to changes in the credit quality of obligors are offset by the credit option payments, which therefore reduces risk exposure and enables lenders to manage their credit risks. Whereas options were once limited only to the capital markets, they have become integrated in all aspects of credit. Under modern credit risk, options represent the many choices that prevail in the market to transfer credit risk from one investor to another. Essentially, an option is a contract to either buy or sell a security for a specified price on a designated date. The price for this option that must be paid is called the premium, and to use this contract requires that an exercise or strike price must be paid. Making the choice of the type of option that is desired means deciding on whether to apply the two most common types of options, which are known as a **call** or **put**. For a certain time period, a call option can be purchased to buy a financial instrument at a set price, which is known as the strike price. A premium is paid, in addition to the strike price, by the holder of the call option for the right to buy the instrument, up to the time that the option expires. The premium is also the market price of the option and equal to the "intrinsic value" and the "time value of money." As illustrated in Figure 4.15, if the owner of the call option decides to purchase the instrument, the seller or writer of the option must provide the security at the established contract price. Owning the option gives leverage to realize a higher risk return while transferring the risk from the owner to the option seller. If the option is sold before it expires, then the investor accepts the risk from the option buyer. These products are typically used as substitutes for

FIGURE 4.15

The Call Option

Security	Expiration	Exercise Price	Type	Premium
ABC	November	$30	Call	$3

■ The buyer of the call pays the Premium of $3 = $300 to purchase the security at $30 before or at the expiration (Long position in the option).

■ The writer of the call promises to sell the security at the exercise price regardless of what the market price is if the option is exercised. (Short position in the option contract)

buying stock and are cheaper as well as less risky than owning the stock. The option of having the call is only good if the price rises before it expires, or it will be worthless and may even leave the holder with a loss. The key to buying a call option is timing and speculation.

The inverse to the call option is the put option, because it relies on the price of the asset to decline in order for it to be profitable. This credit product allows the owner to sell the instrument by a certain time period for a certain price. Similar to the call option, the owner pays a premium to have the right to sell the asset up to its expiration date. Purchasing a put is similar to selling short, as illustrated in Figure 4.16. Using this choice means that there is

FIGURE 4.16

The Put Option

Security	Expiration	Exercise Price	Type	Premium
ABC	November	$30	Put	$3

■ The buyer of the put pays the premium of $3 = $300 to sell the security at $30 before or at the Expiration to the writer of the option (Long position in the option).

■ The writer of the put promises to buy the stock at the exercise price regardless of what the market price is if the option is exercised. (Short the option contract)

T A B L E   4 - 2

Three Most Active Sectors for April 2006

United States	Europe	Asia
Auto manufacturers	Fixed line telecom	Financial services
Banks	Banks	Banks
Financial services	Publishing	Electrical equipment

Source: RiskCenter.com

both unlimited profit and unlimited risk potential. The value of the option varies according to what the perceived market price will be when it is exercised. Similarly, credit options are commonly used in this manner to hedge the risk of any changes to a borrower's credit quality when lenders are exposed to financial loss. For example, a bond investor that purchases credit options on the debt to receive payment on the bond if it defaults is only trying to offset the potential for credit loss. If the bond does not default, the credit option would not be used, although payments would continue to be made to the option holder. This has been the situation for both General Motors and Ford Motor Company, both of which have continued to dominate the market for credit derivatives among creditors and investors. As noted in Tables 4.2 and 4.3, the most active sector in the United States for credit derivative trading is the automotive industry, and in Europe and Asia the most active sectors are telecommunications and financial services. Although the risk of the debt for General Motors and Ford requires higher returns to investors, concern continues to prevail among the holders of debt

T A B L E   4 - 3

Five Most Active CDS for April 2006*

United States	Europe	Asia
GMAC	KPN	Aiful
Ford Motor Credit	VNU	Takefuji
General Motors Corp	Kaupthing Bunadarbanki	Softbank Corp
Computer Sciences	Deutsche Telecom	Sony

*CDS are for credit default swaps, which will be discussed later in the chapter.

Source: RiskCenter.com

for these two auto firms because of the rising gasoline prices and potential labor instability. By using credit derivatives, lenders have purchased an optional funding strategy and investment tool to help reduce their credit risk exposure through this type of credit protection. The distinction between the two instruments is that although options transfer risk from one investor to another, the credit derivatives provide insurance that transfers the risk to a guarantor if default occurs. Another major distinction is that options allow holders the choice to buy or sell assets when their price exceeds or falls below the strike price, which gives them the opportunity to make money. On the otherhand, a credit derivative pays the holders in the event of default to prevent them from suffering the risk of financial losses. This practice of purchasing insurance as a funding strategy against risk has become a growing phenomenon among lenders, and one that has led to a growing credit derivatives market.

4.14 CREDIT DERIVATIVES: A GROWING MARKET

The market for credit derivatives consists of customized products that contract to transfer credit risk between participating parties so that investors can buy and sell a form of insurance against corporate and business defaults. Although most derivative and option products are based on some other underlying credit product or instrument (e.g., currency derivative values are derived from the foreign exchange market, equity derivatives are derived from the stock market or interest rates), the value of a credit derivative is intangible, because its worth is derived from and based on a borrowers' creditworthiness. In general, credit derivatives are typically applied on a debt obligation after a facility is underwritten for a single borrower to reduce the risk of credit exposure. Suppose, for example, that a leveraged finance transaction is approved and the lender wants to enter into a credit derivative contract to hedge against the risk of default by a high-risk borrower. The lender can enter into a bilateral contract as the protection buyer, which transfers to another party known as the protection seller the credit risk in the debt asset or the counterparty. The bank, as the protection buyer, has therefore mitigated its risk exposure in the event that the leveraged company defaults. If the counterparty defaults on the asset, the protection seller will pay the protection buyer a preagreed principal amount. In other words, the lender has purchased a form of insurance by hedging the borrower or counterparty's risk of default on its debt obligations.

Credit derivatives are priced to reflect the credit quality of the borrower, which is also an incentive for the protection seller to assume the credit risk. Suppose a credit derivative is entered into with a protection seller for an investment-grade-rated counterparty to provide compensation with a premium in the event of a downgrade. In this example, the protection seller anticipates the borrower will have a positive credit event and negotiates for an upgrade, downgrade, or both in the contract for the hedged credit event. The upgrade would therefore be a positive credit event that would reduce the credit risk exposure and result in a profitable return to the protection seller. This is an example of the market environment that prevailed during the period 2001–2004, when the low interest rate environment encouraged corporate bond issuers to recall their high-yield bonds in exchange for lower priced term loans. For some creditors, the redemption of the high-yield bonds was a positive credit event that resulted in enhancing their credit portfolio returns. Aside from purchasing protection, a lender will also sell credit protection in order to gain exposure to a corporate name. A final reason why lenders enter into credit derivative contracts is to reduce the cost of capital by limiting their balance sheet credit exposure to increase lending capacity. If we refer to our example from Chapter 2, which is illustrated in Figure 4.17, we see that credit risk is assumed and managed by transferring exposures through hedging and the capital markets.

The phenomenal growth of the credit derivatives markets that has occurred over the past few years resulted in a 128% increase alone, to an estimated $12 trillion dollars in notational outstanding trades between June 2004 and June 2005.[10] Concerns, however, have emerged over the rate of the growth. Regulators, for example, feel that inadequate market prices and infrastructure has impeded the efficiency of the credit derivatives market. Given that these products are traded over the counter, the rapid growth in their volume has not kept pace with the required technological infrastructure that is needed to process them. Many trades continue to be processed manually rather than electronically, thus increasing the probability of manual errors and exposure to operational risk as the market continues to grow.[11] In a recent survey by the International Swaps and Derivatives Association (ISDA), it was

FIGURE 4.17

Managing the Credit Risk Transaction

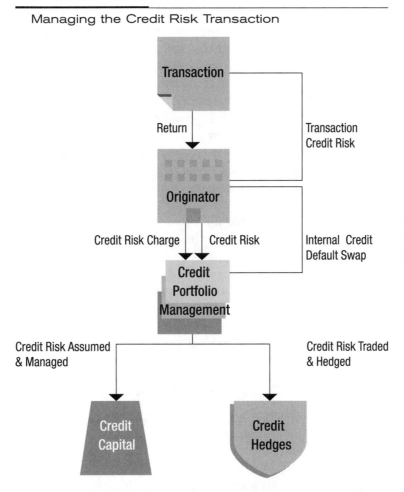

found that around "one in five credit derivatives trades made by banks in 2005 initially contained errors, which was double the rate from what it was in 2004."[12]

Although primarily used to hedge against corporate defaults, credit derivatives have also been adapted for other segments of the capital markets. For example, credit derivatives for asset-backed securities were introduced to the market in June 2005 and more recently in 2006 to the shipping industry. As credit derivatives were initially introduced on corporate loans as opposed to other funding assets, they have become a structured finance funding strategy that has continued to be reflected in the ongoing convergence of loan and trading books. Although the global banks continue to be the net buyers and sellers of credit derivative products, there has been an explosion of nonbank credit derivative investors in both the United States and Europe. According to the Fitch Rating Agency, the top 25 counterparties of credit derivatives in 2003 were represented by 10 institutions, which held 69% of total counterparty exposures, essentially unchanged from the same banks' counterparty position of 70% in 2002.[13] In addition to banks, the investors who purchase and take the credit risk are in essence selling protection or a form of insurance on a particular borrower's creditworthiness and are primarily composed of asset managers, hedge funds, insurance companies, and pension funds. These investors seek to enhance their portfolio returns by accepting the credit risk in an asset in exchange for a fee and the potential returns or yields. The transfer of risk by the protection buyer is essentially a process through which the creditor bank, for a fee, can reassign the risk of certain credit events that may occur.

Among the most common credit derivatives products are credit default swaps, asset or total return swaps, credit-linked notes, and collateralized debt obligations (CDOs), of which single-named credit default swaps have become the most widely used. Each of these credit products will be discussed in the next section.

4.14.1 Credit Default Swaps

A credit default swap is a financial guarantee whereby, for a fee, the protection seller agrees to compensate the protection buyer if a counterparty defaults or is downgraded in a credit event. Typically, banks use single named credit default swaps to hedge the credit risk exposure on a single borrower by providing credit protection or insurance for both bonds and loans in the event of the issuer or borrower's default. Credit default swaps are also commonly used by lenders that fund specific industries or geographical areas. Specifically, these instruments allow lenders to exchange their loan repayments with each other, by reducing the amount of credit risk. To further illustrate, refer to Figures 4.18, in which a corporate borrower obtains a $10MM credit facility from Bank A, who is also known as the credit protection buyer. The credit protection buyer purchases a credit default swap on the credit obligation related to the specific borrower (known as the Reference Entity or Third Party) for a fixed payment amount that is paid on a periodic basis. The price or fee, which is usually quoted in basis points, is

FIGURE 4.18

Credit Default Swap

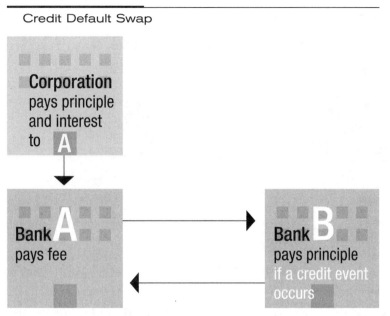

calculated based on $1,000 of premium for each $10MM of debt that is being insured against default. Thus a price of 40 basis points means the protection buyer will pay $40,000 annually to insure $10MM of debt. The credit obligation, which is referred to as "borrowed money," may comprise a variety of obligations, such as all of the debt belonging to the reference entity or particular company. Most of the time, the obligations will be equivalent or pari passu to all of the entity's senior unsecured debts. The payment to transfer and accept credit risk from the protection buyer to the protection seller will be contingent upon credit risk events that might occur. If the event occurs and the protection buyer is the lender, Figure 4.19 shows that compensation by Bank B or the protection seller will be made for the loss based on a price that was originally agreed upon when the parties entered into the contract. In the event of default on the bond or loan, where the lender has also purchased a single named credit default swap, the protection seller will take delivery of the defaulted obligation at either the contracted price, or will pay the difference between the agreed price and the current market value. What defines a credit event is also agreed upon when the parties enter the contracted transaction agreement. For example, the agreement may state that "the credit event can

FIGURE 4.19

Credit Event Outcome

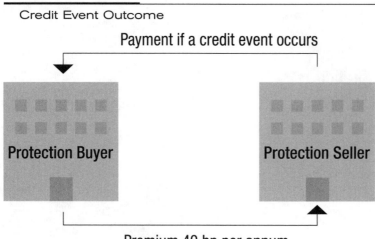

only be for the event of downgrading as well as default by the reference entity." In general, the ISDA defines credit events to consist of the circumstances noted in Figure 4.20. Should no event occur during the life of the facility, then at maturity, the protection buyer will have fully repaid the premium and the protection seller will discontinue the contract. In other words, the protection seller of credit risk can take either a short or long position on a company's credit quality.

When lenders buy credit risk, they are taking a short position with the assumption that the reference entity's credit quality has a weak outlook. Should default occur, the creditor will subsequently be paid the par value amount on the hedged credit exposure. In contrast, if the lender sells credit risk through a credit-default swap, it is taking a long position with the assumption that the reference entity's credit quality is strong. As an over-the-counter market product, the pricing for credit derivatives usually tends to be more transparent than what would have traditionally been the case in the loan markets. This has changed, however, with the advancement in pricing applications under modern credit that find the convergence of debt and equity becoming integrated and applied in credit assessment. Credit specialists can therefore use the credit default swap pricing to support their credit assessment, because it is also tied to the market's valuation of the borrower. For example credit specialists estimate that

FIGURE 4.20

Defined Categories of Credit Events

Bankruptcy	A formal bankruptcy proceeding is commenced as to the reference obligor or the obligor formally admits to insolvency.
Failure to Pay	The reference obligor fails to pay principal or interest when due and payable after expiration of any applicable grace period.
Restructuring	A transaction or governmental announcement or decree results from a deterioration in the creditworthiness or financial condition of the obligor and results in a reduction in the rate or amount of interest, a reduction of principal, a deferral of interest or principal or subordination of the reference obligation.
Obligation Acceleration	Any obligation becomes due and payable before it would otherwise have been done and payable as a result of a default or similar event other than a failure to pay.
Obligation Default	Any obligation becomes capable of acceleration as a result of a default or similar event other than a failure to pay.
Repudiation/ Moratorium	The reference obligor or a governmental authority challenges or disaffirms the validity of the reference obligation or declares or imposes a deferral of payments.

General Motors is trading at around 20% or 2,000 bp* for five-year protection against default, and Ford is trading at around half that level or a 10% probability of default (PD).[14] Based upon this industry data, some analysts and experts are predicting defaults for both companies unless revenues are stabilized, which many consider unlikely

*A basis point is one-hundredth of a percentage point and used in the context of interest rates.

given falling sales and declining consumer demand. This also suggests why supporters of credit default swaps claim that the value of these products serves as an "early warning sign" to a borrower's deteriorating credit quality. The contention is that "because they isolate pure credit risk, they are a more sensitive indicator of a company's underlying performance than other measures."[15]

4.14.2 Credit-Linked Notes

Credit-Linked Notes (CLNs) essentially provide debt lenders with insurance against loan repayment defaults. This funding strategy combines regular coupon paying notes such as a bond with some credit risk feature, in return for a higher yield to accept the risk by the investor. Although more often used for portfolio purposes to meet regulatory capital requirements, these credit products are a byproduct of securitization that can also be used on single transactions. Lenders can shift the credit risk exposure of an individual loan transaction to a credit investor(s) without affecting the original lender borrowing relationship. Unlike credit default swaps, credit-linked notes can be sold to a multitude of investors by transferring the credit risk exposure for a single transaction to a special purpose vehicle (SPV), as illustrated in Figure 4.21. Although there are a number of variations to the structure of credit-linked notes, the diagram represents

FIGURE 4.21

Structure of Credit-Linked Note

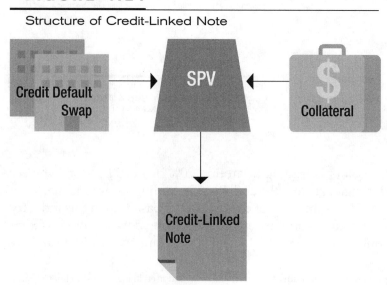

the structure for a credit default note, which is among the most common types of this facility. The credit default note is typically used to reduce credit default risk by using a credit default swap on a bond transaction by creating a synthetic credit exposure. The lender (protection buyer) transfers the credit risk to the protection seller through the SPV intermediary, who subsequently issues the CLN to the investor. The investor now has direct credit exposure to the original borrower (Reference Credit) in the form of a synthetic or manufactured exposure. The manufactured exposure is a result of the credit default swap, as the CLN is contingent on the performance of a specified borrower or reference entity. The CLN is manufactured with an embedded credit default swap in a funded asset to form the SPV whose credit risk and cash flow characteristics are similar to interest and principle repayments for a bond or loan. Provided that the reference credit has no defaults, investors usually receive a higher return than the borrower's corporate bond, and the note is also backed by high-quality collateral such as Treasuries. However, should a credit event occur that affects the creditworthiness of the original corporate entity, the investor will bear the risk of the losses. Settlement terms on these products require that investors only receive the actual bonds in the event of default of the underlying company in lieu of the Treasuries. This can result in significant losses if the bond's value declines significantly.

Another product variation of a credit-linked note is exhibited in Figure 4.22, in which the fee from the swap accrues a higher

FIGURE 4.22

Credit-Linked Note

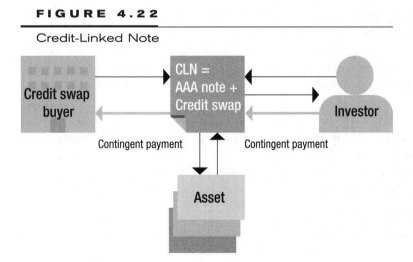

return on the credit default linked note. The $2.4BN CLN under-written by Citigroup on Enron in 1999 to a SPV known as Yosemite is an example of a CLN that had significant loss. The facility was contracted by Citigroup to reduce exposure to the energy-trading company on $1.7BN, which represented four times the bank's internal limits. However, subsequent to the default by Enron, Citigroup became embroiled in litigation relative to the transaction, as investors claimed that the bank was aware of accounting fraud by the company and helped to mislead them.[16]

4.14.3 Total Return Swap

Another commonly used credit-linked note or derivative structure is the asset or total return swap, which is designed to mitigate credit risk exposure from noncredit events such as exchange or interest rates volatility. A lender (total return payer/buyer) funds a debt instrument and then transfers the credit risk exposure and interest in the facility to an investor (total return receiver/seller). Although the investor does not have legal ownership of the asset nor a rela-tionship with the Reference Entity, the total return swap transaction has created a synthetic or manufactured credit exposure. The pay-ments on these transactions by the lender are typically linked to the return on a loan transaction or portfolio, because the protection sell-er ties them to some reference rate or benchmark such as the yield on Treasuries or a spread above LIBOR. Lenders will often use these funding strategies for regulatory capital purposes. If you recall the example earlier in the chapter on a $1BN syndicated loan facility with JPMorganChase, assume that the syndication was undersub-scribed with $650MM sold. Suppose further that because the bor-rower is a long-standing and profitable customer, the bank wants to retain the balance of the loan, but the concentration exposure from doing so would be over the lending limits and 8% internal capital requirements. By entering into a total return swap with another OECD Bank, JPMorganChase would then be able to fund the loan balance by swapping this asset from its balance sheet to the investor in favor of the borrowing relationship.* As compensation for the funding costs of buying the balance of the asset, the bank pays the total return receiver the appropriate equivalent LIBOR. The result is

---

*The Organization of Economic Cooperative Developing Countries (OECD) consists of governments from over 100 number countries around the world that are committed to democratic banking and market best practices.

FIGURE 4.23

Total Return Swap

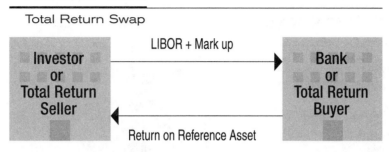

that the arranger has now created an off-balance-sheet exposure and incurred lower capital requirements. An illustration of the total return swap is exhibited in Figure 4.23, which outlines how the basic features of this product operates through the cash flow payments that are directly returned to each party. The total return receiver is paid a return on the reference asset and the investor pays the bank to purchase an asset that it has not had to fund and that covers all interest charges and the assets market value. Similar to bonds, however, these funding strategies are exposed to market risk, because if the price of the asset rises, the receiver is paid the appreciation and, if it declines, payment to the buyer is equivalent to the depreciation in value. The facility terminates if a credit event occurs prior to maturity.

4.14.4 Collateralized Debt Obligations

Collateralized debt obligations (CDOs) comprise a range of structured transactions that have come to be used more often for portfolio selection risks. The CDOs are a diverse basket of different types of structured finance debt assets. The pool of assets can consist of a variety of bank loans or corporate bonds that are bundled together in a CDO and rated for their marketability in the capital markets. The assets in the CDO, which may include credit default swaps, leveraged loans, high-yield bonds, and emerging market debt, are issued through an established SPV that is bankruptcy remote to the originator of the securities.* Typically, the assets in the pool are mixed with different tranches of risk classes that

---

*Goodman (2002); The first synthetic CDO was concluded by Swiss Bank Corporation, who served as the issuer on Glacier Finance Ltd. The transaction was funded by JPMorgan under the name of BISTRO and JP Morgan.

FIGURE 4.24

Collateralized Debt Obligations (CDOs)

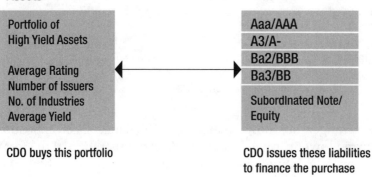

Assets

Portfolio of High Yield Assets		Aaa/AAA
		A3/A-
Average Rating Number of Issuers No. of Industries Average Yield		Ba2/BBB
		Ba3/BB
		Subordinated Note/ Equity

CDO buys this portfolio

CDO issues these liabilities to finance the purchase

encompass a range of securities from highly rated AAA senior facilities to unrated credit instruments, all of which are packaged according to the risk appetite of investors. To illustrate a CDO, refer to Figure 4.24, which shows the various types of debt tranches. The primary structural feature of the CDO is that it serves as a credit enhancer by allowing higher quality debt (e.g., AAA rated) to be issued relative to lower rated underlying collateral (e.g., single B rated). Usually there is an equity tranche that is also linked to the CDO that is exposed to high risk, but priced to produce high returns. The senior debt level of the tranche is often considered to be less risky, with lower returns, and a mezzanine debt tranche lies in the middle.

Given that this funding strategy has become a common derivative structure, it should be noted that the name CDO is used interchangeably with other derivative products in that they are all dependent on the type of underlying asset and collateral that it supports. The CDOs are alternatively referred to as collateralized loan obligations (CLO), collateralized bond obligations (CBO), or collateralized structured obligations (CSO). They can be **funded** for balance sheet and regulatory purposes in order to transfer the risk of existing loans or bonds, and they can be **unfunded**. Under a funded structure, a protection seller (investor) will pay the protection buyer (purchaser) a notional amount at the beginning of the contract, which will be subject to a write down or reduction of the principal in the event of default during the contract. The protection seller is paid a fee throughout the maturity of the contract that reflects the risk of the tranche, equivalent to LIBOR plus a spread. The investor also receives a fee that is placed into a collateral account and invested in low-risk government securities. In contrast to funded CDOs, no sum of money is exchanged at the beginning of the contract on unfunded CDOs, because the protection seller is expected to pay in the event of default, at which time the contract is terminated. Because the protection buyer does not receive payment at the beginning of the contract and relies on the protection seller's ability to pay into the vehicle, it creates counterparty risk that must be managed. The protection seller does, however, receive a spread during the life of the contract, and in the event of default will pay the obligated debt on the portfolio reference entities. Unfunded CDOs are usually motivated by an arbitrage profit opportunity on investment-grade or high-yield bonds and loans. Although, initially, banks entered into CDO contracts for balance sheet considerations, recent trends have shown arbitrage profiting to be the motivation behind this growth.

Banking regulators, however, have remained skeptical about the inherent risks that CDOs hold, along with other credit derivative products, particularly because of their novelty and increased volume growth over the past several years. Since they started in 1997, the volume of CDOs has been phenomenal, with an estimated $120BN sold in 2004 alone.[17] As illustrated in Figure 4.25, the notional amount of synthetic CDOs between 2002 and 2004 according to their collateral asset types was represented by an average monthly total issuance of $37BN. Although much of this growth has been attributed to the low-interest-rate environment for structured finance investment-grade credits, activity in this credit product continued through 2005, despite the rise in interest rates and corporate default ratings downgrades.

Nonetheless, regulators are making tremendous efforts to learn about the types of risks these products hold, especially those that may expose the financial market system to a systematic risk. Given that these products are tied to higher yielding debts for higher returns, they are exposed to market and credit cycle changes that could lead to pressures on the overall economy. Currently, the market lacks any indications on what the worst-case ramifications and risks would be. For those that utilize this funding strategy, such as arbitragers, they have been able to create profit opportunities to some of the market imperfections that are associated with illiquid bonds and loans. Lenders have been able to use this type of

FIGURE 4.25

Synthetic CDO Issuance by Type of Collateral

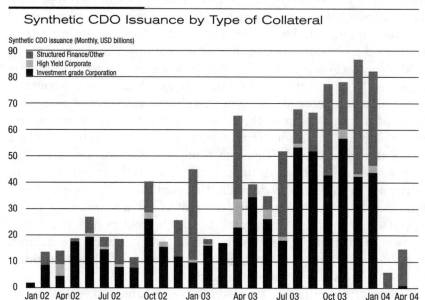

Source: www.cred.tflust.com

securitization to aid them in reducing their concentration risk to
selected borrowers and also to obtain balance sheet benefits.
However, the concern is that the structural complexities and degree
of credit risks can also outweigh the gains. This is because CDOs do
not always effectively mitigate risk exposure, especially when the
securitized assets result in greater risks than the actual debts supported. For example, assume that a SPV is formed by a lender to act
as a conduit for securitized loans in the form of asset-backed securities, with a highly rated tranche that is sold to investors. To obtain
the high credit rating, it is determined that the transaction will need
some kind of credit enhancement from the originating or sponsoring bank. Under this scenario, the originating bank still retains the
major credit risk components and has actually only substituted
the value of the underlying debts with a securitized asset. In return,
the sponsoring bank receives the residual spread on the loan yields
along with all of the interest and other costs, but not any benefits
from mitigating credit risk exposure. The question then becomes
whether the portfolio of assets is appropriate for securitization,
because problems in measuring exposures can arise on asset securities of unfunded facilities such as revolving credits, counterparty

risk from credit derivatives, or unfunded commitments. The reason that is attributed to this is that companies may not always use their revolving facilities, but prefer to have them ready in the event that they are needed, and often, they are drawn when they have financial trouble. Quantifying the default probability of these structures therefore requires that an estimate of the default probability is made on imprecise exposure amounts. For example, suppose a SPV is formed to act as a conduit for securitizing $100MM of unfunded loan commitments in the form of asset-backed securities. The conduit plans to issue $80MM in senior securities to the public, with the remaining $20MM to be sponsored by the issuing bank. Generally, a letter of credit by the originating bank is required to provide credit enhancement to the deal in order to attain a high credit rating so that the assets can be sold to the public. In effect, the letter of credit and $20MM is actually providing credit protection to the $80MM debt investors, who will not realize any negative consequences unless the loan losses exceed the 20%. The amount of credit risk that is retained in the securitization is therefore based on the level of lower tranche securities, which can be highly risky. Although a high credit rating on the senior securities makes the possibility of default unlikely, the point is that the originating banks still retains the credit risk from the securitized asset. This is why the use of asset securitizations must have a clear distinction between the exposure and the credit obligation, in order to mitigate the risk of credit loss. For this reason, arbitrage regulatory capital requirements are issued on CDO structures such as these, because lenders often will still retain the credit risk exposure on these securitized vehicles. As we will discuss in Chapters 7 and 8, statistical credit scoring and credit ratings have become widely used in these matters, to better measure the probability of default on the securitized assets.

4.14.5 Credit Assessment

Analysis of a CDO begins by assessing the various counterparties that may include the protection seller or asset manager. Credit specialists will also be concerned about the structural characteristics for the types of underlying asset classes and the designated collateral mix to mitigate the risks. Because there is limited liquidity, the analyst will want to review the cash flow stability for the CDO, especially on the more junior tranches, to determine timely repayment and probability of default. Another major risk is that because these product structures are still relatively new and the market is still learning about their risks, credit specialists must consider how one asset within the pool of debt instruments can affect the other assets in the pool. This is important, because CDOs are priced on the effect of correlation, and limited data are available on whether any deterioration can lead to a chain reaction that will affect another asset class. In addition, because many CDOs are held by the same protection buyers and sellers, which are integrated throughout the credit markets, this ultimately could have a snowball effect should the participants panic and engage in a rapid sell-off.

4.15 CONCLUSIONS

Firms need commercial bank loans and other traditional debt products to ensure that sufficient financial resources are available to meet daily working capital needs. Companies need asset conversion loans to meet their production cycles when cash flows have been mistimed. Capital investment expenditures are also required for strategic growth and to maximize the company's competitive value and future market position. Funding strategies are furthermore needed for companies that find themselves stifled by high borrowing costs and want to replace existing debt with cheaper funding sources. Lenders use various credit products according to their term to maturity relative to a company's short-, medium-, and long-term funding needs. These products range from the use of traditional loan products to the capital market products such as CDOs, which have come to serve as an indicator and enhancement for evaluating the financial performance and repayment ability of single borrowers. Many products, however, are filled with a broad range of option-like characteristics, which should be understood by credit specialists in all business credit sectors.

CHAPTER DISCUSSION QUESTIONS

1. What credit products would the lender use to provide working capital and finance an acquisition?
2. What are the three types of credit funding strategies that lenders typically finance?
3. What is the difference between a credit default swap and a total return swap?
4. What credit product would the lender provide to build a toll highway?

5. Distinguish between a bridge loan and a subordinated loan?

6. Why do some debt suppliers prefer the use of a standby letter of credit?

7. Distinguish a club versus a bilateral syndicated loan extension?

8. What is structured finance?

9. Suppose Sea Way Bank has significant credit risk exposure to Field Company, an automotive manufacturer. Although Field Company has been a profitable and long-standing customer to Sea Way, the bank now anticipates a downgrade as a result of the cyclical automotive industry and operating problems due to production costs, labor costs, and health-care employee benefits. Many of its contracts from major suppliers have also been delayed or postponed while industry restructuring is undertaken. Field Company approaches Sea Way regarding a new facility to purchase new machinery. Although Sea Way does not want to decline a long-standing relationship, how would you propose that the loan officer propose the credit request?

10. A top-rated multinational company requires short-term unsecured finance for general working capital requirements that can vary, but can be in excess of $100M at any one time. What type of funding strategy would you suggest for this firm?

11. What type of credit facility will guarantee the obligations to a supplier of an operating company?

12. Assume that Bank A finances the media industry and Bank B finances the telecommunications industry, and Bank C acts as an intermediary between these banks to mitigate their risk exposure. Bank A receives interest payments on $10,000,000 of outstanding loan receivables, which it pays to Bank C as the intermediary. Bank B also receives $10,000,000 in interest payments for outstanding loan receivables that it sends to Bank C, which switches the payments between Bank A and Bank B. Under this arrangement, Bank A receives the interest payments from Bank B, while Bank B receives interest payments from Bank A. What type of credit funding product does this facility structure represent?

BIBLIOGRAPHY

Batchelor, Charles, "Derivatives 'fixing' to spur growth" *Financial Times*, March 23, 2005, p. 27.

Bavaria, Steven, "A Rated Market, at Last!" Standard & Poor's *CreditWeek, 27 Feb. 2002,* www.lsta.org/assets/files/ Home_Page/MilkenLevLoanPrimer1004.pdf.

Berger, Harris, S., Gearin, William, F., "Due diligence: two important words for all those who wear the white hats," *RMA Journal*, 87, 2, Oct. 2004, p. 39(6), article A123561384.

Caouette, John, B., Altman, Edward, I., and Narayanan, Paul, *Managing Credit Risk, The Next Great Financial Challenge,* Canada: John Wiley & Sons, Inc., 1998.

Capital Eyes, Bank of America Business Capital Monthly e-newsletter, April 2006.

Dahiya, S., Puri, M., and Saunders A., "Bank Borrowers and Loan Sales: New Evidence on the Uniqueness of Bank Loans," *Journal of Business*, 76, 4, 2003.

Dresdner, Kleinworth, Wasserstein Research, "Credit Derivatives Research Report," September 2002.

Finnerty, John, D., *Project Finance, Asset-Based Financial Engineering*, New York: John Wiley & Sons, Inc. 1996.

Francis, Jack Clark, Frost, Joyce, A., and Whittaker, Gregg, J. *The Handbook of Credit Derivatives*, New York: McGraw-Hill, 1999, p. 13–16.

International Swaps and Derivatives Association, "Interest Rate Swap Example," International Swaps and Derivatives Association Inc., retrieved October 9, 2005. www.isda.org/ educat/pdf?IRS-Diagram1.pdf.

James, C. and Smith, D. "Are Banks Still Special? New Evidence in the Corporate Capital-Raising Process," *Journal of Applied Corporate Finance*, 12, 4, Winter 2000, p. 8–19.

Kiff, Jim and Marrow, Ron, "Credit Derivatives," Financial Markets Department, Bank of Canada Review, Autumn 2000.

Kothari, Vinod, "Credit Derivatives: A primer." Vinod Kothari's Credit Derivatives Website. www.credit-deriv.com/creprime.htm.

Lopez, Jose A., "Financial Instruments for Mitigating Risk," FRBSF Economic Letter, Nov. 23, 2001, retrieved October 4, 2005, www.highbeam.com/library/docfree.asp?

Madura, Jeff, *Financial Markets and Institutions*, 7th edition, Belmont, CA: Thomson South-Western, 2006, p. 393–394.

Manuel, Ammann, *Credit Risk Valuation: Methods, Models and Applications*, Berlin: Springer Verlag, 2001.

Ranson, Brian, "The Growing Importance of Leveraged Loans," *The RMA Journal*, May 2003.

Risk Glossary, "Interest Rate Swap, Contingency Analysis." www.riskglossary.com/link/interest_rate_swap.htm.

RMF Investment Consultants, "Leveraged Loans, An Introduction to an Asset Class," Investment Summary, RMF, 2001.

Rosenthal, James A., *Securitization of Credit: Inside the New Technology*, New York: Wiley, 1988.

Rule, David, "The Credit Derivatives Market: Its development and possible implications for financial stability," G10, Financial Surveillance Division, Bank of England, Financial Stability Review, June 2001.

Satyajit, Das, "Credit Derivatives CDOs & Structured Credit Products," 3rd edition, John Wiley & Sons (Asia) Pte Ltd, 2005.

Tett, Gillian, "CDOs Have Deepened the Asset Pool for Investors but Clouds may be Gathering," *Financial Times*, April 19, 2005.

Thinkorswim Inc. "Calls, Puts & Covered Writes," Thinkorswim Inc. retrieved October 2005, www.thinkorswim.com/tos/displayPage.tos.jessionid=AFFAD6AC47BE70A885FCIEE19D958FB5?webpage=companyInformation.

Yahoo Finance, "Basic Option Concepts: Call Options," Yahoo!Inc, retrieved September 29, 2005, https://biz.yahoo.com/opt/basics3.html.

Company-Specific Financial Performance

5.1 INTRODUCTION

In Chapters 3 and 4, we described the preliminary loan approval process that credit personnel should address prior to undertaking further assessment on new transactions and presented a general framework to evaluate particular credit products relative to a company's funding strategies. The goal of this chapter is to provide an overview to the fundamental analytical applications that are used to assess a borrower's credit and financial performance.

5.2 IDENTIFYING THE HIERARCHY OF RISKS

All corporate banking and commercial lending transactions have a hierarchy of risks that need to be identified, assessed, and ranked in order to structure and underwrite credit facilities. Credit risks have to be evaluated and analyzed according to the specific risks of a borrower's general creditworthiness relative to the type of credit product that is proposed. Individual credit facilities have to be appropriately evaluated for their exposure amounts, as well as for the structural complexities that a credit request may entail. To assist in this phase of the credit assessment, a common approach that can be used is to apply a risk evaluation framework as a guide in the credit analysis and measuring process. What distinguishes the risk evaluation framework under modern credit risk is that it integrates the applications of fundamental credit analysis into sophisticated internal rating systems by escalating the effect of a single transaction's assessment into the overall credit portfolio returns.

Credit department specialists and analysts have historically performed fundamental credit analysis on individual loan transactions across industry specializations in a classical credit assessment flow. After reviewing the purpose for a credit request, the credit analyst would analyze the financial performance according to the company's financial statements, while also applying a range of standard analytic techniques to make the appropriate adjustments according to their personal perspective. The adjusted financial statements would subsequently be trended and spread in the financial projections, inclusive of stress tests assumptions on the identified risks to a firm's industry and operating position. This process also guided the lender's facilities structuring and pricing conditions, in that the credit analyst was forced to cast a suspicious eye over all aspects of the borrower's provided information in order to protect the bank's position for future repayment ability. The weakness in this approach was that it focused too much on the borrower and only considered the facility at a minimal level, neither of which process in fact attempted to quantify the transaction's overall default probability.

As commercial lenders increasingly have become more reliant on internal credit risk rating systems under the modern approach, credit assessment and analysis is now designed to support the measurement of risk rather than to simply identify and assess risks. Besides providing a conceptual framework to guide the loan origination and credit process, risk rating systems are also used to monitor portfolio concentration limits, as well as for customer profitability analysis and management reporting. At the same time, in using these systems to quantify default probability, they in effect build upon their predecessor and go beyond solely evaluating the borrower's characteristics. Although we will discuss internal risk ratings and their implications further in Chapter 9, it should be noted that, at most of the larger banks, these systems now serve as a risk evaluation framework for which credit decisions can be made to capture specific risk factors for firms such as those highlighted in Figure 5.1. At the same time, it should also be noted that although the advancements in internal risk rating systems have most certainly minimized the number of grinding details that were required under the traditional applications, they are nonetheless not a substitute or replacement for the fundamentals of traditional credit analysis. This is because the credit specialist must understand the components methodology from which

FIGURE 5.1

Summary of Credit Risk

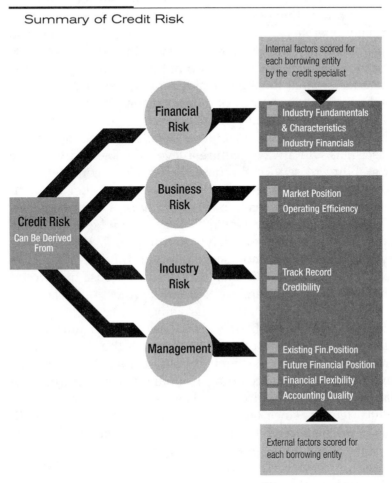

ratings are derived and have the ability to interpret and assess their results.

The specific risks that affect an individual company's creditworthiness, including the probability of default, will usually vary depending upon the borrower's relevant financial and operating characteristics. In conjunction with traditional credit analysis, a borrower's credit assessment will often require intuitive and perceptive analysis. This is also the case in the use of risk ratings, which can be subjective and hold degrees of bias, because the factors is assigning ratings and the corresponding weights that are given to each factor are still based on human judgment. In addition, the qualitative risks relative to the environment in which the company operates and the market trends that it faces are also subjective and based on perception. In fact, a major weakness of quantitative measures is that they do not always account for the qualitative factors that must be considered when extending credit, such as the human psychology of a firm's management.

Because the basis for any credit assessment must encompass both the quantitative and qualitative details of the transaction, credit decisions will always require a level of subjectivity for the obligor's ability to service the debt. Roger Hale, considered by some classical credit practitioners to be the grandfather of credit analysis, stated in his publication *Credit Analysis: A Complete Guide*, that "Credit decisions are personal." "They cannot be made solely on the basis of guidelines or analytic techniques." "Each lending officer must exercise common sense and good judgment."[1] Hale further advocated that credit analysis was an expertise that would be "enhanced and refined throughout one's professional career as a result of the experience and skills gained in reviewing many transactions." Because each transaction has its own unique features, Hale advised credit officers to approach them accordingly and wrote that a credit assessment "is your decision, and you must feel comfortable with it according to your own judgment." The foundation of Hale's philosophy has not really changed for commercial lenders since the early 1980s, as extensions of credit continue to be predicated on a subjective assessment of borrowers among different lenders. Aside from the varying perceptions about the degree of certain risks that may prevail among different analysts, there is also the assigned rater's opinion about how such risks should be rated. Rather than accepting the rating as a simple spreadsheet that calculates the financial indicators from the input data, credit specialists should look beyond the face value of reported financial data, as it is usually not a firm's true economic condition but only an approximation.

A company-specific risk evaluation can therefore serve to highlight the key credit issues of a borrower's financial and operating conditions as well as the strengths and weaknesses it faces in the external market environment. By focusing on specific key credit questions in the risk evaluation process, the credit specialist will be able to identify areas that need to be further investigated and analyzed in individual transactions.

5.3 CONSTRUCTING A FRAMEWORK TO RISK-EVALUATE TRANSACTIONS

The framework for developing a company-specific risk evaluation to assess credit transactions is similar to the example that is illustrated in Figure 5.2. When credit transactions are extended, renewed, or amended, lenders want to know about these key credit questions and issues relevant to the borrower. Analytical risk measures are applied to identify and evaluate the specific financial, business, industry, management, and facility risks related to a borrower and the proposed credit exposure. Among the financial measures and risk-rating objectives are the overall financial analysis on the adequacy of future cash flows and the borrower's debt service capacity to repay the credit facility. This includes identifying the liquidity position from cash flows in addition to those that will be affected by additional off-balance-sheet and contingent financial obligations. Additional components to also be considered are the firm's profitability, working capital, and need for capital, along with a conceptual understanding for fundamental accounting theories and applications to evaluate the firm's financial flexibility and accounting quality. Asset valuations also need to be considered,

FIGURE 5.2

Risk Evaluation Framework

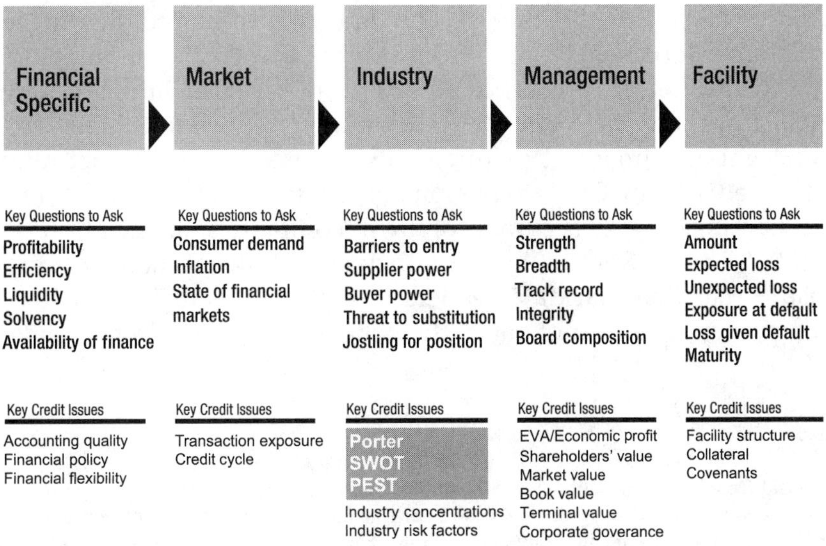

Financial Specific	Market	Industry	Management	Facility

Key Questions to Ask	Key Questions to Ask	Key Questions to Ask	Key Questions to Ask	Key Questions to Ask
Profitability	Consumer demand	Barriers to entry	Strength	Amount
Efficiency	Inflation	Supplier power	Breadth	Expected loss
Liquidity	State of financial	Buyer power	Track record	Unexpected loss
Solvency	markets	Threat to substitution	Integrity	Exposure at default
Availability of finance		Jostling for position	Board composition	Loss given default
				Maturity

Key Credit Issues	Key Credit Issues	Key Credit Issues	Key Credit Issues	Key Credit Issues
Accounting quality	Transaction exposure	Porter	EVA/Economic profit	Facility structure
Financial policy	Credit cycle	SWOT	Shareholders' value	Collateral
Financial flexibility		PEST	Market value	Covenants
			Book value	
		Industry concentrations	Terminal value	
		Industry risk factors	Corporate goverance	

particularly in working capital transactions and as a secondary means of repayment. Although the qualitative factors for evaluating a firm's industry, market, and management risks will be covered in Chapter 6, the focus in the remainder of this chapter will be on how the key financial credit issues are evaluated for credit risk.

5.3.1 Evaluating the Borrower's Financial-Specific Performance

A company-specific financial risk evaluation highlights the borrower's operating conditions from the reported financial statements and supplementary data. When analysts evaluate financial statements, they are seeking to determine the purpose for which the borrower wants financing and whether it will have the debt capacity to repay the facility in the future. Conclusions drawn from the income statement, balance sheet, and statement of cash flows of a borrower will be a key credit risk if the financial data are not transparent. This was evident in the whirlwind of corporate scandals during 2001 and 2002 for several major public firms like Enron and Worldcom. Because the lack of transparency by these firms was alleged to have been so aggressive, it led the U.S. Congress to introduce stringent legislation and subsequently pass the 2002 Sarbanes–Oxley Corporate Responsibility Act (SOX). Authored by Congressman Michael Oxley of Ohio, in conjunction with Senator Paul Sarbanes of Maryland and Senator Richard Shelby of Alabama, the SOX has given new meaning to the phrase "the buck stops here." Aside from officers and corporate directors now being held to higher standards, the bill also imposes new restrictions on the ethics of auditors and corporate lawyers. The legal and financial requirements covered under the act now ultimately require CEOs to personally certify, with their signatures, the legitimacy and accuracy of their company's financial statements.* The SOX seeks to strengthen reporting mechanisms and ensure that financial data readers have transparent information. Companies that do not meet the guidelines are subject to have

---

*Under Section 403 of the bill, CEOs and CFOs are required to verify their company's financial records and are held liable if they misrepresent the truth about their company's finances. Section 404 also requires that companies create extensive internal controls and processes that document and verify material information concerning financial results.

"material weaknesses in their audited financial statements that can lead to higher credit risk and incur higher financing costs." In other words a material weakness indicates to the public that the financial statements may not be accurate and legally exposes borrowers as well as lenders to possible litigation. From a credit perspective, companies whose auditors identify material weaknesses in their financial reports ultimately expose the lender to the risk of a decline in their stock price, capitalization, reputation, and potential legal liability.

In general, lenders will be concerned with the accuracy and reliability of the reported financial statements; in particular, a firm's earnings, assets, liabilities, and cash flows are a concern if they are mis-stated. However, it is difficult to measure and quantify control deficiencies by internally risk rating a firm with material weaknesses, because it is only in the details of the quantitative and qualitative analysis that credit issues are usually found. Credit personnel that assess transactions and assign risk ratings have to investigate and use their analytical judgment to determine how severe control deficiencies may be. They must determine if a reported material weakness represents a complete financial failure that will impair the company's access to financing, or whether it is a trivial problem that has little bearing on the reported earnings. A rule of thumb that credit specialists can apply is to determine whether or not the material weakness represents the type of financial failure that bears on the borrower's reported earnings and financing access. Controls that are expected to impact a borrower's financial and operational results are the primary emphasis to lenders, although credit specialists must still scrutinize and investigate on all reported matters. Table 5.1 summarizes the types of credit issues that are usually considered by creditors when evaluating identified material weaknesses, and Table 5.2 gives a list of early warning signs that can be problem indicators. The components of these indicators will be discussed in the next section.

5.3.2 Interpreting the Details in the Financial Statements

Credit specialists must be cognizant of the fact that assessing and analyzing the credit risk of a borrower ultimately relies upon their individual analysis and due diligence on behalf of the lending

TABLE 5-1

Material Weakness Indicator

Credit Issues to Review	Matters of Concern
Revenue recognition and measurement	How are future revenues booked in the current period for long-term contracts?
	How is unrealizable revenue calculated?
	Does the borrower have any swap transactions that overstate revenues and that do not have any realizable value?
	Evaluate how currency value affects earnings?
Accounting quality	What type of accounting policies and methodologies does the company practice?
	Does the company use conservative or aggressive accounting policies?
	Are derivative positions valued correctly at Mark-to-Market Accounting?
	What is the valuation rationale?
	Does the rationale for derivative accounting have a material impact on the financial statements?
Leverage	Is the company managing leverage with additional debt?
	Does the firm have any convertibles that appear to be equity but are actually a debt or credit trigger?
Mergers and acquisitions	Determine if the firm has any mergers or acquisitions that will impact the firm's future debt position and the debt/capital risk ratio?
Loss on derivatives	Does the firm appear the have any complex hedging strategies in place that are not real hedges?
	Are the derivatives liquid and are there any naked positions?
Off-balance sheet transactions	Does the company have any operating leases that should be capital leases or any capital leases that should be operating leases?
Special-purpose entities and joint ventures	Is the firm engaged in financial engineering with Special Purpose Entities (SPE) and Joint Ventures (JV)?
	Determine if the firm is engaged in assisting in product financing to its parent company customers and, if so, how is capital
Capitalization	How is the firm capitalized and does it have reliable access to future capital. What are the borrower's sources of capital and how are the capital sources structured?

(*Continued*)

TABLE 5-1 *(Continued)*

Material Weakness Indicator

Credit Issues to Review	Matters of Concern
Goodwill and intangible valuations	How does the company value its assets and at what price?
	Has the company had any significant write-offs or are any expected in the future?
Pension liability	What are the company's estimated pension needs and how does it compare to the projected returns?
	Are the projected pension returns realistic?
	How does the company treat its options?

TABLE 5-2

Early Warning Signs Checklist

Income statement	Sustainability of earnings
	Rapid growth
	Change in margins
	High fixed cost structure components
	Investment income
	Extraordinary items
Balance sheet	Rapid change in receivables
	Rapid change in inventories
	Increases in overdrafts
	Goodwill—what is it really worth?
	Capitalized expenses
	Pension liabilities
Footnotes	Related party transactions
	Lease liabilities
	Contingent liabilities
	Changes to accounting policies
Nonfinancial	Borrower communications
	Change in auditors
	Change in strategy—movement into unrelated businesses
	Delayed financial information
	Insider selling
	Changes in key management

organization. Although audited financial statements and internal ratings are intended to provide greater transparency, it is even more incumbent upon the lender to be thorough in their credit evaluation by looking beneath the numbers. At the same time it should also be noted that many credit decisions have been wrong when they were based strictly on financial statements. In the first place, this is because financial statements are by nature subjective, and do not look at all of the risk factors, which can lead to pertinent questions going unnoticed about borrowers' true credit conditions. For example, assets on the balance sheet may be more illusory than the credit analyst initially thinks. Good credit specialists have to look beneath the surface to really grasp the value of a company's assets in the event that it becomes a secondary source of repayment. Secondly, the lender should always consider that financial statements represent historical information on conditions that have already transpired. A review of a company's financial statements at December 31 is no longer accurate by January 15 or by the time it gets in the hands of a lender. The company's asset market valuations or cash position, for example, will have already changed by January 15, thereby making the reported financial data differ from what is reported on December 31. When evaluating the credit risk of a borrower, the analyst should therefore look beyond financial reports by reviewing all company available and supplementary information. Third, a company-specific risk evaluation should be accompanied by an investigation of events that have occurred since the annual report was prepared. This is why publicly traded companies are required to file and report the 10-K annually and the 8-K and 10-Q quarterly. The 10-K, which entails greater detail than the annual report, is due 90 days after the close of a company's fiscal year, and the Securities and Exchange Commission (SEC) requires the 10-Q to be reported within 45 days after the close of each quarter. As major events can occur during the interim of the financial reporting period that have a significant impact on earnings, companies are required to report them in the 8-K. This includes events such as acquisitions, divestments, bankruptcies, or even management changes, which must also be reported for any adverse effect that it can have on a company. Lenders must determine what effect an acquisition or divestment has on a company's financial condition and whether it has an adverse effect on the borrower's debt repayment. Newspaper articles, surveys, and interviews with company and industry sources familiar with the firm are additional resources to monitor, along with investment and analyst reports and the company's website.

Credit analysts should also be apprised of and review proxy statements, particularly relating to details on executive compensation, perks, employment arrangements, and related party transactions. Sarbanes–Oxley has also placed a ban on loans to officers and directors, thus making any appearance of impropriety a call for circumspection. The 2002 charges that the former CEO of Tyco Corporation, Dennis Kozlowski, purchased art and property with company funds for his own personal use served to expose the issue of abuse and mismanagement of corporate funds by executive management. When reviewing a company with executive perks that seem to extend beyond the benchmarks, credit specialists should undertake further investigation. If company earnings are below expectations, the analyst must consider whether management compensation could become a future credit risk issue. In addition there are companies that have had significant insider and affiliate transactions, such as Enron or Adelphia, for example, which have proven to be low-credit-quality borrowers for lenders.

Another credit factor that should also be evaluated in a financial specific risk evaluation is a company's accounting quality and the risks that are relevant to its historical and future financial performance. These details are needed to apply and outline the historical trends in forecasting future financial performance. Undertaking a financial analysis also requires that credit specialists are familiar with basic accounting concepts and principles.

5.4 ACCOUNTING CONCEPTS AND PRINCIPLES

Credit specialists must be able to understand the accounting methodologies and practices that borrowers use to generate and report financial data. The increasing growth in cross-border transactions, inclusive of exotic funding strategies such as credit derivatives and structured finance, requires analysts to also be knowledgeable about fundamental accounting principles and standards globally. Global companies have different reporting standards for how transactions have occurred that must be reconciled to the standards used by a commercial lender's home country. The Financial Accounting Standards Board (FASB) sets out the fundamental accounting concepts that are relied upon and used in the United States. As a nongovernmental body, FASB establishes the accounting principles and standards known as GAAP (Generally Acceptable Accounting Principles) that are applied to all publicly traded companies and that are required by the SEC. The International Accounting Standards Boards (IASB), which is also a nongovernmental body similar to FASB, establishes the fundamental accounting concepts outside of the United States. The IASB has established a Board of International Accounting Standards Committee to develop a uniform set of accounting principles and standards for these countries, which is known as the International Accounting Standards (IAS). The IASB also publishes a series of interpretations on the international accounting standards developed by the International Financial Reporting Interpretations Committee (IFRIC) and that are approved by IASB.

5.4.1 Differences Between GAAP and IAS

Although GAAP and IAS represent formalized systems for reporting companies' financial histories and economic events, an ongoing struggle has prevailed over the years between the users of these two systems. Although GAAP has historically been perceived as more subjective and "rule-based," in contrast, IAS has been viewed by its users to have more substance because it is based on "principles." Opponents of GAAP state that their rules are too narrow, but the counter-argument by the opponents of IAS is that the principle guidelines used in their financial reporting are much too broadly defined and should be more specific. IAS proponents have also argued that the standards originally developed by GAAP have been inconsistent in that they have enabled a number of alternative accounting methods to be used. European firms have further claimed that GAAP standards are more difficult to use and too costly to implement, as well as suggesting that they lead to attempts at circumventing the standards while encouraging scandals like Enron. In contrast, U.S. firms and supporters of GAAP feel that principle-based or IAS accounting standards are difficult to compare in financial reporting and that, without having a structured approach as found in rules-based accounting, too much flexibility and manipulation is provided to auditors. Rather than detail how the accounting principle should be applied, GAAP users advocate that IASC only identifies how the principles are used, while allowing companies to indicate their compliance with IASC standards without having comparable financial statements.

Historically, the United States and, particularly, the SEC, have not recognized IASC standards for publicly traded companies that did not conform to GAAP. Rather, publicly traded non-U.S. companies that were listed on the U.S. stock exchanges were required to file a Form 20-F (in lieu of Form 10-K) and reconcile their financial reports to GAAP.* Although less restrictive, form 20-F is similar to an annual report, but only requires that companies detail their financial reporting accounting methods and reconcile net income and stockholders' equity with GAAP. However, as more companies seek to be listed on overseas stock exchanges, lenders should verify how the distinctions between the two systems will impact a debt transaction. Credit specialists that evaluate borrowers using different accounting standards must be familiar with the basic distinctions between them in order to adjust, risk rate, and grade borrowers.

It does, however, appear that changes and conformity between the two standards may be unfolding. Since the early 2000s, the U.S. FASB representatives have been working with IAS to adopt consistent international standards with the intent to move towards full convergences globally by 2007. European companies specifically see uniform accounting standards as a means to better compete globally. Many of these companies have faced severe competition and constraints by having to pay a few basis points in higher financing costs due to the differences in accounting standards. In addition, central banks and foreign governments have become strong advocates of the conversion towards the principles-based rules approach in recognition of how a systematic collapse of the global financial system could slow capital flows. This has become increasingly more evident, as accounting standards have not kept pace with many of

---

*Until recently, an exception to this has been between the United States and Canada, who have a multi-jurisdictional disclosure system, which has been aided by the fact that Canadian companies also use GAAP standards that are established by the Canadian Institute of Chartered Accountants. Although the standards differ between countries, the agreement requires that U.S. and Canadian companies that issue securities in Canada or the United States are to be reconciled to the respective country. The reconciliations between U.S. and Canadian GAAP standards, can be found in the footnotes of the companies' financial statements or summary description of the accounting policies used. However, in 2006, Canada announced that it would be formally changing to the IAS sometime in 2007.

the innovative financial instruments that are on the market today. It further supports the cliché that "while finance is a technique, accounting is an art." To obtain a true picture of an individual oblig- or's credit risk, there must be confidence about the transparency of information, beginning with accounting quality and the method- ologies used in the reporting. Obligors can change their risk profile instantaneously with an interest rate swap, credit default swap, or by acquiring options or forward contracts to hedge their future credit exposure, as well by changing the quality of accounting methodology that they use. Until these accounting standards are converged or harmonized, credit specialists will have to rely on rec- onciling the differences at the time, and, despite the efforts that are under way to move closer to harmonization of GAAP and IAS, it remains to be seen how they will develop.

5.4.2 Reviewing Accounting Policies and Reporting Methodologies

Credit specialists must also review the accounting policies of a firm to appropriately risk rate them. Commercial banking credit analysts have traditionally been trained and skilled in identifying weak accounting quality and reporting methodologies.* Seasoned and experienced lenders have known from decades of detailed credit analysis that companies inflate their financial reports by using accounting methods that resulted in reporting the financial performances sought by investors and creditors. In response, banks would make the appropriate adjustments in pricing credit facilities when existing deviations surfaced. At the same time, commercial lenders are also apprehensive about companies that use aggressive accounting policies, particularly as history has proven that there is a tendency for them to be accompanied by aggressive behaviors, which risks lenders usually want to avoid. Because of compliance guidelines like Sarbanes–Oxley, financial statement readers and, in particular, lenders of credit, have a greater degree of comfort when companies apply conservative

---

*Research by Bharath, Sunder and Sunder (2004) states that "there is anecdotal evidence that banks discern the quality of borrowers better than bond markets. The authors also note research evidence from Beatty, Ramesh and Weber (2002) that "demonstrates that banks charge interest rates to take into account the accounting changes for financial statement deviations and also in monitoring loan covenants."

TABLE 5-3

Critical Financial Performance Measurements

Accounting quality	The need for capital
Financial policy	Financial flexibility
Capital structure	Working capital
Asset valuation	Profitability
Off balance sheet	Cash flow adequacy
Financing	Ratio analysis

rather than liberal accounting principles. Notwithstanding this, the type of accounting policies used by firms is also an important indicator about the type of management a company has in place, because it can reveal the ethical practices of firms. Although the use of liberal accounting policies may fall short of actually engaging in accounting deceptions, credit specialists and other commercial lenders have also found them to represent less than unscrupulous motivations.

A borrower's accounting quality should be measured along with a variety of financial performance measurements. Table 5.3 highlights some of the critical financial performance measurements that should be reviewed when undertaking a risk evaluation. Aside from having an effect on all other key credit issues, they serve as financial indicators that should be further investigated and serve as early warning signs. Many of these measurements can initially be glimpsed in the ratio analysis, which is also a critical emphasis in credit analysis that continues to remain under modern applications. In fact, credit analysis has always applied the practice of ratio analysis as a technique to highlight areas about borrowers that should be further investigated. The next section will discuss this practice and the role it continues to play in credit risk management.

5.5 RATIO ANALYSIS

Because financial statements alone do not render a complete description of financial performance, credit analysis uses ratio analysis to build upon the assessment of a firm's cash flow position to further examine the borrower's operations. Ratio analysis integrates isolated financial information into a common format in order to evaluate a firm's historical financial performance over various business cycles. This also serve as a relationship indicator that helps to identify risks and potential growth prospects that can subsequently be used to forecast a firm's future debt repayment. As we will also discuss in Chapter 6, ratios are used to evaluate industries, and in particular compare the composition of sector competitors relative to their sales and costs structures as well as their relationship to assets and liabilities. To derive the most information from the analysis, credit analysts use several approaches depending on what they want to determine. One approach is to evaluate the change in a firm's size over time in common size financial statement format by comparing data between firms of different sizes and presenting financial statement analysis components as a percentage of a relevant base ratio. The second type of ratio analysis is the cross-sectional analysis, which compares a company's financial ratios to the industry or median value ratio averages of other firms in the industry. Another approach is the review of trends in a time series analysis of a company's performance over a period of time such as five years, typically to reveal weaknesses derived in year-to-year comparisons that highlight trends.

However, there are several points to keep in mind about ratios. First, financial ratios are "flags" indicating areas of strength or weakness. One or even several ratios might be misleading, but when combined with other knowledge relevant to financial performance, ratio analysis can tell much about a borrower or its industry. Second, there is no single correct value for a ratio. The observation that the value of a particular ratio is too high, too low, or just right depends on the perspective of the analyst. Third, a financial ratio is meaningful only when it is compared with some standard, such as another industry trend or ratio trend for the specific metric and industry being analyzed. Credit specialists must also remember that although ratios provide an historical snapshot of companies, as a tool, they cannot be relied upon alone. Although they serve as an analytical tool to evaluate the risk exposure to a company, there are limitations to using them alone to determine a borrower's creditworthiness. They do not define the company's value, as that depends on the present value of future cash flow projections and, alternatively, creditworthiness requires that projected cash flows are able to exceed the debt service capacity to repay the loan. In addition, because ratios report historical financial performance, they do not reflect the company's condition throughout the year. Their usefulness is even more limited when based on a single year and they really require a trend analysis that can be compared to the industry. Notwithstanding that, firms also have the ability to manipulate ratio results in their reporting process. Unless the financial statements have been appropriately adjusted, they can be distorted if, for example, items such as off-balance sheet liabilities are not accounted. Another distortion that can be prevalent in ratios is that the industry comparisons will often have operating segments outside of the borrower's industry. It is difficult, for example, to make an industry comparison for a company like 3M, which has multiproduct lines. A more realistic picture can be found, for example, with the airlines industry, which tends to provide a single product line in delivering air transport services.

5.5.1   Ratio Categories

Although lenders use a variety of ratios, which may be calculated differently and subject to their preference, the table of ratios presented in the Appendix at the end of this chapter presents some of the more common that are used, which fall under the following six categories.

5.5.1.1   Profitability

Credit analysts evaluate earnings and profitability to gain insight into how decisions are made about a firm's ongoing operations and whether those policies will have a sustaining impact on the quality of its earnings. The importance of earnings and profitability to lenders is not so much about the absolute profit amount increases that a firm earns but rather that the profits generate sufficient cash flows to serve as a source of debt repayment. In general, profitability ratios examine the quality of earnings as well as operating efficiency and how a firm's earnings are employed relative to sales, assets, and equity by comparing the profits earned to the resources invested in the firm. Lenders prefer companies that generate higher profitability margins and equity capital because they are better able to internally generate equity and attract external capital. A company with strong profitability is also better able to respond to business adversity, as they generally will have stable earnings that are growing. One should not assume, however, that because a company is profitable it has the ability to service its debt. Profitable companies have been known to default on loans and become bankrupt after running out of sufficient cash to meet their financial obligations.

5.5.1.2 Performance

Performance ratios are a link between income statement and balance sheet items. Performance ratios serve as indicators for how well management is generating profits with the company's capital. Although they are not specifically credit ratios, they can provide another clue to the borrower's performance. The ROA (return on assets) measures the amount of profit that is earned relative to a firm's total assets or the profit margin and how many times the company's assets turnover. To measure the amount of profit generated by each dollar of equity in the firm is the purpose of the ROE (return on equity), whereas the ROS (return on sales) measures how much profit is produced per dollar of sales on sales. Examination of the firm's performance can be further analyzed with the Dupont Analysis. By separating the basic components of the ROE, ROA, and ROS, the Dupont Analysis can identify strengths and weaknesses about the company's profit and asset efficiency as well as its leverage. To help simply this concept, we can use the Dupont Equation (see Appendix) to illustrate how the ROE can be used to analyze the efficiency of profit margins, capital structure, and asset utilization of a business. Although the ROE is an indicator of a firm's efficiency to generate profits from sales, this ability is also linked to how well it utilizes assets to generate those profits. The effectiveness of asset utilization is furthermore tied to the amount of assets that a firm generates for each dollar of equity. These inter-relationships can be seen in the example in Figure 5.3 for Wrigley and Keebler, both of which are consumer product firms. Suppose you are reviewing a credit request for Wrigley and determine that Keebler, along with other industry competitors, have a higher ROE than Wrigley. As the analyst, you would quite naturally want to delve further into why Wrigley has a low asset turnover, because it could suggest potential problems in the level of sales that Wrigley's assets are producing. For example, Wrigley's ROE appears to be attributed to a low leverage position compared to Keebler's high leverage position. At the same time, Keebler's high leverage has actually helped to generate a high ROE and compensated it for having a low profit margin compared to Wrigley. Credit specialists can use the Dupont Equation to study the firm's expense items and turnover and consider key credit issues and questions relative to the firm's production and marketing efforts.

FIGURE 5.3

Wriggley and Keebler, Examples of ROE

Keebler: ROE = Margin   x Productivity x Leverage

$$= \frac{95MM}{2,226MM} \times \frac{2,226MM}{1,659MM} \times \frac{1,659MM}{329MM}$$

$$= 4.27\% \quad \text{x } 1.34\% \quad \text{x } 5.04$$

$$= 28.84\%$$

Wrigley: $$ROE = \frac{308MM}{2,062MM} \times \frac{2,062MM}{1,548MM} \times \frac{1,548MM}{1,139MM}$$

$$= 14.94\% \quad \text{x } 1.33\% \quad \text{x } 1.36$$

$$= 27.02\%$$

5.5.1.3 Liquidity and Solvency Ratios

One can think of liquidity as a relative and solvency as an absolute. Liquidity ratios indicate how quickly a company can convert the operating assets into cash. Solvency is the ability to meet cash obligations as they become due (e.g., pay wages or supplies). Lenders examine solvency ratios to see if the firm has over extended itself with high levels of debt that result in adverse business conditions. The standard test of liquidity in most industries is the current ratio or current assets divided by current liabilities. It stands to reason that the current assets have to be greater than current liabilities, otherwise the company will be insolvent. A current ratio greater than "1" is usually an indicator that the company has positive working capital as well as sufficient liquidity to cover its short-term maturing obligations. As current assets are inclusive of inventory that may not be converted quickly into cash, the quick ratio is used to give a more meaningful liquidity measure. Companies that do high-volume cash business and have a high inventory turnover, such as supermarkets or gas stations, will usually have current and quick ratios below 1. However, the analyst should still compare these ratios with the company's industry average.

As liquidity and solvency are both crucial to a firm's profitability and viability, the lender also needs to determine whether the company has sufficient liquidity or cash and cash equivalent resources to meet short-term maturing obligations in one year or less. This assessment is also important when evaluating a firm's working capital condition. Liquidity questions can be relatively easy to analyze because of the short-term time frame. Solvency, however, requires that the firm has adequately and strategically planned to have sufficient cash generation for the next three, five, ten, or more years to service its obligations during that time. In essence, liquidity problems can lead firms into bankruptcy due to inadequate long-term solvency planning.

5.5.1.4 Efficiency Ratios

Firms want to maximize their profits for any given level of risk by operating efficiently, and use efficiency ratios to measure how working capital resources are handled. Lenders want to know how credit is extended to a borrowing firm's customers? Do they have policies of timely collections or do they have lax credit policies that results in significant write-offs and late collection of accounts receivables. Is the inventory appropriately managed with timely sales, or does it remain in storage too long and become obsolete, which results in an opportunity cost as the goods do not sell rapidly. What types of cash management decisions do they apply upon payment for their products? Do they pay down their debt or simply earn interest on the cash received? Does the company collect its receivables in a timely manner.

5.5.1.5 Leverage and Debt Ratios

Lenders want to see firms with capital structures that are well managed and not too reliant on debt because debt increases the company's risk. The capital structure represents the proportion of a company's debt and equity financing mixture that comprises its total capitalization. It demonstrates how the firm raises external funding sources and how the asset mix of these sources are appropriate for the degree of leverage. It is also the composition of the capital structure that determines the cost of debt or cost of capital. When a company issues debt it becomes obligated to repay fixed interest and principal payments. This is why the income statement components EBIT (Earnings Before Interest and Taxes) and EBITDA (Earnings Before Interest Taxes Depreciation and Amortization) are relevant to credit specialists, because it represents the funding source that will make these payments. Because interest costs are tax deductible, debt is usually a cheaper external financing source than equity, and investors tend to be accepting of a rise in debt as the firm will benefit from the higher operating cash inflows or returns. In addition, the cost of capital for debt is also cheaper, but increases earnings per share. At the same time, lenders feel that they are exposed to less risk than investors because they have a higher claim on the cash flows that service the firm's debt. The tax deduction derived from interest expense makes it cheaper to use debt as a financing source rather than equity, and it also results in a lower cost of capital or discount rate. In other words, as long as the increased debt level results in higher profitability or increase in earnings, investors and lenders are accepting of it in the firm's capital structure. Companies will therefore aggressively use debt as a preferable financing source because the higher debt levels results in higher shareholder value and firms find that, up to a point, it is more beneficial for a firm to issue debt than equity.

Financial leverage is the degree of financing that the firm elects to fund its operations from debt financing that locks it into fixed interest charges. The more debt a company bears, however, the more it will begin to impact the firm's business and financial risk and lead to higher financial leverage. Debt legally obligates the firm to annual interest payments that represent fixed costs to the firm. The ability to service this debt is based on the amount of EBIT it has to repay these fixed obligations. As long as the company is expanding and earnings are rising, a degree of financial leverage is acceptable. However, when the economy starts to contract and earnings decline, investors and lenders become concerned about the company's ability to continue to repay the fixed obligations. This is why credit specialists have to consider the firm's financial flexibility and how borrowers will respond to adverse business conditions relative to their ability to meet debt obligations if existing credit circumstances change. If fixed obligations become more than EBIT, the firm's solvency becomes an issue, because leverage and risk increase when it locks in a set of fixed costs. Note that, when revenues rise, costs tend to remain level and profits will rise rapidly, but when revenues decline, costs continue to remain the same and profits will fall quickly. Therefore, if the return from invested capital exceeds the current interest rate on borrowed funds, then the firm's owners benefit when the company borrows because the owners are able to profit from the use of other people's money.

Lenders, particularly, may be hesitant to extend credit at any cost, because they know that too much debt will only increase the probability of default by the company. An example of this was seen when Delta Airlines was denied financing by lenders in 2004 in an effort to avoid bankruptcy. Lenders perceived that the carrier's fixed obligations were greater than its ability to service them over the long term, and questioned its future solvency. This position subsequently forced Delta to seek relief beyond the traditional means.* Although the level of fixed obligations for the carrier was attributed to the structural changes that had transpired in the airline industry, nevertheless, concern prevailed for Delta's highly leveraged position, along with its lack of financial flexibility and inability to meet projected earnings and loan covenants.

It is because of leverage and the need for financial flexibility that credit specialists are concerned with the extent to which a firm derives its cash resources from debt versus equity, because the more debt the company has versus equity, the more highly leveraged it becomes and the less financial flexibility it has. Preferably, the analyst wants to see a firm that minimizes its weighted average cost of capital (WACC) and that is able to attract alternative sources of capital at a reasonable cost by having an optimal capital structure. As a company's value is maximized at its minimum cost of capital, the WACC is used as the target capital structure. A desirable capital structure is the optimal capital structure in that it strikes a balance between risk and the lower costs of financing. This is why credit specialists look at market fundamentals to determine when the company is reaching the optimal capital or Debt/Capital level. If companies are exposed to increased business risk and have operations and earnings sensitive to a decline, then lenders prefer that they have lower debt exposure or the cost of borrowing becomes higher along with stricter credit terms and conditions.

Lenders also assess a borrower in comparison with its competitors. If all of the industry participants have experienced a decline in bond or credit ratings, there is hesitancy about the amount of credit exposure that the lender may want to bear. Financial flexibility is a firm's capacity to adjust how they use their real and

---

*Delta received financial assistance from American Express, which is a nontraditional financier to the aviation industry and also was a limited choice among lenders that were willing to accept credit exposure to the air carrier.

financial resources under conditions of uncertainty in order to meet evolving goals of long-term value creation. Highly leveraged firms may be forced to lower investments and volatility of cash flows can sometimes lead to lower investments due to higher frequency of cash flow shortages.

5.5.2 Evaluating Financial Flexibility

Lenders want to see performance measures that demonstrate how management has prioritized the company objectives without having negatively impacted the firm's long-term performance. Financial flexibility indicates the options available to firms and how management will respond to adverse business situations. Having sufficient accessibility to cash inflows from operations along with excess borrowing capacity and assets that can quickly be converted into cash will give the firm the resources and flexibility to face challenging circumstances.

Companies need financial flexibility to respond to new investment opportunities or to unexpected changes in the external operating environments. An inverse relationship exists between financial flexibility and risk. The greater a company's financial flexibility, the lower the risk becomes to extending credit. Conversely, the lower the financial flexibility, the higher the risk becomes. Along with determining the total real debt obligations (both on and off balance sheet) for a borrower, the analyst wants to know what optional financing sources the borrower has available to it? Does the company have funding sources able to support unexpected contingent losses? In other words, the lender wants to avoid being a lender of last resort. The credit specialist also wants to consider any recent changes the company has undergone that could affect future repayment ability. Is the company exposed to environmental liabilities or potential legal problems that could affect its existing capital structure and financial flexibility in the future? Given any potential contingencies that the company may face, what would serve as a source of comfort to mitigate such factors? A company's size and role in the national economy can be a mitigating factor if it has accessibility to greater resources. Other factors are a firm's ability to sell assets and its affiliations with other entities or subsidiary companies. Having accessibility to the various capital markets and financial instruments will also mitigate concerns about a firm's financial flexibility.

Lenders must also understand what the company's future financial flexibility will be as it relates to investment strategies and plans, as these are the factors that will affect future cash flows. An examination must be made on how cash flows will be affected by any organizational structural changes as well as expansions, diversifications, or other capital commitments. How will any changes affect a firm's business and financial risk exposure, especially as it relates to the firm's liquidity and solvency. Factors that could change the existing financial structure are also a concern. An example may be plans a company may have under way to change its current production operations in order to lower the fixed and variable cost structure. High operating costs include the use of vertical integration and high technology by companies in their effort to remain competitive. When investments are undertaken, they lower the firm's debt capacity by facilitating an increase in risk. However, the company also faces risk from operating leverage or from the degree to which the firm chooses to lock in noninterest fixed costs, which is often done to leverage the profits during good times.

5.6 ASSET VALUATION

The valuation of assets is important because they relate to expected cash flows that will contribute to the company's debt service capacity including a secondary repayment source. To understand how asset values interact with the firm's cash flows, we should start with a basic fundamental that the "value of any asset is the present value of the expected cash flows from the asset." The related cash flows that are to be derived from the assets are a function of the amount that a particular asset will generate, the timing of when the cash flows will occur, and what types of uncertainties relate to receiving the cash flows. Because the expected cash flows will differ for individual assets, the lender needs to value them based on their estimated life and degree of certainty.

A concern that lenders have when valuing assets is how they are valued. Therefore, if a firm values its assets based on the amount paid at the time of purchase, there is little doubt as to the objectivity of the valuation. However, as firms want to get the maximum values, many companies use valuation methods other than the historical costs, which is why companies use differing valuation methods that can also determine how the values are to be used. If, for example, the asset is for sale, the value will be based on the future profits that the asset is expected to generate. Should the asset need to be replaced, it is valued at the cost replacement value, which is different from the historical cost. As lenders recognize the need for inflation, the price-level-adjusted historical cost is used to reflect the general inflation rate in order to derive the net realizable value or amount the company would obtain from the asset sale, which is net of any related sales costs. Valuations also have to be placed on assets to justify their net present value. For example, suppose a company wants debt financing to buy a building that it had originally leased and requests for the facility to be structured as a revolving term loan that could be used for expansion purposes. The lender would most likely not only take a lien on the building, but on all of the equipment in the factory, and want to attain a realistic valuation on the collateral.

The question is also asked many times why lenders should be concerned about the total value of a company when they are financing for loan purposes. Lenders need to know the value of the company's net worth in the event of bankruptcy or liquidation. Usually, the market value of a firm's stock is the measure of what the market believes the company is worth. This is why the aggregate market value of the firm's stock is used as a measure of the total value of the owners' equity or net worth. Private companies must also be valued, and many entrepreneurs are quite concerned about what their companies may be worth. The asset valuation of securities such as bonds is usually relatively easy to value because of the certainty that the bondholder will receive the promised cash flows in the future. However, the cash flows on stock are more uncertain, because investors are only entitled to residual cash flows that exist after all others with claims against the firm have been paid and can be more or less than what is expected. An alternative is to value the entire firm based on the cost of capital, which encompasses the cost of equity and the cost of debt.

Finding a value for a company is no easy task, but lenders seek the value on large corporations because they want to know how the market views a company in the event of liquidation and where they lie in recovering their funds based on the facility structure. A similar reason is valid for medium or middle market companies where a lender has a better chance of recovery and usually a better position. If there are fewer lenders with claims on the company, then they all try to claim a senior secured position on the company's assets. The value of these assets serves as an indicator to projecting the future cash flows in their recovery efforts. Valuing companies, especially middle market companies, can be complex as it is easy to destroy value with ill-judged acquisitions, investments, or financing methods. How a business is valued depends on its purpose, and is why there are different methods with which credit specialists should be familiar. Applying these methods, however, will be pertinent to the different contexts in which a facility is extended, such as valuing a private company, an acquisition target, or a company in distress.

5.7 CASH FLOW RATIOS

Cash flow ratios are used to further assess a company's solvency and liquidity, and vary among lenders and in the calculation. These ratios are also useful for evaluating borrowers with weak cash flows and for lender derived cash flow statements, because they tend to provide more information than traditional balance sheet liquidity and working capital ratios. Although traditional working capital ratios will indicate the level of cash held by the company at the historical date, cash flow ratios will determine the amount of cash that can be generated over time and compare that to near-term obligations and how the company can meet them. The value of cash flow ratios can become evident when traditional ratio analysis does not reveal severe liquidity problems and a company finds itself filing for bankruptcy. Free cash flow ratios, for example, serve to determine a company's ability to survive cyclical downturns and price wars. The importance of having a basic understanding of cash flows is why this concept is discussed in more depth in the next section. First, a review on the importance of cash flow analysis to credit lending specialists will be discussed followed by the principles of cash flows as a risk evaluation tool. This will be followed by a review on how to interpret and analyze the information that the statements of cash flows provide relative to a credit evaluation. Finally, the direct and indirect methodologies to construct cash flows will be reviewed along with a suggested format to derive cash flows when they are not provided by the borrower.

5.8 CASH FLOW ADEQUACY

A primary objective in the credit risk evaluation of nonfinancial firms is to analyze a borrower's cash flows and to assess the firm's ability to generate adequate cash inflows to repay external funding obligations in the future. A point to remember is that although the evaluation of cash flows is not a replacement for financial, operational, or ratio analysis, it is, however, an important tool to measure risk and one upon which credit specialists have come to rely.

5.8.1 Why Cash Flows Are Important

Because cash is the primary debt repayment source for principle as well as interest, a borrower's cash flow adequacy is in fact the single most important factor in evaluating creditworthiness. Traditionally, and under classic credit risk, the extension of credit by most commercial lenders up to the 1950s had primarily been for short-term working capital facility lines, which were analyzed for leverage and liquidity measures. When the industry transitioned from short-term to term lending sometime in the late 1950s, bankers also began to recognize the limitations of these measures, because it was cash and not earnings that repaid debt facilities. Using balance sheet assets for liquidation purposes was also not without problems such as accessibility to the security and current collateral market valuations, neither of which guaranteed repayment on existing loan values. Thus, banks began to undertake cash flow analysis in response to this, although it was not until some time in 1988 that the statement of cash flows became a reporting requirement under both GAAP and IAS. Cash flow analysis is at the heart of corporate credit analysis, in so much as it is used as a measure to understand firms' historical and current financial conditions, capital structures and serve as a basis to project future cash flows. It becomes even more important when the credit quality of the borrower is weak or when a company has healthy profits but weak cash flows that can lead to bankruptcy. More importantly, in examining a borrower's cash flows, the credit specialist gains a better understanding not only of the company's financial flexibility and capital structure, but also of the factors that contribute to its real financial position. This is done by restating a firm's reported financial information on a nonaccrual basis according to the cash flow position, so that analysts can identify what lenders really care about—the actual net cash that flows into the firm and how that cash is being generated and consumed.

5.8.2 Deriving a Firm's Cash Flows

A firm derives sources of cash from its ongoing operations as well as from the investments that are made in the overall business. It also generates cash from asset sales and from debt and equity sources provided by lenders and investors. The company uses cash to make new business acquisitions and to purchase fixed assets. Cash is also used for expansion purposes and to pay dividends, interest, and taxes. Sources of cash are generated **into** the company and uses of cash are consumed **out of** the company. For example, if a company decides to raise $1,000,000 in equity funding, this is a source of funds into the company. After receiving the equity, the decision by management to spend $300,000 on new office furniture becomes a use of funds that are going out of the company. As a result of these transactions, the firm's total cash flows are comprised of generating $1,000,000 in cash while consuming $300,000 of the cash and resulting in net cash flows for the period of $700,000. To better illustrate how credit analysts can distinguish between a firm's sources and uses of cash, refer to the classifications on outflows and inflows of cash in Table 5.4. Sources of funds are usually reflected as a profit on the income statements and indicate increases in liabilities and equity or decreases in assets. In contrast, uses of funds are reflected as a net loss on the income statement and indicate decreases in liabilities and equity or increases in assets. The point to understand about the above example and its relationship in cash flow analysis to the sources and uses of funds is that, although the transactions described would not necessarily affect the company's profits, they do, however, affect its cash position. For example, the $300,000 purchased office equipment that we outlined above was for a use of funds that increased the firm's assets from the $1,000,000 equity funding source and also resulted in a $300,000 decline in equity. If we continue with our example above we can see in Table 5.5 that "cash is king" in evaluating a borrower's repayment ability, because it pays the bills and is not the same as profits. In addition to the $1,000,000 in equity funding, the effect of transactions on the company's profits is not necessarily the same as its sources of cash to meet its debt repayment. Cash flows measure a firm's viability, because it helps to determine whether the firm can meet its obligations as well as generate sufficient cash over the long term.

TABLE 5-4

Cash Inflows and Outflows

Origins and Flows of Cash	Operation	Investment	Financing
Inflows (sources of funds +)	Sales of goods Revenues of services Interest-bearing asset returns Dividends	Sales of property, plant and equipment Sale of debt and equity of other entities Returns from loans (principal) to other	Proceeds from borrowing Proceeds from Issuing equity securities
Outflows (uses of funds −)	Payment for inventory Payment for operating expenses Payment for noninventory suppliers Interest for lenders Taxes	Acquisitions Purchase of debt equity security of other entities Loan (principal) to others	Repayment of debt principal Repurchases of firm's own equity security Payment of dividends

5.8.3 Classifying the Statement of Cash Flows

As suggested earlier, because cash and profits are not necessarily equal at a given point and time, credit specialists find cash flows to be more relevant because the accounting quality used in financial reporting is exposed to subjectivity in how profits are valued. Principally, the statement of cash flows identifies the net effects of operating transactions on earnings and operating cash flows, and reconciles net income and net cash from operations by demonstrating that cash at the beginning of the year balances to the reported cash at the end of the year. The cash flow question that credit analysts must answer is "where does the company's cash come from and how is it spent?" This is done by restating the net effects of the firm's reported operating, investing, and financing activities in order to explain changes in its cash for the period in question.

Because a borrower's debt service capability is usually either stronger or weaker than may be apparent from earnings, credit analysts will separate and evaluate the cash flows by identifying the origins and flows of a firm's sources and uses of cash. Principally, this is done by restating the inflows and outflows of cash to reflect changes in the firm's cash position that are related to its operations, investments, and financing activities.

TABLE 5-5

The Effects of Transactions on Profits Versus Cash

Company raises $1,000,000 in equity capital.

The company buys office furniture for $300,000 that has a 5-year economic life and straight-line depreciation is used.

Old computers are sold to employees for a sales price of $25,000 that is equivalent to the net book value.

The receipt of $350,000 is recorded as cash sales.

An invoice for $200,000 is paid for cost of goods sold.

A10% repayment is made on a $1mm, 5-year bank loan.

	In ($)	Out ($)
Cash Flow		
Equity capital	1,000,000	
Office furniture		−300,000
Sale of fixed assets	25,000	
Revenues	350,000	
Cost of sales		−200,000
Principal repayment		−100,000
Total cash flow	1,375,000	−600,000
Net cash flow		775,000
Profit		
Equity capital		
Office furniture		−60,000
Sale of fixed assets		
Revenues	350,000	
Cost of sales		−200,000
Principal repayment		
Total profit	350,000	−260,000
Profit		90,000

5.8.4   Structure of Cash Flows

Cash flows are structured according to their sources and uses into one of three broad categories that consist of cash flows from operating activities, cash flows from investing activities, and cash flows from financing activities. The sum of each of these cash flow categories equals the change in cash balances over a firm's financial accounting period.

5.8.4.1   Operating Activities

In general, cash flows from operating activities detail the cash effects of transaction and other events that determine income and is an indicator of whether the firm has been generating cash or requiring cash infusions. A firm's operating cash flows represents the cash inflows or revenues received from the primary business operations as a result of producing and delivering goods and providing services. Companies obtain cash from **operations** by earning revenues for delivering or producing goods for sale or services rendered. This means that a company's cash that is used in operations may include expenditures for wages, inventory purchases, advertising, and so on. Cash is also used in ongoing operations for fixed assets purchases as well as for acquisition or expansions, and for taxes that must be paid on the earned profits or as dividends to investors and interest to lenders for debt financing. As illustrated in Table 5.6, a company's cash operating cash flows begins with net income to which any expenses that do not require cash, such as depreciation, are added back. Added or subtracted to these activities are plus the increase in accounts payables, and increases in prepaid expenses and account receivables are added. Because these adjustments can be complicated, credit specialists should be aware of what the activities indicate such as the increase in accounts receivables is subtracted from net income because the matching principal assumes all revenues that are recorded have been received. A summary of these activities is presented in Table 5.7. In general, positive cash flows will usually indicate that the

TABLE 5-6

Operation Activities (Year Ended December 31 2005)

Operations	
Net income	$7,346
Cumulative effect of accounting change	$375
Depreciation, amortization, and other noncash items	$1,536
Net recognized (gains)/losses on investments	$2,221
Stock option income tax benefits	$2,066
Deferred income taxes	($420)
Unearned revenue	$6,970
Recognition of unearned revenue	($6,369)
Accounts receivable	($418)
Other current assets	($482)
Other long-term assets	($330)
Other current liabilities	$774
Other long-term liabilities	$153
Net cash from operations	$13,422

TABLE 5-7

Operating Activities (Summary, Year
Ended December 31, 2005)

Operations	
Net income	$7,346
Depreciation, amortization, and other noncash items	$1,536
Unearned revenue	$6,970
Accounts receivable	$(418)
Other	$(2,012)
Net cash for operations	$13,422

firm is stable and viable, and negative cash flows could represent a problem. However, there are no set rules for interpreting the results, as there can be many factors contributing to a firm's cash flow position, which is why the credit specialists must get behind the numbers.

5.8.4.2 Investments Activities

Cash flows from investing activities include acquiring and disposing of property, plant and equipment, along with other productive assets. Cash flow from investing also includes any gains or losses on marketable securities or other financial investments. Investing cash flows therefore consists of activities related to asset sales that will be used over the long term in the production of goods or services by the firm. Cash can also be sourced from asset divestments and the sale of other firms' securities. Sales of fixed assets and maturing investments are a source of funds, but the purchase of marketable securities is a use of funds. Table 5.8 presents a summary of a firm's investment activities.

TABLE 5-8

Investing Activities

Additions to property and equipment	$(1,103)
Purchases of investments	$(6,346)
Maturities of investments	$5,867
Sales of investments	$52,848
Net cash used for investing	$(8,734)

TABLE 5-9

Financing Activities

Financing	
Common stock issued	$1,620
Common stock repurchased	$(6,074)
Sales/(repurchases) of put warrants	$(1,367)
Preferred stock dividends	—
Other, net	$235
Net cash used for financing	$(5,586)

5.8.4.3 Financing Activities

The financing activities of a firm indicates changes to the capital structure as it relates to the firm issuing equity, paying out dividends, repaying debt, as well as taking on additional debt. Financing cash flows includes the proceeds from stock issuance and dividend payments to investors for providing the funding sources, along with principal debt repayment to lenders and stock repurchase for the firm's own outstanding shares. Debt borrowings and stock equity issuances represent sources of funds that will increase inflows, but the payment of dividends is a use of funds and outflows that are subtracted. Table 5.9 presents a summary of these activities.

5.8.4.4 Cash Flows from All Activities

To derive the cash flows from all activities, the net increase or decrease in cash should be obtained for the statement of cash flows. This is done by adding the cash inflows and subtracting the cash outflows from operating, investing, and financing activities to obtain the net increase in cash, as illustrated in Tables 5.10 and 5.11.

TABLE 5-10

Cash Flows from All Activities

Net change in cash and equivalents	$(898)
Effect of exchange rates on cash and equivalents	$(26)

TABLE 5-11

Change in Cash Balance for the Period

Cash and equivalents, beginning of year	$4,846
Cash and equivalents, end of year	$3,822
Cash flow for the year	$(924)

5.9 DERIVED CASH FLOWS

In general, companies will use one of two methods to derive cash flows—the direct or indirect methods. The indirect method is the format most commonly used by lenders, particularly when using the income statement, balance sheet, and supplemental information in the financial statement footnotes to derive the firm's operating cash flows. Table 5.12 highlights each of these methods. Beginning with the indirect method, one can derive the cash flows by taking net income and

TABLE 5-12

Cash Flow Approaches

Direct Method	Indirect
(+) Collections from customers' disbursements	(+) Net income
	(+) Depreciation
(−) To merchandise suppliers	+/−Change in working capital
	(−) Accounts receivable
(−) To employees	(−) Inventories
(−) To creditors	(−) Other current assets
	(+) Accounts payable
(−) To other suppliers	(+) Other current liabilities
	(=) Cash flow from operations
(=) Cash flow from operations	
	(+) Capital expenditures
	(=) Cash flow from investing
	(+) Increase in long-term debt
	(+) Issue of common stock
	(=) Cash flow from financing
	(+) Change in cash
	(+) Cash at the beginning of the year
	(=) Cash at the end of the year

adding back depreciation or all cash and noncash charges that involve no cash flow; cash flow from operations are then derived by also adding to the above, the adjusted period-to-period sum of the changes in working capital balances from the prior year. This is similarly done for cash flow from investments and financing after recasting the income statement and balance sheet changes. Notice that the increase or decrease in cash position (the period-to-period change in cash and cash equivalent) can be used as a final check to verify this process as the sum of all cash flows that equals the reported balance sheet cash position. It should also be noted that the SEC has found the indirect method to be the preferred choice to present and evaluate the statement of cash flows. The direct method, which is more laborious, compares the cash-based numbers to accrual results by taking the accounting ledger transactions and categorizing them as an operating, financing, or investing activity. The sum net total of these transactions at the end of the period will equal cash flow from operations.

For companies that provide insufficient financial statement data, from which the lender is still unable to make a sound assessment of cash flow adequacy, the credit specialist will restate the data into a lender's cash flow format, similar to Table 5.13. This is often done with private companies who do not present lenders with prepared cash flow statements or when financial statement detail is lacking in the reported data. Lenders also derive cash flows to highlight key cash flow information such as the breakdown of core and noncore earnings, and in order to calculate cash flow ratios. Because of the need to determine movements in working capital and investments, a lender's cash flows are also used to distinguish between a firm's core and noncore activities, as well as enable analysis of mandatory long-term debt repayment.

5.10 HOW LENDERS EVALUATE CASH FLOWS

The focus of the credit specialist when analyzing a borrower's cash flow statement is to first identify the quality of the company's core earnings and determine whether they are positive or negative. A firm's earnings ability is important in cash flow analysis to determine whether earnings are being generated from ongoing operations or from nonrecurring gains. By identifying on a trend basis the composition of earnings generated, the analyst can assess profitability and identify the amount of working capital cash used in the company's

TABLE 5-13

Lender's Derived Cash Flows

EBITDA
− Interest paid
− Taxes paid
= Gross operating cash flow
+/− Change in inventory
+/− Change in A/R
+/− Change in A/P
+/− Other W/C changes
− Net operating cash flow
− CAPEX
+/− Investments
− Free cash flow
− Debt payments
− Dividends
+/− Change in short-term debt
+/− Change in long-term debt
+/− Change in equity
+/− Other
= Net change in cash

Abbreviations: A/P, accounts payables; A/R, accounts receivables; CAPEX, capital expenditures; EBITDA, earnings before interest taxes depreciation and amortization.

current operations to sustain or grow the business. Cash flows are also analyzed to determine the available funds to service debt and repay dividends. Because companies may be pressured to declare dividends for investors, lenders want to be comfortable in knowing that dividend payments will not conflict with debt repayment. Finally, the credit specialist wants to identify the available internal cash sources the firm will have to finance its fixed assets and long-term investment growth.

5.11 CONCLUSIONS

A company-specific financial performance evaluation identifies the borrower's hierarchy of risks by asking key credit questions. The key credit issues assess a range of financial-specific areas relevant to a borrower, although many of the details can be gleaned from the ratio and cash flow analysis. The range of ratios can vary according to the lender, but usually encompasses profitability, performance, efficiency, leverage, and cash flow analyses. Cash flows are also important to understanding how the borrower will support future debt repayment. Typically, lenders will use either the direct or indirect method for large public companies. When company-provided financial statements are limited to the income statement and balance sheet, without the accompanying cash flow statements, lenders can construct a corporate cash flow or what is also known as the banker's cash flow statement.

CHAPTER DISCUSSION QUESTIONS

1. Mrs Peter is the owner of Cinemax Universal, a holding company for a chain of 12 movie theaters and a small TV station in New Orleans. Although the company is privately owned, Mrs Peters and Cinemax Universal have been a long-standing client of Buena Vista Broadcasting, with the relationship dating back to 1990. Mrs Peters has recently approached Buena Vista regarding her expansion efforts to purchase a 23-store commercial office building that is expected to be fully occupied (10 leases are contracted with tenants for up to five years with provisions for renewal and step-up rental income). Mrs Peters plans to operate one of the stores as both a distributor and retailer for children's accessories, and wants to gain a direct retail license from Disney as well as a $10MM line of credit. Rent rolls on the building are expected to yield $180,000 per month. Mrs Peters also projects that distribution revenues can yield from $75,000 to $100,000 per month and retail sales of $30,000–$50,000 per month. Mrs Peter has asked for the $10MM line of credit as part of her working capital needs and says she would be willing to pledge an assignment of rental proceeds as collateral. Create a Risk Evaluation for the facility request to use in evaluating the credit-specific fundamentals of the respective credit request.
2. Select a company to review the cash flow statements and identify what, in your view, are the key cash drivers for the company? What type of credit risk do you feel

the company is exposed to based on the cash flow analysis?

3. Jackson Tool and Die Co. is a middle market manufacturer of plastic and metal products that also designs and manufactures industrial packaging equipment and consumables for the automotive industry. A credit request is made by the company to consider extending a $50MM Revolving Credit Facility to Jackson Tool and Die. As the credit analyst, your primary concern in making this decision is whether or not the company has the ability to generate enough cash to repay the loan. According to your evaluation of Jackson's cash flow statements (Table 5.14), what conclusion do you draw from answering the following questions relative to the company's cash flow adequacy given the following questions?

a. How successful has the company been in generating cash from operations over the last three years? How confident are you in the company's ability to generate cash flow in the future and repay its loan? What could lead to cash flow problems for the company?

b. What are the primary internal sources of cash from operations?

c. Has the company been able to finance fixed assets with internally generated cash? Quantify.

d. How has expansion of the business been financed? To what extent is the company dependent on outside financing?

e. Is internally generated cash adequate to pay existing debt and dividends?

f. Is operating cash flow adequate to finance future internal growth via small and medium business acquisitions?

4. Select a company and calculate the key profitability, performance, liquidity, debt service, leverage, and efficiency ratios. Summarize your results for two years in Table 5.15, provided below. Based on your data, what does the firms' ratio analysis tell you about the company?

TABLE 5-14

Data for Jackson Tool and Die Co.

	For the Years Ended December 31 (in Thousands)		
	2005	2004	2003
Cash provided by (used for) operating activities:			
Net income	$712,592	$805,659	$957,980
Adjustments to reconcile net income to cash provided			
by operating activities:			
(Income) loss from discontinued operations	(2,672)	(3,210)	11,471
Cumulative effect of change in accounting principle	221,890	—	—
Depreciation and amortization and impairment of goodwill			
and intangible assets	305,752	386,308	391,565
Change in deferred income taxes	(60,471)	38,612	(16,238)
Provision for uncollectible accounts	21,696	21,862	10,198
Loss on sale of plant and equipment	6,146	11,106	7,479
Income from investments	(147,024)	(139,842)	(151,692)
Noncash interest on nonrecourse notes payable	39,629	42,885	44,871
Loss on sale of operations and affiliates	4,777	4,389	6,014
Other noncash items, net	1,853	(7,479)	(7,704)
Change in assets and liabilities:			
(Increase) decrease in—			
Trade receivables	8,058	156,794	47,622
Inventories	71,844	158,502	(13,493)
Prepaid expenses and other assets	10,981	(18,757)	(50,975)
Net assets of discontinued operations	1,433	36,054	31,410

(Continued)

TABLE 5-14 (*Continued*)

Data for Jackson Tool and Die Co.

	For the Years Ended December 31 (in Thousands)		
	2005	**2004**	**2003**
Increase (decrease) in—			
Accounts payable	14,455	(105,758)	(69,522)
Accrued expenses and other liabilities	(9,649)	(62,401)	(94,455)
Income taxes payable	87,422	26,288	11,209
Other, net	44	14	(169)
Net cash provided by operating activities	**1,288,756**	**1,351,026**	**1,115,571**
Cash provided by (used for) investing activities:			
Acquisition of businesses (excluding cash and equivalents) and additional interest in affiliates	(188,234)	(556,199)	(798,838)
Additions to plant and equipment	(271,424)	(256,562)	(305,954)
Purchase of investments	(194,741)	(101,329)	(14,651)
Proceeds from investments	77,780	210,669	84,102
Proceeds from sale of plant and equipment	29,208	20,000	28,595
Proceeds from sale of operations and affiliates	211,075	14,015	7,758
Other, net	3,079	7,432	(5,539)
Net cash used for investing activities	**(333,257)**	**(661,974)**	**(1,004,527)**
Cash provided by (used for) financing activities:			

Cash dividends paid	(272,319)	(249,141)	(223,009)
Issuance of common stock	44,381	54,699	25,410
Net proceeds (repayments) of short-term debt	(231,214)	(351,743)	302,076
Proceeds from long-term debt	258,426	4,122	1,125
Repayments of long-term debt	(30,707)	(16,035)	(264,929)
Other, net	2,790	1,330	(493)
Net cash used for financing activities	**(228,643)**	**(556,768)**	**(159,820)**
Effect of exchange rate changes on cash and equivalents	**48,607**	**(1,355)**	**(32,882)**
Cash and equivalents:			
Increase (decrease) during the year	775,463	130,929	(81,658)
Beginning of year	282,224	151,295	232,953
End of year	$1,057,687	$282,224	$151,295
Cash paid during the year for interest	**$73,284**	**$79,541**	**$92,062**
Cash paid during the year for income taxes	**$474,954**	**$338,864**	**$507,783**
Liabilities assumed from acquisitions	$34,267	$96,963	$282,891

TABLE 5-15

Ratio Table

	2004	2005
Profitability		
Gross margin		
EBITDA margin		
Net margin		
Performance		
ROA		
ROE		
ROCE		
Liquidity		
Current ratio		
Quick ratio		
Coverage ratios		
Interest cover		
Fixed charge cover		
Leverage ratios		
Leverage		
Gearing		
Debt repayment		
Efficiency ratios		
Asset turnover		
Inventory turnover		
Collection period		
Days sales in cash		
Payables period		
Fixed asset		
Turnover		

BIBLIOGRAPHY

"Business Credit," *Publication of National Association of Credit Management*, 89, 11, December 1987.

Cossin, Didier, *Advanced Credit Risk Analysis*, Chichester (England); New York: John Wiley & Sons, 2001.

Coyle, Brian, *Framework for Credit Risk Management*, Chicago, IL: Glenlake Pub. Co., 2000.

"Credit Analysts Get Back to the Fundamentals," *Euromoney*, April 2002, www.euromoney.com.

Credit Research Foundation, *Analysis and Evaluation of Credit Management Function*, New York: Credit Research Foundation, 1953.

Fiedler, Edgar R., *Measures of Credit Risk and Experience*, New York, National Bureau of Economic Research, Columbia University Press, 1971.

Groppelli, A. A. and Ehsan, Nikbakht, *Barrons Business Review Books—Finance*, 4th edition, Ballons, Hauppauge, New York, 2001.

Knowledge @ Wharton, "Operational Risk - Benefits and Challenges of Sarbanes–Oxley Compliance," June 10, 2005, www.riskcenter.com

Miller, Donald E., *Improving Credit Practice*, New York: American Management Association, 1974.

Miller, Donald E., *Using Credit to Sell More*, New York: New York National Association of Credit Management, 1974.

Simmons, James G., *Creative Business Financing: How to Make Your Best Deal When Negotiating Equipment and Business Loans*, Englewood Cliffs, NJ: Prentice-Hall, 1982.

Standard and Poor's, "A Credit Policy Update," in Rating Direct Research on Sarbanes–Oxley Section 404, and "Standard & Poor's Approach to Evaluating Control Deficiencies," November 22, 2004.

APPENDIX: KEY RATIOS

Ratio	Calculation	Definition	Analysis
Profitability Ratios			
Gross margin	$\dfrac{\text{gross profit}}{\text{net sales}} \times 100$	Gross margin is the difference (spread) between the cost of producing the goods and the price at which they are sold.	An increasing ratio may indicate better control of production costs. It may also be the result of higher prices due dimply to inflation, not management ability. A decreasing ratio may indicate problems with cost control or production efficiency, or the need to reduce prices due to competitive pressure.
Operating profit margin	$\dfrac{\text{operating profit}}{\text{net sales}} \times 100$	The percentage of profits retained from each sales dollar after the cost of goods sold plus operating expenses have been deducted.	This ratio should remain stable or increase over time. Understanding changes in the ratio requires a detailed breakdown of SG&A.
EBITDA margin	$\dfrac{\text{EBITDA}}{\text{net sales}} \times 100$	A proxy for cash flow to sales.	This ratio should remain stable or increase over time.
Net profit margin	$\dfrac{\text{net profit}}{\text{net sales}} \times 100$	Net profit margin measures ther business' ability to generate profit from eachsales dollar.	In general, this ratio should move in the same direction as the gross and operating profit margins. Variance require a closer look at nonoperating expenses and the company's ability to manage its tax position.
Dividend payout ratio	$\dfrac{\text{dividends}}{\text{net profit}} \times 100$	Measures percentage of earnings, after taxes and extraordinary items, paid to stockholders.	Over time, this ratio indicates the division of earnings between payments to stockholders and reinvestment in the business.
Direct cost and expense ratios	$\dfrac{\text{Cost of goods sold}}{\text{net profit}} \times 100$	Indicates the percentage of each sales dollar used to fund expense.	Upward trends in any of these ratios may indicate reasons for declining profitability.

Ratio	Formula	Indicates	Analysis
	$\dfrac{\text{SG\&A}}{\text{net sales}} \times 100$	Indicates the percentage of selling expenses used for net sales.	Downward trends may indicate successful cost control measures or economies of scale.
	$\dfrac{\text{interest expense}}{\text{net sales}} \times 100$	Indicates the % of interest costs for each of sales.	

Efficiency Ratios

Ratio	Formula	Indicates	Analysis
Sales to assets	$\dfrac{\text{net sales}}{\text{total assets}}$	The sales to assets ratio indicates the dollar amount of sales generated by each dollar invested in assets.	To understand changes in this ratio, you need to analyze how efficiently management handles specific categories of assets (e.g., receivables, inventory, and fixed).
Inventory days on hand (inv. DOH)	$\dfrac{\text{inventory}}{\text{cost of goods sold}} \times 365$	Inv. DOH is an indicator of management's efficiency in managing inventory. As a general rule, low or declining DOH means greater operating efficiency than high or increasing DOH.	Analyze the breakdown of inventory. Raw materials and finished goods are easily liquidated. Work in process is more difficult to sell if liquidation becomes necessary. An increase may also indicate a deliberate management decision to make a bulk purchase in anticipation of a sales surge or disruption in the supply of raw materials.
Accounts receivable days on hand (ARDOH)	$\dfrac{\text{net acc. receivable}}{\text{net sales}} \times 365$	Indicates management's collection and credit-screening abilities. As a general rule, low or declining DOH means greater operating efficiency than high or increasing DOH.	Analyze accounts receivable to determine if there are any concentrations (accounts representing 10% or more of total (ARDOH) receivables). This represents a higher degree of risk even with a low DOH ratio. Analyze receivables aging schedule. Evan with a low DOH ratio, if most past due receivables are 120 days or older, there is a greater likelihood of charge-off.

(Continued)

APPENDIX: KEY RATIOS

Ratio	Calculation	Definition	Analysis
Accounts payable days on hand (APDOH)	$\dfrac{\text{accounts payable}}{\text{cost of goods sold}} \times 365$ Note: time period needs to be adjusted when looking at 3, 6, or 9 month results.	Measures trade creditor financing of inventory. Indicates management's paying habits. Increasing DOH may be indicative of cash flow problems.	Compare DOH calculation to the company's terms of Sale: How fast are the paying their bills? Are they taking advantage of discounts? Are they incurring service charges? In general, a firm with cash flow problems leans on its trade creditors first.
Working investment on sales	$\dfrac{(\text{A/R} + \text{Inv} - \text{A/P} - \text{accured exp})}{\text{sales}} \times 100$	Measures how effectively the working capital accounts are being employed.	A declining ratio indicates more efficient operations
Sales to net fixed assets	$\dfrac{\text{net sales}}{\text{net fixed assets}}$	Indicates how efficiently a business uses its fixed assets. Shows how many dollars of sales are generated by each dollar of fixed assets.	A declining ratio may indicate recent additions to fixed assets or excess capacity. An increasing ratio may indicate reliance on old plant and equipment.
Performance DuPont Formula			
Return on sales (ROS)	$\dfrac{\text{net profit before taxes}}{\text{net sales}} \times 100$	Measures operational efficiency for the amount of profit produced for each dollar of sales	
Return on assets (ROA)	$\dfrac{\text{net profit before taxes}}{\text{total assets}} \times 100$	Measures the return on investment represented by the business' assets.	Always remember to use net profit before taxes to eliminate the effects of different tax rates on profit; otherwise, any comparative analysis could be distorted.
Return on equity (ROE)	$\dfrac{\text{net profit}}{\text{tangible net worth}} \times 385$	Measures the rate of return on sharesholders' equity.	This ratio provides a good gauge of management's ability to operate a profitable business.

Debt Capacity Ratios

Ratio	Formula	Description	Notes
Debt to assets	$\dfrac{\text{total liabilities}}{\text{total assets}}$	Indicates the degree to which assets are funded by external creditors.	The lower the ratio, the greater the cushion against creditor losses in the event of liquidation. Remember, the greater the business risk, the larger the equity cushion required.
Total liabilities to net worth	$\dfrac{\text{total liabilities}}{\text{net worth}}$	Measures how many dollars of outside financing there are for each dollar of shareholders' equity.	This ratio compares all debt to permanent captial. It indicates the firm's ability to leverage (do additional borrowing). A high ratio means high leverage and high risk.
Bank debt to net worth	$\dfrac{\text{bank debt}}{\text{net worth}}$	Measures how many dollars of bank financing there are for each dollar for shareholders' equity.	A low ratio means the firm has greater flexibility to borrow in the future.
Debt to tangible net worth	$\dfrac{\text{total liabilities}}{\text{tangible net worth}}$	A more accurate measure of creditors' ownership.	Intangible assets are subtracted from net worth as they are not physical assets and their liquidation value can be negligible.
Interest coverage	$\dfrac{\text{net profit before tax} + \text{interest exp.}}{\text{interest expense}}$	Measure the degree to which earnings can decline without affecting the company's ability to meet annual interest costs.	This calculation does not include leased assets and obligations under less contracts.
EBITDA/Interest expense	$\dfrac{\text{earnings before interest taxes depr. \& amort}}{\text{interest expense}}$	Excludes other income and/or expense that may distort the ratio.	
Debt/EBITDA	$\dfrac{\text{debt}}{\text{earnings before interest taxes depr. \& amort}}$		

(Continued)

APPENDIX: KEY RATIOS

Ratio	Calculation	Definition	Analysis
Liquidity Ratios			
Current ratio	$\dfrac{\text{current assets}}{\text{current liabilities}}$	Indicates current asset dollars available to pay current obligations.	This ratio does not take asset proportions into account. It assumes asset convertibility into cash, on time. Because it relates only to balance sheet accounts, it measures only one moment in time. Look at seasonality and mismatches in financing and cash flow.
Quick acid (acid test)	$\dfrac{\text{cash} + \text{marketable securities} + \text{net A/R}}{\text{current liabilities}}$	More accurate measure of current liquid assets available to pay current obligations.	This ratio still does not take collectability or timing of accounts receivable into account. It does eliminate reliance on sale of inventory in meeting obligations to short-term creditors.
Cash Flow Ratios			
Cash flow/ interest expense	$\dfrac{\text{cash flow}}{\text{interest expense}}$	Where cash flow = net income + depreciation + change in deferred taxes	
Cash flow/ long-term debt	$\dfrac{\text{cash flow}}{\text{long-term debt}}$	Measures time firm needs to repay long term debt from its cash flow	
Cash flow/ total debt	$\dfrac{\text{cash flow}}{\text{total debt}}$	Measures time to repay total debt obligations with cash flow	High or increasing ratio is an indicator of debt repayment ability

CHAPTER 6

Company-Specific Risks: Business, Industry and Management

6.1 INTRODUCTION

In Chapter 5 we introduced the concept of a risk evaluation framework to serve as a guide in company-specific credit assessment. In this chapter we will continue with part 2 of the process by focusing on the qualitative factors that are inherent in a transaction's credit risk exposures. Similar to the company's specific financial risks, an industry risk assessment evaluates the environmental factors that are likely to affect ongoing and future business operations. The first part of the chapter will focus on risk evaluation of the general industry environment. We will look at the industry dynamics that must be examined, starting with the market within which a borrower operates. This is important to support the company-specific analysis so that the high-performing firms can be identified in the industry. Next we will present several techniques that are used to identify the critical risk factors facing sector borrowers and that also serve as a basis to ask key credit questions about the quantitative factors.

6.2 INDUSTRY DYNAMICS

"Industries are like cities—They have their own characteristics and dynamics forces. In some cities, such as Hong Kong or New York, the risks are high, but the rewards for success are rapid and substantial. Some are full of bustle but achieve little; others are slow or dull but efficient. Some cities, such as Paris, hardly seem to change, yet they survive; others appear almost overnight in a burst of speculating growth, but in a few decades, they can come to resemble the ghost mining towns of the old American west."[1] All industries have their own unique fundamental characteristics which are driven by industry metrics and measurements that are specific to their needs. In retail, for example, a key performance measurement is sales per square foot, but a key metric in the automotive industry is the number of labor hours it takes to assemble a car. Credit specialists therefore need to know the impact that such metrics will have on the creditworthiness of a particular company and how the exposure will affect the composition of the overall portfolio. A common industry risk metric technique that was discussed in Chapter 5 is to analyse the relationship of a firm relative to its competitors in an industry ratio analysis. To derive a meaningful assessment for borrowers or firms in a particular industry sector, the comparison should be targeted to those firms that are within the same peer group category. For example, the risk evaluation for an independent power company should not be compared with an integrated oil and gas company. Despite the fact that the firms are in the same industry sector, one firm is an individual or small independent firm, but the other is a large, integrated oil company. An integrated oil company will usually have downstream and upstream operations that are engaged in exploration and production activities, and which are integrated with refining, transporting, and marketing of the product to consumers. The independent oil producing firm, however, is typically involved in providing upstream activities for exploring and producing the commodity.

An industry-specific ratio analysis can include every conceivable financial ratio and statistic to provide a framework for firms as well as be derived from a number of sources. A common approach is to evaluate the metrics that are used to quantify industries' performance relative to the measurement characteristics of the individual industries. As industry fundamentals vary significantly among individual sectors, companies become exposed to a range of risks that are distinctive to the sector within which that particular borrower operates. Airline companies, for example, are risk-evaluated according to their revenue passenger miles (RPMs) and available seat miles (ASMs), both of which are important to the revenues earned and the companies' market share. The RPMs gauge the revenues that are earned by the carrier for each passenger, based on the number of miles flown by individual customers. The ASMs estimate the potential revenues that can be earned by taking the ratio between the total seat numbers and the distance that is traveled

TABLE 6-1

Operating Margin

American	0.01%
Continental	−0.3%
Delta	−9.8%
Northwest	−0.9%
United	−2.3%
US Airways	−5.5%
ATA	−3.8%
Air Tran	5.0%
America West	1.0%
JetBlue	11.4%
Southwest	8.5%

Source: Moody's.

given a carrier's capacity. However, comparing the RPMs and ASMs of a major air carrier to a small commuter carrier would not be accurate because of their differences in size and peer group participants. Intuitively, a risk evaluation for the global airline industry would certainly indicate exposure by companies to high oil prices that have become exacerbated by structural changes in the industry. The assessment would further reveal, at least among the larger carriers, that the RPMs and ASMs have been impacted by industry structural changes, which have benefited low-cost airlines. As detailed in Table 6.1, the operating margins among low-cost carriers at September, 2004, for U.S. firms reflected increasing growth at the expense of declining negative growth for the larger firms. Table 6.2 highlights how the structural changes in the industry have

TABLE 6-2

ASM Figures of Major and Low-Cost Airlines

ASMs	FY00	FY01	FY02	FY03	LTM
Total majors	747,519	736,959	692,645	654,694	690,119
Total LCCs	127,958	136,687	149,350	165,294	176,993
Percent share LCCs	17%	19%	22%	25%	26%

Source: Moody's.

FIGURE 6.1

Average Fuel as a Percent of Total Costs, Moody's Rated
U.S. Airlines

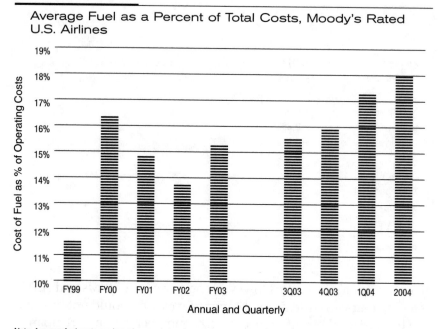

Note: Average fuel costs are based on annual and quarterly percentages for 2003 and 2004.
Source: Moody's.

impacted the dynamics for the major carriers, who have lost market
share to their low-cost competitors (LCC). The structural changes are
supported by the larger carriers' dependence on the high-cost structures of hub and spoke systems, which has led to increased competition among most of the major airlines in favor of carriers like
Southwest, JetBlue, and Air Tran. Figure 6.1 and 6.2 further highlights that the high industry cost structure on a global basis has also
been attributed to the high cost of fuel, which represents about
15–20% of airline operating costs. Despite attempts to protect earnings by hedging, in some cases, up to 90% of fuel requirements, the
already weak credit metrics combined with an already weak liquidity position does not bode well for most of the large national airline
carriers. These industry fundamentals are examples of how market
environmental factors will inherently impact specific credit risks
and are tied to companies' industry market environments. Credit
specialists should understand how the economic structure of borrowers can affect their creditworthiness and how transactions are
underwritten in order to minimize some of the inherent risks of
credit loss.

FIGURE 6.2

Average Fuel as a Percent of Total Costs, Moody's Rated European Airlines

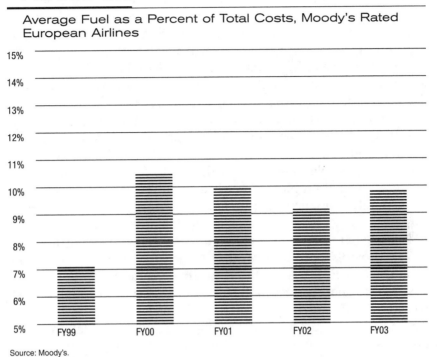

Source: Moody's.

6.3 INDUSTRY MARKET ENVIRONMENT

The industry risk evaluation begins with examining the general industry environment and then moving on to the analysis of individual borrowers in the environment. Credit specialists want to know the specific structural risks that can impact a company's business operations for the duration of a credit facility. The underlying economic structure of an industry is driven by market environment factors, many of which are external to a firm such as changes in demand, input costs, new regulations, taxes, and so on. The impact of inflation, for example, is a key credit issue that needs to be considered for how inflation will impact individual firms within the economic environment. Some industries, such as banking, will be more sensitive to inflation or interest rate fluctuations because, in general, the trend is that rising prices will lead to higher inflation and lower consumer spending. The consequence of this will be lower revenues for businesses or, in the case of the financial services, for higher credit defaults that are accompanied by higher interest rates and lower bank returns. An industry's economic structure is also closely tied to a firm's business cycle, which can become relevant to the industry outlook. Some firms may become exposed to cyclical, seasonal, or secular factors that contribute to the volatility in earnings. Discount retailers find that sales over the long term continue to steadily increase, even when the economy declines, unlike electronic firms, which see a rise in sales when the economy is strong. Economic indicators such as the gross domestic product (GDP), along with a variety of market and industry data sources, can provide insight into firms' business cycles. Wherever possible, analysts should try to forecast a company's financials over a complete industry economic cycle. Understanding the general economic structure and business cycle can be used to ask specific key credit questions in the borrower's financial projections that are relevant to future credit issues. For example, if a borrower provided projections that forecasted a 40% growth in revenues and EBITDA for the next three years, the lender would have to ask what changes in the industry structure and competition would permit growth that is so far above the historical trends. Among the key questions that might also be asked relative to the business cycle is one about the firm's market demographics.

An industry's business cycle rotates around its market demographics, which exposes sector participants to both the highs and lows of key credit risk issues. For example, companies that cater to families and children benefit more in emerging markets where birth rates still tend to be high. In regions where the populations are aging, there will be a strong demand for pharmaceutical companies or nursing homes. Demographic factors reflect the inherent risks to businesses as they relate to specific characteristics that may be unique to a sector's firms' survival and competitive market positions. Companies that have high inherent industry risk factors and low profitability, like those outlined in Table 6.3, survive by adapting to the challenges of the industry and being able to manage the uncertainty of future profitability. The chart in Table 6.3 also identifies examples of industry sectors that have above- and below-average growth prospects. Companies that have above average-growth prospects are experiencing either increasingly positive demographics or changing market trends. Steel, for example, has become an inherently high-risk industry since the onslaught of global competition from low-cost steel-producing countries and

TABLE 6-3

Group 1 (Above-Average Growth)	Group 2 (Below-Average Growth)
Aluminium	Steel
Wireless communications	Wired communications
Nonpetroleum energy	Oil and mining
Discount retailers	Neighborhood supermarkets
Holistic and herbal pharmaceuticals	Traditional pharmaceuticals

substitute products like aluminum. The growth of nonpetroleum energy products is quickly starting to show a greater demand as Western countries realize their dependency on limited petroleum resources and the need to have alternative fuel supplies.

In addition to the demographic factors that drive an industry, are the specific variables inputs relative to the size and product mix used by the sectors within which firms operate. The specific variables that dictate an industry's structure and dynamics constantly change for a firm, based on the intensity of competition that it faces. A company's ability to generate a return for its various sources of capital is dependent on its position in the industry and the health of the industry itself. In particular, internal factors may affect a borrower's revenues and cash flows within the context of the industry and its credit quality. The types of variables that affect the automobile industry, for example, are illustrated in Figure 6.3, and include the marketing, strategic, production, and financial inputs that impact the industry and individual firms within it. Auto manufacturers have to apply significant resources and effort to determine the marketing inputs for design and product quality that meet consumer taste preferences. When new designs enter into the market, billions of dollars must then be invested in research and development costs. The inability of sector firms to be competitive within the dynamics of an industry's structure is also why some major industry firms are unable to survive and find themselves in bankruptcy.

Firms that operate and survive in unprofitable industry sectors are also affected by its product mix and size. A larger company in a declining market sector has a demonstrable advantage over a smaller firm because of the strength of resources that it has to access, which serves as more of a buffer to withstanding

FIGURE 6.3

Variables in an Automotive Industry Analysis

Marketing Variables

Product quality
Product line comparison
Price
End sales financing
Dealer network
Advertising
Market share

Production Variables

Capacity
Operating leverage
Degree of integration
Automation
Sourcing
Economies of scale
Labor relations

Financial Variables

Size of assets
Profitability
Debt capacity
Support
Access to capital markets
Ownership
Capital spending requirements
Characteristics of banking group
Foreign exchange effects

Strategic Variables

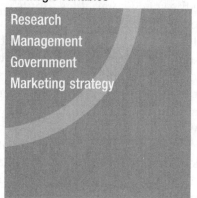

Research
Management
Government
Marketing strategy

adversity. Companies that survive the adversity are those that adapt their capital structure to industry challenges and manage the uncertainty of future profitability.

Credit specialists should also evaluate the diversity of a company's product line(s) and how they will affect the firm's future market position. Companies dependent on one product or production facility can be placed at greater risk when demand for that product changes. Evidence of this has unfolded in lending to middle-market manufacturing companies that only produce one product line and have been forced to outsource either portions or all of their manufacturing and production processes to control costs. Alternatively, the diversity of revenue sources that are generated by companies with multiproduct lines is not as affected by a decline in a particular product line.

The industry risk evaluation for diversified companies, however, should be analysed by segment to effectively monitor a borrower's risk exposure. For example, the industry risk evaluation for 3M, a U.S. global manufacturer that operates in seven business segments, would not be inclusive without undertaking a comparative analysis for each of its business lines, which are noted in Table 6.4. Because of the company's broad-based activities in health-care, industrial, display and graphics, consumer and office products, electro and communications services, safety, security and protection services, as well as transportation sectors, the earnings volatility and cash flows for each of these industry sectors within which it operates must be individually evaluated. Although diversified companies such as 3M have a range of revenue sources to mitigate any declines that a particular product line might incur, by analyzing the company on a per segment basis, the lender can monitor its exposure concentration to better realize overall portfolio optimum returns. For example, given that approximately 20.7% of 3M's revenues sources are derived from its health-care operations, a lender that already has a large credit exposure to this sector may want to either syndicate out a portion of the facility or consider entering into a credit-linked note. Although 3M is a highly successful company and an example of one that has grown from having a diverse range of product lines, some multiproduct firms have also been known to experience business failures because of this very reason. The economic downturn that shocked the Asian foreign exchange and equity markets during the Asian currency crisis in the late 1990s, for example, ultimately forced many Korean chaebols* (conglomerates) to divest from businesses outside of their core industries.[†]

Lenders use various techniques to measure a firm's industry position as well as assess how it responds to the changing external trends within the environment. A common technique, discussed in the following, is the Porter Model. Porter evaluates and categorizes an industry's market environment based on "the rules of

---

*A chaebol is a conglomerate of businesses that are usually owned by a single family and operated under one parent company in Korea. Similar structures are referred to as keiretsus in Japan.

[†]The Asian currency crisis refers to the period when the East Asian currencies faced a sharp decline, all of which were unable to withstand devaluation pressures and floating rates along with other measures that the governments attempted to implement.

TABLE 6-4

Comparative Analysis of 3M's Business Lines

Business Segments (Dollars in millions)	2005			2004			2005 vs. 2004 % Change	
	Net Sales ($)	% of Total	Oper. Income ($)	Net Sales ($)	% of Total	Oper. Income ($)	Net Sales (%)	Oper. (%) Income
Health care	4,373	20.7	1,215	4,230	21.1	1,123	3.4	8.2
Industrial	3,806	18.0	735	3,444	17.2	610	10.5	20.5
Display and graphics	3,558	16.8	1,159	3,416	17.1	1,133	4.2	2.3
Consumer and office	2,986	14.1	576	2,861	14.3	542	4.4	6.3
Electro and communications	2,333	11.0	463	2,224	11.1	342	4.9	35.4
Safety, security and protection services	2,292	10.8	553	2,125	10.6	491	7.9	12.6
Transportation	1,772	8.4	461	1,674	8.4	426	5.8	8.1
Corporate and unallocated	47	0.2	(153)	37	0.2	(89)		
Total company	21,167	100	5,009	20,011	100	4,578	5.8	9.4

competition," by evaluating the industry structure in conjunction with the market position and product mix.

6.4 THE PORTER MODEL AND THE FIVE COMPETITIVE FORCES

A common technique that has come to be used to evaluate competition is the Porter Model, which was developed in 1980 by Michael Porter, a Harvard Business School professor; the model is also widely known as the "Five Competitive Forces" or simply the "Porter."[2] The basis of the model is to analyze a firm's industry position according to five competitive forces that Porter defines to be critical factors in determining the long-run profitability and industry attractiveness of a borrower. As we discuss in the next section, Porter's theory behind the model is that the long-term sustainability in an industry is contingent on how the sector participants respond to the five competitive market forces, which are illustrated in Figure 6.4.

6.4.1 Threat of New Entrants

Industries revolve around the number of firms that exist within a common group and serve as the basis of competitive rivalry between them. The greater the number of firms within the group, the more intense the competition becomes. Prior to the 1970s, rivalry among global auto manufacturers, for example, was primarily confined within the domestic country or region within which each firm was headquartered. Global market share was predominately held by Toyota in Asia, the Big Three (General Motors, Ford, and Chrysler) in the United States, and, although slightly more fragmented, European firms held the dominant positions in their respective domestic markets of Germany, France, and Italy. Competition at that time tended to be somewhat of a gentleman's approach that revolved around each producer following the others' lead. This started to change during the late 1980s and early 1990s, when foreign auto producers around the world began to enter into each other's markets, with the Japanese leading the race to erode into the industry's global market share. Competition was brought to a new level, as U.S. and European firms responded by seizing market share away from each other and entering the markets of their domestic and overseas rivals. Suddenly, the threat of new entrants changed the market environment to increase the degree of competition while reducing the industry's attractiveness.

FIGURE 6.4

Understanding Industry Dynamics—the Porter Model

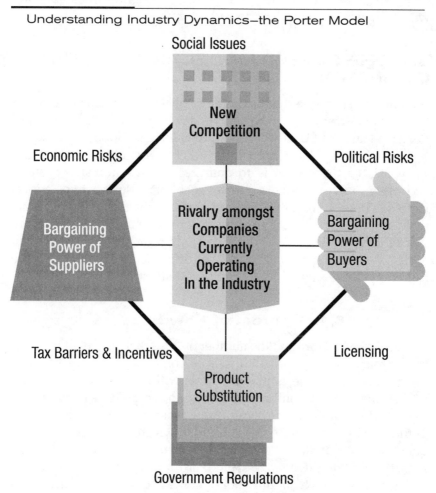

The threat of new entrants largely depends on the barriers to entering the industry. Barriers exist due to the large capital outlays that must be laid out to enter some industries and risk reaction from existing firms and possible loss as they seek to protect their positions. Shipbuilding, for example, requires huge financial resources to enter, which can serve to keep out new competitors, unlike real estate or some other business services in which there is easier accessibility for market entry. An industry can impose barriers to entry by achieving economies of scale in all business functions (e.g., research and development, purchasing, distribution, manufacturing, and so on). A firm with economies of scale will achieve operational efficiency while also lowering the cost per unit to produce, at the same time that it realizes higher production. Achieving economies of scale, however, has also started to motivate some entrants to seek joint venture partners in order to reduce the response by existing competitors and avoid significant losses. This has been the method that China has used to circumvent barriers to entry in the automotive industry. By engaging in joint venture partnerships with Western automotive companies such as General Motors and Volkswagon, China has developed an infant industry through the use of foreign technology and foreign financial resources, combined with its own cheap labor market. Having accessibility to proprietary technology by joint venturing with overseas auto producers, along with reduced capital outlays for intangible items such as research, branding, advertising, and so on, has given Shanghai Automotive Industry Corp. (SAIC) a significant cost advantage over its competitors. This approach has resulted in SAIC having reached number 461 on *Fortune Magazine's* list of global companies, allowing it to expand into other Asian markets, with plans to begin exporting to the United States in the future.[3] New entrants can also face barriers of entry independent of economies of scale. Established firms such as Volkswagon and GM were able to benefit from the barriers to entry that foreign firms typically encounter in China. Because of their proprietary technology at the time, these auto companies were able to enter into a large undeveloped market without facing cost disadvantages.

Another barrier to entry can exist when existing industry firms control the channels of distribution, making it difficult for new entrants to enter into the market. The lack of shelf display space is a reason that is attributed to new magazine failures, as the lack of visibility makes it inaccessible to consumers. New entrants can also be deterred by the advantage that existing firms have from the experience of being in an industry. The cumulative experience that an established firm gains over the years from remaining in business gives them a cost advantage over time. Because competition is also based on quality and price, when firms do not offer a differentiated product from competitors, new entrants can more easily enter the market. At the same time, a new entrant must offer a price high enough to earn a profit or it will not be able to compete over the long term. Such was the case with the U.S. airline People's Express during the 1980s, when it attempted to grab market share by offering below-industry-standard air fare prices to consumers. Although, at the time, the idea of low-fare carriers with few frills was initially receptive to passengers, it was the high-cost hub and spoke cost structure that eventually led to the airline's failure. Many of the established airlines had also built customer loyalty through advertising, customer service, and other unique product advantages, thereby exposing People's Express to significant costs barriers at that time.

6.4.2 Threat of Substitutes

Porter contends that the threat of substitute products can also create competitive rivalry by offering cheaper, alternative products that perform effectively for the same purposes. We have already noted earlier in this chapter that the substitution of aluminum in automobiles in place of steel is one example. A primary reason why aluminum substitute products have been so effective in competing with steel is that their price and performance is just as effective and even cheaper. Customers' brand loyalty and relationship with firms can impact the success in the market of substitute products. This has been the case with wireless telecommunications, as it has proven to be less costly than wired phone service, forcing an erosion of the dominance that was once held in wired telephony. The lack of brand loyalty by consumers to an industry that at one time held a monopoly in many states and regions around the world has over time led to the industry becoming intensely competitive. This is primarily attributed to the fact that new market entrants have come to provide lower wireless per-minute charges, which have reduced phone bills.

6.4.3 Bargaining Power of Suppliers

Competitive rivalry can also prevail in the bargaining power of suppliers or from the businesses that supply materials and other products to industries. The bargaining power of suppliers relates to the number of industry buyers there are compared to the number of sellers. If there are more industry buyers than sellers, the cost of raw materials and components can result in the buyers having a significant impact on the sellers' profitability. As an example, because there are so many original equipment manufacturers (OEM) and a finite number of automobile manufacturers, an OEM will typically supply the various component parts to one or two automakers. If Toyota or another auto manufacturer were to switch to a new OEM, it is likely to bankrupt the displaced supplier, which is why OEMs hold very little bargaining power as auto industry suppliers. This position, however, has started to change in the United State, for pharmaceutical firm suppliers, as their bargaining power has grown because of consumers wanting and sourcing generic and lower cost brands through the Internet, or because of supply access from Canada and Mexico. Suppliers also gain bargaining power when they provide undifferentiated, highly valued commodity products like oil.

6.4.4 Bargaining Power of Buyers

Buyers can also have bargaining power when they are the primary customer or buy in large bulk and volumes. Similar to the example that we used above for OEMs, the bargaining power of buyers exists when a single industry, company or person can significantly impact the margins of a company. This is also a reason why credit specialists prefer for borrowers not to be too dependent on any one buyer. If, however, the borrowing customer is a dominant player in a market with many sellers, the credit position is then stronger.

6.4.5 Intensity of Rivalry

The intensity of competition among firms is tied to the industry's structural features relative to the size, growth rates, fixed and overhead costs for the number of participants. For example, when competitors are equivalent in size, the rivalry among them can be fierce, as we have seen in the telecommunications sectors or when one player becomes a clear market leader such as is the case with discount retailers in the United States, which has seen Walmart dominating as the market leader, followed by Target and Kohl. The degree of competition that has unfolded among the other retail discounters has led to extreme rivalry in this market.

Although the Porter model defines an approach to risk-evaluate competition, it does not point out how to determine whether a firm will survive competition over the long run. The ability of a firm to succeed can be assessed by evaluating its strategy, which is also important regarding how it will handle competition. A company's strategy should therefore be evaluated for each segment and market in which it operates. Identifying the strategy and how well management implements it is a qualitative assessment factor for which Porter has defined three generic components (See next section).

6.5 WHAT IS THE CORPORATE STRATEGY

The company's strategy must be identified and evaluated on its philosophy and on the basis of how well implemented it is by management. Michael Porter has identified three generic corporate strategies that can be applied in risk evaluation. The **low-cost producer** uses economies of scale (or some other proprietary mechanism) to meet or undercut competitive prices while maintaining fairly high profit margins. If necessary, a low-cost producer often accepts lower margins, but tends to be larger in size and have the benefit of economies of scale. Another strategy is for a company to **differentiate** some part of its product or service for which consumers are willing to pay more, whether it is for quality, ease of use, or design. Businesses that have adopted a differentiation strategy tend to be smaller and earn higher margins compared to low-cost producers. For industries that have high returns, this can attract new competitors to enter the market and erode the margins without having the benefit of scale. Although a differentiation strategy will generally lead to higher profit margins, this rarely supports the size of a low-cost producer. An example of a firm with a differentiated strategy is the car manufacturer Rolls-Royce. Few new or existing auto competitors will seek to compete with the upscale design that Rolls-Royce offers, given the start-up costs and large losses they will face along with the high level of risk that cannot be recovered. The third strategy is to have **focus**, by attacking smaller markets either through differentiation or low-cost production. Focused companies are generally among the smallest in size and can have either high or low margins, depending on the focus. These firms will typically attempt to achieve a high or dominant market share in smaller business segments to protect their credit quality. An example is the German pen maker Montblanc, which is known for its Meisterstuck brand and has now expanded into making Montblanc-branded wristwatches. The company's growth strategy is to become a leading brand global luxury watch manufacturer. Firms in this industry have historically been dominated by manufacturers with a nineteenth-century pedigree that were known to meticulously design their own innards, a meticulous and expensive process that tends to take years.[4] Montblanc, however, has circumvented this approach by implementing its strategy of outsourcing the watch work to Switzerland's Swatch Group. The company has displayed some modest success by using nontraditional means and starting out in the United States, where it has its largest market share, while also entering the industry fairly quickly. By outsourcing to Swatch for the watch works, Montblanc has taken an easier route to market entry by obtaining the Swatch parts and then setting them into their own Montblanc watch bodies. For Montblanc or any firm to develop a strategy that enables it to enter into a new industry fairly rapidly, a risk evaluation should identify its competition along with the environmental risks that it faces. In the following sections are some of the most common techniques that are used to evaluate this process.

6.6 PESTEL ANALYSIS

The PESTEL analysis evaluates the external forces that can impact an industry and gauges the future market potential for the growth or decline of a product or firm. Many of the environmental factors that companies face, such as those in Table 6.5, are ones over which firms have limited control. The company's response to these risks, however, is an indicator of the strength of its management and whether it has a consistent strategy to support the firm's market position. Among the factors that can significantly affect the attractiveness of a company and industry are the political, economical, social, technological, environmental, and legal influences. **Political decisions** that impose mandatory requirements and safety laws can affect a company's earnings and future cash flows. The decision by the U.S. government to break up the telecommunications monopoly that was once held by American Telephone & Telegraph (AT & T) subsequently transformed how we communicate, with innovation in telecommunications. Compared to over 30 years ago, consumers now have a choice of long-distance carriers as a result of this government policy. The market is also affected by **economical factors** and their impact on how consumers will respond. A weak economy tends to lead to higher unemployment and less spending by businesses. Conversely, consumers have more confidence when the economy is growing and generally will respond by purchasing products that they had chosen to defer when the economy was depressed. **Societal** changes will pressure businesses and industries to offer products that reflect changing consumer demands and taste preferences. The focus on better health and diets has led fast-food companies such as McDonald's to change their menus to include

TABLE 6.5

Pest Analysis

Political (incl. Legal)	Economic	Social	Technological
Environmental regulations & protection	Economic growth	Income distribution	Government research spending
Tax policies	Interest rates & monetary policies	Demographics, population growth rates, age distribution	Industry focus on technological effort
International trade regulations & restrictions	Government spending	Labor/social mobility	New inventions & development
Contract enforcement law Consumer protection	Unemployment policy	Lifestyle changes	Rate of technology transfer
Employment laws	Taxation	Work/career & leisure attitudes Entrepreneurial spirit	Life cycle & speed of technological obsolescence
Government organization/ attitude	Exchange rates	Education	Energy use & costs
Competitive regulation	Inflation rates	Fashion, hypes	(Changes in) information technology
Political stability	Stage of the business cycle	Health consciousness & welfare, feelings on safety	(Changes in) Internet
Safety regulations	Consumer confidence	Living conditions	(Changes in) mobile technology

more nutritional product offerings such as salads and grilled chicken. Perhaps the biggest impact on how business operates has been **technology.** Companies must be able to remain technologically competitive in order to deliver their products and services. Technology has created new advances with the evolution of wireless cell usage, and with the advent of digital subscriber lines (DSL) and fiber-optic connections in place of copper-wire connections. In addition to changes in technology, businesses are affected by a changing **environment** in which businesses strive to respond to any new emerging trends. We can use the same example of the telecommunication sector, which has provided a range of voice, data, and video applications to enter both homes and businesses, thus paving the entry into the market of new firms. Another example is research and development into solar energy as an alternative fuel source over the years, which has fostered new changes in the fields of health and education. Many of these technological decisions have also been the fuel for **legal** influences, as a result of new government legislation and policies. Legal influences can occur from a host of political processes that affect a firm's industry position. The financial services industry has seen the evolution of modern credit risk management along with other compliance requirements as a result of legal influences, which now place greater demands on financial regulators. Legislation such as the upcoming Basel II Accords in 2007 will also bring new changes to lenders, in a similar way to how acts of terrorism led to the USA Patriot Act to implement new standards for monitoring credit relationships.

6.7 SWOT ANALYSIS

A complementary model to PESTEL is what is known as the SWOT analysis, which can be used to assess a firm's business strategy as well as product line. The origins of the SWOT analysis stem from the Stanford Research Institute in Menlo Park, California, when a research team during the 1960s and 1970s were funded by Fortune 500 companies to undertake a study to determine the causes of corporate failures and what could be done to prevent them. The team divided the analysis into four segments. The first objective is to identify the **strengths and weaknesses** of a company that are under management's control, which refers to the firm's people and products. The second objective is to examine the **opportunities and threats** that firms face, these being the external forces over which

FIGURE 6.5

SWOT Analysis

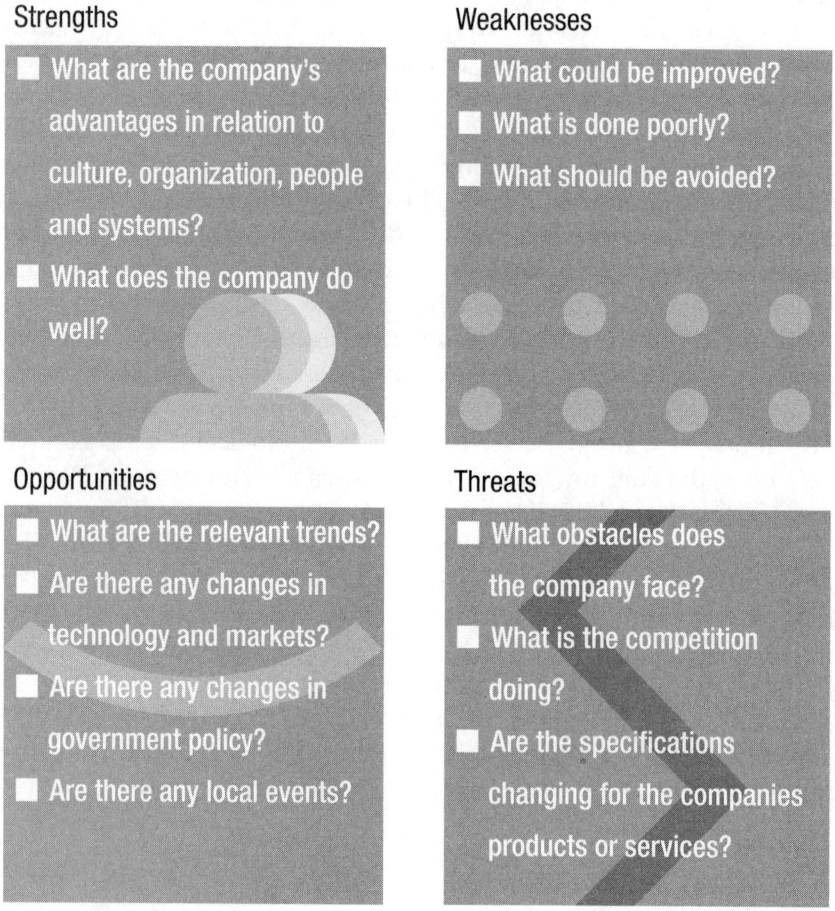

Strengths

- What are the company's advantages in relation to culture, organization, people and systems?
- What does the company do well?

Weaknesses

- What could be improved?
- What is done poorly?
- What should be avoided?

Opportunities

- What are the relevant trends?
- Are there any changes in technology and markets?
- Are there any changes in government policy?
- Are there any local events?

Threats

- What obstacles does the company face?
- What is the competition doing?
- Are the specifications changing for the companies products or services?

management may not have control. Figure 6.5 is an example of the concept behind a SWOT analysis.

6.8 INDUSTRY LIFE CYCLE

Another qualitative technique in a firm's risk evaluation that is applied to the industry and business risk is the industry life cycle. This technique is used on many specific products and product lines to interpret a firm's financial position. The life-cycle stages of an industry can impact its financing needs and repayment ability, as well as determine a firm's attractiveness according to what life-cycle

FIGURE 6.6

Product Life Cycle

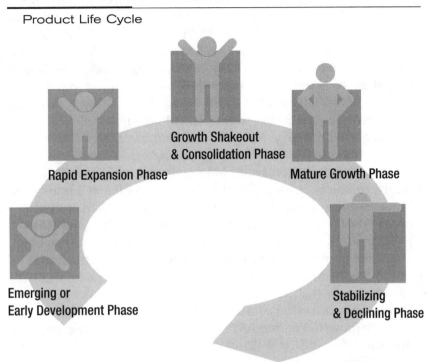

Growth Shakeout
& Consolidation Phase

Rapid Expansion Phase

Mature Growth Phase

Emerging or
Early Development Phase

Stabilizing
& Declining Phase

stage the product is in within the industry. In general, industries have five stages to their economical life cycle, as shown in Figure 6.6. The stages begin with a firm's early development and move on into its rapid expansion, then the shakeout or consolidation stage. A mature growth stage follows leading to a point of stabilization or into a decline phase. Some industries will move through these stages slowly, but others will move rapidly, and some may even skip a stage. There are also situations in which an industry can revert back to an earlier stage of growth rather than moving ahead, similar to what happened in the telecommunications industry. During the 1970s and early 1980s, telecommunications was defined and known to be a stable, low-growth industry. However, by the 1990s, the industry had been pushed into a fast growth stage due to the advent of deregulation, the Internet, and mobile phones. Nonetheless when we look at the **early development** stage, we see that most companies in an industry are usually in their infancy.

The birth of new industries is usually founded in this early development stage as a result of some type of change or discovery, such as when photocopier technology was developed for use in the fax machine. A company usually experiences erratic sales growth and minimal or no profitability at this point, although its growth prospects may be high. Consequently, credit analysts find it difficult to forecast the industry or firm's future prospects in this phase, which is why these companies tend not to rely on bank credit, but instead on equity or venture capital as their major financial support. When lines of credit are a funding source, it will be a minimal part of the firm's financing strategy. For products that are perceived to have rapid growth potential, this stage will attract new entrants and lead to a significant degree of rivalry among competitors. The additional entrants, combined with high business risks, results in some of the existing competitors having to face uncertainty. Firms may therefore choose to depart from the industry or be forced out by competition.

Companies that do survive the early development phase will advance to a **rapid expansion stage**, where, following the failure of others, a few firms emerge as dominant industry leaders. Industry revenue growth will tend to boom, profit margins will rise, and, depending on the sector, capital investments will be needed to sustain future growth. The product or service quality will also improve as the surviving industry firms continue to perfect their business models. Companies will now start to seek business credit and are viewed to be better lending prospects than they were in the early development stage. The credit assessment at this stage can still be particularly difficult, especially for below investment grade and smaller firms or if the industry is not asset intensive and relies on specialized equipment. Credit extensions will usually require that debt repayment is solely based on future cash flows because of the limited company assets to serve as a secondary repayment if the borrower defaults. At the same time, because of the ongoing working capital and capital investment needs, free cash flows may continue to be negative, even while profits rapidly grow.

During the growth of the **shakeout/consolidation** stage, some companies are acquired or bought, and others voluntarily leave the industry. Often, the leading firms in the industry will tend to buy out the remaining industry players in response to competition, and some will succeed in remaining to become a dominant player. This contributes to a heavy use of debt finance by these firms, which may also start to access the money or capital markets to meet their funding strategies. Although most of the profits still need to be reinvested back into the company, dividend payments are now a priority for the firm's investors, but only at levels that are sustainable for the firm. It is not until a company reaches its **maturity growth stage** that industry and company profit margins start to peak. At this time, the market has most likely become fairly saturated by the industry, but revenues continue to grow, albeit at a slower rate. Capital investments start to decline while costs remain level or slowly start to fall. During this phase, the overall product or service market demand may also stop growing, causing companies to try and seize market share from competitors in an effort to stimulate growth. Often, bank loans are the largest source of capital at this stage, and most industries will usually have sufficient assets to support the loan financing. As most of demand represents product or service, the credit analyst can more easily attempt to forecast future earnings and cash flows, which are usually based on estimating sales or demand in the overall general economy. At some point, the firm's capital expenditures will start to slow down and further reduce external financing needs. Depending on the industry, revenues will also start to stabilize as consumers choose to either replace worn-out or obsolete models. For example, a consumer may hold onto a refrigerator for 25 years, but buy several new televisions during the same period as technology is still evolving. By the time the industry starts to stabilize and enter into a **declining stage**, substitute products and new technologies are gaining market acceptance. This was seen in the steel industry throughout the United States and in Western Europe. In both of these regions, the industry had a flat global demand as a result of lower cost competition primarily from Southeast Asian producers, which resulted in lost market share to traditional producers. Notwithstanding that aluminum had also become an acceptable substitute and cheaper alternative to steel products. As we have also noted earlier for above- and below-growth industries, without new replacement models for product lines that become obsolete over time, most businesses are likely to decline. The result in this situation, as we have seen with wired telephone companies, will be a decline in product demand along with decreasing revenues accompanied by higher accelerating costs.

6.9 MANAGEMENT

An industry analysis would not be complete without the assessment of a firm's management, which is essentially responsible for how well a firm performs and what is its future survival. This begins with an assessment of a firm's strategy, an evaluation that should not be conflicted by how much the credit specialists or relationship manager favours a firm. A company's management establishes the firm's strategy, and lenders need to determine how consistent it is to the core business and whether the managers can effectively implement it. Determining if a company's management is excellent, competent, or truly wretched is one of the most challenging undertakings for lenders. This is because a principal factor in any credit decision is the credibility of a firm's management. Credibility is not, however, limited to integrity, but also to whether management has the requisite skill sets and character traits. At the same time, the evaluation of management is very much a subjective analysis, particularly for middle-market and small borrowers that have fewer resources than large corporations.

A company's management should be able to guide its strategic efforts in a manner that yields steadily growing revenues and ongoing profitability. This was subject to question when IBM appointed Sam Palmisano in 2003, regarding his implementation of IBM's strategic efforts to capture outsourcing as an integral part of the company's future. After years of struggling to find a niche market while operating without direction in sectors that had been captured by Microsoft and Hewlett-Packard, lenders and investors questioned whether IBM's management could "get it right."[5] This is important because management must be able to successfully lead a firm through business adversity in order to maintain an entity's competitive position. The failure by Michael Eisner to maintain Disney's stock price at an expected level, subsequently led to accusations that he had failed to implement an appropriate corporate strategy. What was perceived by Eisner as his lack of strategy resulted in a loss of confidence for his management ability. After several months of internal conflicts, Roy Disney led the demand that, rather than wait, Eisner should not only retire immediately but neither should he have the authority to name a successor, and Eisner was ultimately forced to announce his retirement (although he did name his successor).

Companies that possess a respectable management team are usually given the benefit of the doubt during troubled times. There is less concern when a company like Microsoft is faced with numerous litigation issues such as the millions of dollars in fines by the European Community that they have been charged with for not sharing certain intellectual property rights with European system users. Because of Microsoft's dominant leadership position and management strength, it has displayed the type of leadership qualities that lenders respect. One of the best gauges of management quality is whether managers do what they say they are going to do. Plans and policies have to be judged for their realism. One way to assess this is by checking actual performance figures against budget targets. How well the company's plans are implemented can be a guide that helps to assess management's consistency and credibility. A management's track record is an indication of how well it understands and knows the marketplace. One approach to evaluate the management track record is to review presentations that are made to equity research analysts and investors, whose opinions are formed during meetings; this can be an important tool in risk evaluation.

Another tool when assessing management is to determine the depth of experience that they have in an industry. Questions may arises about leadership ability when managers transfer from outside of a particular industry, as was the case when Burger King appointed Gregory D. Brenneman, a former Continental Airline executive, to be its new CEO for the chain in 2004.[6] Because Burger King's sales and profitability had been languishing for years, many observers wondered if his airline background had provided Brenneman with the intellectual effectiveness to demonstrate the needed conceptual thinking for a fast-food company. Although management's track record may appear to offer a more objective basis in a firm's risk evaluation, making an assessment of the results that contribute to a management's skills can be difficult to determine. Lack of objectivity has caused credit specialists to question if, for example, good results are a result of a firm having good management, being devoid of management influence, or achieved in spite management. The issue of management competency has also evolved to now encompass the health of management. The death of McDonald Corporation's Chairman and Chief Executive Jim Cantalupo from an apparent heart attack while at the company's annual convention in April 2004, followed by the death from colon cancer of Charles Bell, the successor to Cantalupo in January 2005, now has creditors asking if firms are responsible for management's health, because it affects performance?[7]

In addition, the composition and competency of a board of directors has also become important in the age of corporate governance. Questions are now asked about the knowledge and experience of individuals that serve on boards compared to traditional practices that focused on the social contacts of these members. Character has also become important. When Michael Eisner stepped down at Disney as Chairman of the Board in 2004 after a 43% shareholder rebuttal of his re-election, he responded by naming George Mitchell, a former U.S. senator, to replace him as chairman, although Eisner himself continued to retain the position of CEO. The appointment of Mitchell, however, was not without complaints, many of which related to his past relationship with two failed firms. Leading the complaints were the two primary shareholders, Roy Disney and his partner Stanley Gold, who complained about Mitchell's lack of experience and management depth based on his historical management failures. Herein lies another case in which lenders want management changes to include clear succession planning. This is because they do not want to have problem credits that result from key management changes, which may impact corporate strategy due to a lack of succession planning that leads to loan restructuring. One model that is receiving high praises in appointing board members among companies that have good corporate governance is that used by Lucent Technologies. The company does not pay significant compensation to board members, which gives a perception that their relevancy is much more respected as a contribution to the firm.

In addition to financial performance measures, lenders find that management's philosophy regarding leverage, risk tolerance, growth, and acquisitions is equally important. Ideally, a company should have a strong, experienced, independent board of directors that keeps focused on its business. In the worst-case scenario, when a company veers off course, the board may have to replace senior management. Among other considerations that are questioned is whether the organization is significantly reliant on any one individual? This is important not only for governing reasons, but also for the company's security. How sound would an entity that is totally reliant upon one person be if the respective individual were kidnapped, for instance?

Another element considered with regard to risk evaluation of management is the company's effectiveness and approach to handling risk. Are finance considerations given high organizational recognition or is management primarily focused on growth by acquisitions, for example, with little regard to its effect on leverage?

Lenders prefer a management team to possess the staying power to remain at the company over the long term and have sufficient time to demonstrate problem-solving skills and implement decision-making solutions. Although this is not often the case at middle-market firms, it does, however, become an issue when those firms transition from an organizational or family-owned entity into a professional management team. For borrowers that have corporate structures that pose potential problems, the credit applications should either be denied or the loan documentation should be written to ensure that the lender is protected from any shortcomings. Public companies such as Adelphia Cable Company or Hollinger International that are owned by founding families or entrepreneurs and have dual stock listings are also more exposed to more supicion or scrutiny.* The trend is now to hold these firms more accountable or impose restraints on their traditional management prerogatives.

6.10 HOW DOES MANAGEMENT PERFORM GLOBALLY

A risk evaluation for companies should consider management performance on a global level. Companies have to be prepared to meet the challenges of global competition in order to retain their industry positions. Industries across most sectors today are now becoming global, which requires that companies continue to change their business models while increasing efficiencies and reducing their costs to remain competitive. Although some of the most successful companies are those with strong presences in overseas markets, the cost of doing business for medium and small companies has become more expensive, as these firms sell the same products as their larger competitors, at the same or at lower prices. In an effort to control their cost structures, firms will outsource their production operations to lower cost markets, which exposes them to a host of sovereign risks. Such risks can range from having sufficient inventory and stock on hand to adverse currency movements that dictate the foreign exchange equivalent and determine the cost of goods sold. Alternatively, a multinational seeking cheap labor costs in an emerging market, through foreign direct investment, could be hampered by limitations on repatriating cash to its parent company or lenders.

---

*Dual-listed companies are publicly traded firms in which stockholders own dividend yielding having limited voting rights, and the voting power lies with the founder.

Actions by sovereign governments can have a significant impact on
the firm's industry position. Along with tariffs that may be imposed,
credit costs can also be affected by the borrowing jurisdiction in
which companies operate. Because laws, regulations, and accounting practices differ among sovereign territories, firms are exposed to
credit quality issues that can have a significant impact on reported
earnings and profitability after translation of foreign earnings.

Profits can also be impacted globally when overseas operations are under the power of autocratic governments who may be
opposed at some point in the future from revolts. Actions by sovereign governments that require market accessibility only if
investors engage in joint ventures with local companies have
resulted in higher credit risk exposure for borrowers. Management
response to labor situations in foreign countries is another consideration. The debacle overseen by Rebecca Marks, former CEO of
Enron's Dabhol Plant investment in India, led to significant criticism against the American firm for failing to understand the poli-
tics of the country and avoiding the labor unrest.*

6.11 MEASURING MANAGEMENT RESULTS

The ability to risk-evaluate management performance should be
values-driven, beginning at the top-down and across functions.
Financial measures of management have traditionally encompassed evaluating a company's performance according to how the
market reacts. Value drivers range from stock prices, market mul-
tiples, variations of the Dupont Equation, net operating cash flows,
operating profits, and individual projects, which have all been
used to measure management performance. The assumption with
these indices has been that a determination could be made on
shareholder returns who were the real providers of the firm's capital. The limitations with these measures have continued to prevail
over the years. A primary deficiency is that many measures were
criticized for putting too much emphasis on the cost of debt at the

---

*Enron entered India at the request of the country's National Government without realizing
how the local government and community viewed their investment as an attempt to gain
sovereign control. Having few Indian and local companies involved while also outsourcing
many significant contracts to American and overseas firms, further served to create animosity
the community. The result was rioting against the firm's plant and civil unrest that led to less
than desirable public relations for both the company and India and which eventually became
settled through international arbitrations.

exclusion of the cost of capital, such as the ROA, which measures the return on invested assets, at the exclusion of the cost of capital. For example, if a firm's ROA is 12%, but cost of capital is 15%, then the cost to finance those assets is more expensive than the return derived from investing in the assets. If the firm's cost of financing is higher than the cost of capital, this also can be an indicator that it is highly leveraged as well as exposed to other credit risk issues.

An alternative concept that has grown over the years is that of economic profit, which focuses on the value that will be derived from invested capital in the future or from the company's future economic profits. Although economic profit is a generic concept that was developed over 100 years ago, the more common name that has grown to be familiar to the financial industry is Economic Value Added (EVA) and Shareholders' Value Added (SVA). Developed by the management consulting firm Stern Steward, EVA represents a value creation model for firms to measure future returns based on risk and reward. Although it was mainly used to measure the performance of a firm over a long-term period, it has also come to be used to measure management performance and is increasingly being used for management incentive compensation packages. The assumption is that a firm's entire operations are represented by the capital that is invested to function. By emphasizing value drivers such as growing sales, cost controls, and asset management, the firm can determine real or economic versus accounting or paper profits. The primary uses of economic profit include identifying value that is created or destroyed in existing or company wide projects, resource allocations that determine which projects to support, and performance evaluations and management incentive plans. Although EVA is equivalent to the techniques used in the DCF model, it focuses on free cash flows and generic strategies that create value. As illustrated in the following equation,

$$EVA = ROIC - \text{Cost of capital } (\%) \times \text{Capital}$$

the EVA as a tool is the economic profit per the amount or value of the invested capital, which is also known as the return on invested capital (ROIC) minus the cost of capital times the invested capital amount. Another approach, which is known as the capital charge method, is given by the following,

$$EVA = NOPAT - \text{Cost of Capital } (\%) \times \text{Capital},$$

which takes the NOPAT (net operating profits after tax) or the economic earnings generated less the cost of providing the capital, or

FIGURE 6.7

Examples of Capital Charge Method and
Spread Method

Capital Charge Method - Example

Opening capital	300	NOPAT	80
WACC	10%	Capital charge	(30)
Capital charge = 300 x 10%		SVA	50

Spread Method - Example

ROCE (NOPAT/opening capital) :	80/300 = 26.7%
Spread (ROCE -WACC):	27% -10% =16.7%
SVA (Spread x Opening Capital):	16.7% x 300 =50

equivalently, economic earnings generated minus cost of providing capital. To see this more clearly, if the average amount of capital invested throughout the year is $300, and NOPAT is 80 with a 10% WACC, we see in Figure 6.7 that the EVA is 50 for both the capital and spread methods. Some of the criticisms of EVA are that it is too complicated for small businesses. Critics point out that the number of adjustments needed to convert financial statements indicators into EVA equivalents is not realistic. It has also been argued that because EVA advocates less expensive debt to reduce its cost of capital, a small business lacks the ability to utilize such strategies. The contention is that the business environment for small firms changes much too quickly and therefore discourages the ongoing calculations of EVA required for small businesses to measure of historical financial performance. Economic profit is also used in valuations of firms to represent the entire enterprise value and can also be used to value the future profit of the firm.

6.12 CONCLUSIONS

A company's industry dynamics are unique to the fundamental characteristics that drive it. Industry fundamentals vary significantly among individual sectors and are predicated on the industry market environment in which it operates. Several analytical techniques are applied to risk-evaluating a borrower's industry position. The Porter model centers around five competitive forces that analyze a firm's industry position according to its profitability and how it responds to competition. The corporate strategy is also dictated by evaluating a firm's management, the PEST assesses a firm's future market potential, and the SWOT analysis assesses the business strategy and product line(s). Industries can also be evaluated according to the industry life cycle in which they operate. The early development stage is a firm's infancy, as the industry is still emerging. The rapid expansion stage dictates those industry participants that will emerge as dominant leaders in the sectors. The shakeout and consolidation stage finds companies being acquired or leaving the industry, leaving those remaining to move on to the mature growth stage. Those that survive the mature growth stage will subsequently move on to the stabilization and decline stage.

CHAPTER DISCUSSION QUESTIONS

1. Review a company Chairman's Letter in their annual report and describe the firm's management strategy. How do you compare the company's strategy with the industry?

2. What are the fundamental characteristics and industry dynamics for the company you selected above? How does your company's metrics compare with its industry competitors?

3. Prepare an industry risk evaluation on your company and identify the strengths and weaknesses of the industry? Who are the competitors? What substitute products does it have?

4. What are the variables in your input that affect the industry?

5. Compare and contrast two leading competitors in your industry using the industry and business analysis techniques that were discussed in the chapter. Which firms appear to have the strongest fundamentals? Consider the Porter, PEST, and SWOT analyses relative to how well the firms are implementing their strategies?

6. Select a firm that is operating globally and evaluate its international strategy.

BIBLIOGRAPHY

Global Alumino, "Demand for Aluminum," www.
globalalumnia.com/ga_new/industryprofile.

Johnson, Daniel, *Oil Company Financial Analysis in Non
Technical Language*, Tulsa, Oklahoma: Penn Well Publishing
Company, 1992.

FDIC Industry Analysis, www.fdic.gov/bank/index.html.

Credit Risk Measurement

7.1 INTRODUCTION

Up to this point we have focused on the fundamentals of traditional credit practices that have subsequently evolved under the auspices of modern credit practices. For the remainder of the book, we will focus on how these techniques are being applied today as they have become integrated into the new approaches of extending business credit. In this chapter and the remainder of the book, we will focus on the techniques and applications of modern credit risk management. We start in this chapter by defining the role of credit risk measurement and how it is being used by lenders in the banking and financial community. We then present a basic framework to measure credit risk and discuss some applications that have become a standard for quantifying the economic loss from credit exposure.

7.2 THE ROLE OF CREDIT RISK MEASUREMENT IN THE CREDIT PROCESS

The active management of credit risk has become a major agenda at financial institutions over the past several years, whereby lenders now take a proactive approach to individual and credit portfolio transactions. Although primarily motivated by regulatory changes brought about from the upcoming Basel II Accords, for good reasons these developments have become critical to sustaining a sound financial system globally. One reason is the increasingly complex financial risks that lenders now face. Credit providers of all types are exposed to a broad range of financial risks that can result in large financial losses and that need to be managed in part by quantifying and measuring the potential risk exposures. Transaction risks specifically need to be understood within the risk appetite of the organization, relative to how they will impact the portfolio credit risk capital. A second reason is that the stream of financial products in the markets today has made extending credit intimately related to market and operational risks, while also becoming integrated into the entire credit process. For example, a component of credit risk can be derived from the interest spread that is predicated by conditions prevailing in the capital markets and which is also a byproduct of market risk. In addition, there are credit market developments relative to changes in the economy such as productivity, unemployment, business cycles, and so on, which impact the profitability of borrowers and their default probability. The risks associated with delivering transactions can lead to both direct and indirect losses if the internal processes, systems, or staff in the credit process do not perform adequately to service facilities. Operational risks can also transpire from external events such as a systems failure or a natural disaster. Managing these integrated risks requires a systematic and orderly process that can define and measure their loss exposures in all credit and related activities.

A third reason for the application of credit risk measurement is to emphasize risk adversity by identifying and quantifying risks on an aggregate portfolio basis. Along with monitoring risks in a single transaction, the application of analytical metrics can account for all risk sources and consider them on a risk-adjusted basis in order to support portfolio optimization and allocate capital requirements. Meeting these objectives is also what distinguishes the goals of measuring from those of assessing credit risks. Although the measurement goals were introduced in Chapter 2, a review of how the measures of risks fit into the overall credit process is appropriate. The three main goals of credit risk measurement when extending business credit are (1) for the lender to limit credit risk exposure, (2) to earn adequate compensation for the level of risk relative to the facility amount, and (3) to mitigate credit risk from economic loss.

7.2.1 Limiting the Credit Risk Exposure

Like all risks, credit risks are quantified by measuring potential losses of exposure that may occur either directly or indirectly. Extending credit directly to a borrower, obligor, counterparty, corporation, or government that fails to repay their debt obligation, is the most common form of credit loss exposure. In an effort to mitigate any loss, lenders try to structure transactions to reduce their credit risk by taking collateral or putting covenants in the legal documentation, as well as by placing limits on their credit risk exposure. Indirect credit exposure to either a single or multiple counterparties with which there is no direct relationship can also lead to a loss of credit.

The credit exposure to an individual obligor is equivalent to the outstanding amount at risk, and the type of exposure at risk of being loss determines how a transaction is measured. This means that the credit exposure of a single loan, for example, is measured by quantifying the outstanding percentage and par value amount based on how the loan is structured. If structured with credit risk mitigants such as collateral, a guarantee, a credit default swap, or covenant restrictions relative to the terms of the facility, then the amount of credit exposure at risk of loss has been somewhat moderated. This is why credit limits are placed on the total exposure amount or credit line to counterparties and also why collateral is taken in order to control the credit exposure.* Without such limits, lenders will not be protected from relatively significant large credit and high percentage default losses.

Credit risk limits should therefore be established as part of a well-designed credit risk measurement and monitoring system. A credit risk limits system should capture all parties with whom the bank does business and function on the basis that origination cannot begin prior to approval of credit limit exposure to borrowers, obligors, or counterparties. Approval of credit limits also need to be aggregated on a product, industry, and regional or global platform in order to accurately quantify total credit exposure.

7.2.2 Earning Adequate Compensation for the Risks Undertaken

The second goal of credit risk measurement is for the lender to be adequately compensated for the specific risks of extending credit so that earnings and profitability can be maximized along

---

*For credit derivative and trading products, exposure is an estimate of how much a counterparty might owe over the life of a transaction (or portfolio of transactions). It is comprised of current mark-to market of the transaction (immediate cost to replace the contract) plus the potential exposure of a transaction over time given any changes in market rates that could increase the current mark-to-market in the future. Compared to obligor exposure, the magnitude of the potential exposure component is uncertain and can only be estimated by simulation at a certain confidence level.

with increased shareholders' value. When transactions are not adequately priced to compensate for the risks and costs of supporting them, lenders will engage in portfolio selections that become adverse to the overall firm. As a result, earnings will become volatile and threaten the financial institution's economic viability, which will subsequently impact the lender's credit rating. Because a large driver of pricing transactions is the cost of capital to service assets, pricing must reflect the risk/return profile that is risk-adjusted across the credit portfolios on an aggregated basis.

Pricing risks to earn adequate compensation for overall lender returns requires integrated measurement valuation tools that can be applied to both the lending and trading products. This is because the economics of credit has changed the pricing of traditional credit transactions and products, bringing with it an increase in the degree of credit risks. For example, new opportunities in corporate and commercial lending are now accompanied by different types of risks, particularly in the areas of syndicated loans along with project, structured, and leverage finance. The structures of these assets have changed to incorporate an increasing complexity of options that are now embedded in loans, bonds, and credit derivatives. In addition there has been the growth of securitization, credit derivatives, and the secondary loan trading markets. They require risk-adjusted pricing performance assessment at origination as well as for mark-to-market credit portfolio analysis. As discussed in Chapter 4, loan originations in the syndications market have now evolved into an efficient primary and liquid secondary trading market. Similar efforts have been made to standardize documentation and risk-adjust facilities pricing structures with market-flex adjustments.

Credit products must also be priced to reflect borrowers' and counterparties' credit quality based on the current market conditions in order to adequately measure profit and loss implications. The risk that is relevant in pricing an asset or predicting its return is in how much the returns move together with other asset market returns. A variety of credit risk pricing models have become available that are integrated into internal rating systems and adjusted according to established standards that capture both historical and market price data. Pricing tools are also used to provision optimal capital allocations as well as to determine whether the required asset return is greater than the minimum cost of capital to service the asset.

7.2.3 Mitigating Credit Risk Exposure

Mitigating credit risk exposure is a supplement to establishing credit limits in that it attempts to reduce the risk of credit loss by neutralizing, transferring, or removing those risks that contribute to lenders' economic loss. This form of risk mitigation originally came to prominence through the use of securities arbitrage, in which traders would seek to profit from price discrepancies.* The concept of securities arbitrage was transformed into regulatory arbitrage when banks saw a profit opportunity to gain from the economic disparities in transactions compared to the regulatory capital requirements under Basel I. The debates that resulted from regulatory arbitrage reflected attempts by lenders to make strategic risk decisions relative to their overall business objectives by transferring the lower risks off their balance sheets. Transaction hedging would take place on the higher risk loans by retaining them on the balance sheet at the expense of securitizing and removing the safer, lower risk assets. The market differential here is in the requirement for a highly rated investment grade loan with minimal chance of default having the same 8% regulatory capital allocation as a risky speculative graded, fully collateralized loan. Provided that the loan does not default and is appropriately priced, the higher risk asset would result in higher profits to the bank. The problem in doing this is that portfolios that are dominated by high, risky loans can threaten the banks' economic viability, particularly when the economy is in decline.

Effective credit risk management, however, should prioritize the specific credit risks drivers with a targeted program that reduces the amount of credit exposure. A sound credit granting process is therefore needed to capture the drivers of credit risk exposures that encompass sophisticated analytics to analyze and

---

*Arbitrage is the trade of buying low (long or owning the asset) and selling high (short or liable for the asset). When market prices are not in balance, traders recognize the disparity by purchasing the securities in one market to resell them for a profit in another market. As the market becomes aware of this opportunity, more investors will take advantage of this profit combination until prices are converged or return to equilibrium. What makes arbitrage transactions risky is the inability to simultaneously do two transactions, when a change in price on the other transaction does not result in a profit. In addition is the risk that the counterparty does not deliver on the contracted transaction obligation. Because large transaction quantities are required to profit from the small price differentials, the loss exposure can be significant, especially if the transaction is undertaken with borrowed funds.

compute information so that credit decisions are reliable. As illustrated in our review of the Credit Process in Figure 7.1, new transactions originate when the relationship manager interacts and conducts a dialog with the borrower. Credit decisions and approvals are made based on the types of risks that a transaction may hold and the degree of risks that are identified can be minimized according to the defined terms and conditions for the borrower's use of the credit. By defining the facility terms and conditions, the lender can mitigate the risks of default as well as protect the institution in recovery should default occur. The facility terms and conditions, however, cannot be made without the various sources of data required for credit decision making as outlined in Figure 7.2. This includes external information that is provided by the borrower, along with internal supporting information held by the lender relative to the borrower, as well as external credit rating detail. Typically, the borrower- or customer-provided information is quantitative, in the form of financial statements, and the external provided detail will be qualitative in nature, such as industry conditions, external ratings details, all of which will be inputs to calculate and derive the credit measures of the transaction. All of the combined input data will need to be assessed, analyzed, and evaluated for both quantitative and qualitative factors, relative to

FIGURE 7.1

Review of the Credit Process

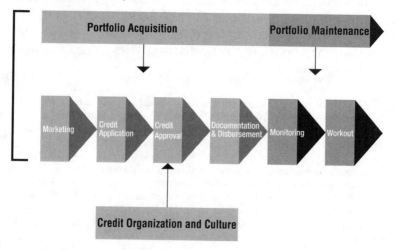

FIGURE 7.2

Credit Risk Drivers

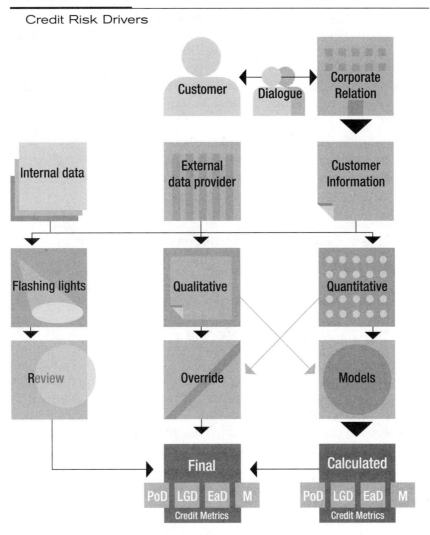

the impact that they will have on a stand-alone and portfolio basis. Indicators in the form of warning signs will serve as flashing lights to the model inputs so that the lender can undertake further review of the credit decision and structuring. Because the basic objective in transaction structuring is to mitigate risks and optimize returns, lenders have a range of options to apply in making their credit decisions that provides them the ability to monitor the debt obligation against the risk of default. Among these options is knowing the degree of risk by applying credit risk measurement analytics to quantify the amount that credit losses are lowered by applying risk-mitigating techniques. When credit transactions are effectively structured, transaction risk can be mitigated against the loss of default by applying several techniques. The most common forms of risk mitigation are collateralization, asset securitization, guarantees, hedging, and netting.* These risk mitigation techniques and applications are used to measure credit risk and the exposure to credit losses, starting with the expected loss for individual transactions, based on the type of facility transaction extended. Measuring the credit risk on different facility types nonetheless begins with a basic framework to quantify losses that are derived from specific credit risk metrics. These basic risk measures therefore provide an indicator for ordinary or expected losses that occur as a normal part of business operations. In addition these are the unexpected losses that take place infrequently, but usually under stressed circumstances, and that have a significantly high impact when default does transpire.

7.3 THE FRAMEWORK TO MEASURE CREDIT RISK

Credit risk is one of the integrated financial risk components that banks and suppliers of business credit face on a daily basis. It is encompassed in all of the activities that take place throughout the entire credit process and defines the risk metrics that are used to measure potential loss exposures. A metric is simply a system of measurement that serves as a tool to facilitate decision making by collecting, analyzing, and reporting the relevance of performance-related data. When financial institutions want to measure the amount of risk to which they are exposed, they therefore need to have the appropriate metrics that can be used to benchmark and evaluate specific credit exposures. In credit risk management, a credit metric is the standard that is used to measure

---

*Netting helps to lower potential credit losses in derivative transactions through the use of bilateral close-out agreements. The agreements are intended to limit the exposure losses by specifying that, in the event of a counterparty default, the lender is only liable for the net amount that is due the counterparty and not the gross sum of all derivative contracts. Financial institutions use these vehicles to prevent defaulting parties from not paying on derivative contracts that have a negative value at the same time that they demand payment on those contracts with a positive value.

a transaction's credit loss in the event of default.* The specific relevant metrics that are used to measure credit exposures are derived from the activities throughout the credit process. If we refer back to Figure 7.1, the components of credit risk exposure are a function of the risk sources that may arise from extending banking, trading, and capital markets credit services. Beginning with senior management, an appropriate credit risk management strategy is implemented that defines the credit granting activities in the credit policy and procedures. This process defines the credit environment and is used by the entire credit organization. Relationship managers particularly need to adhere to a sound credit granting process to originate new business according to the credit policy, which defines the types of customers that are eligible for credit services along with the terms and conditions available to them. Those that are engaged in reviewing and approving credit applications must also adhere to the appropriate credit policy guidelines for the credit process to work effectively. The measurement of risk is also a process of the credit administration function, which oversees the documentation and funds disbursement as part of the back-office procedures. Each of the credit process activities is linked to a specific credit function that may indicate inadequate controls when a loan defaults and becomes the responsibility of the workout group. Lenders therefore need to establish credit control processes that are well defined and effectively managed as part of their credit measurement methodologies and practices. Such practices are the basis for summarizing the credit exposure that is contained in extending transactions.

7.3.1   Measuring the Credit Exposure of a Single Transaction

The amount of credit exposure that could possibly be lost from the default of a single transaction is derived from the credit equation for the expected loss. The expected loss (EL) is a risk measure of the possibility or likelihood of a credit loss that could be incurred should an event of default occur. It is the mean or average loss amount that is anticipated over a given time or risk horizon period and a measure of the average percentage loss for the probability of credit loss on a debt

---

*According to the National Institute of Standards Technology (NIST), published standards that are obtained for measuring risks should be adjusted and tuned to fit specific organizations or situations.

obligation. When we speak of the EL, we are typically speaking of an estimated loss that may occur over a one-year or longer period of time. This estimated loss could be expected from borrowers having similar creditworthiness, credit exposures, debt products, and credit facility structures. Although the time period in which to measure credit risk in the banking book is typically one year, credit products that are traded may require a shorter or even longer risk horizon.

The credit risk metric that drives the EL on individual credit obligations is illustrated in Figure 7.3. As the amount of credit loss that is expected on an individual transaction, the EL is the basic credit equation measurement that represents the cost of extending the credit, which the lender needs to recover when pricing the facility. This credit risk amount is the product of three parameters: the probability of default by a borrower, obligor, or counterparty (**PD**); the exposure amount at default that will be owed should default occur (**EAD**); and the amount of loss given default that the

FIGURE 7.3

Components of Credit Risk

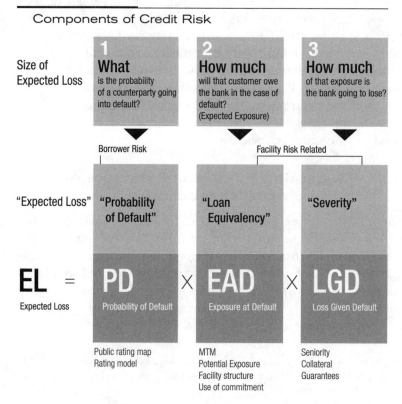

FIGURE 7.4

Linking the Credit Process to the Credit Equation

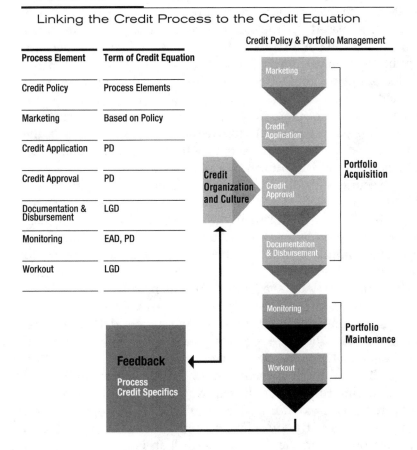

Process Element	Term of Credit Equation
Credit Policy	Process Elements
Marketing	Based on Policy
Credit Application	PD
Credit Approval	PD
Documentation & Disbursement	LGD
Monitoring	EAD, PD
Workout	LGD

lender will lose once default occurs (**LGD**). Notice that each of these risk parameters reflects the operations of the credit process and how the EL is quantified. The relationship between these parameters and the credit process is detailed in Figure 7.4, to demonstrate that the PD reflects the borrower's risk, but the EAD and LGD measure the facility risk.

The PD for the likelihood that the borrower will not repay is generally a function of the bank's internal credit rating, which reflects the borrower's creditworthiness, or a public rating agency can base it on their external credit rating. A borrower's probability of default also represents a frequency measure that attempts to predict a relative default frequency based on historical obligor defaults. LGD is driven by the outstanding balance at the time of default according to the bank or lender's estimate and would be the lost percentage amount of the loan. LGD is also known as the severity rate for the actual amounts the lender can lose if default occurs and is expressed as S. This metric is based on the amount that will be recovered after accounting for collateral support or other risk mitigants. In general, the credit organization does not know when a borrower defaults the full value of the loss until after the workout or bankruptcy period, is completed. Depending on the transaction's facility structure for which a borrower goes into default, the workout term can be for an extended time period, particularly when the liquidation value of the collateral is in question. Facilities that are fully cash collateralized can usually be recovered in a fairly reasonable time period, unlike for property, securities, or other collateral, which requires efforts by the lender to obtain a realizable market value. Such may be the case for collateral that may have more complicated liquidation issues, including those of subordination or accessibility when it resides outside of the lender's control. In addition there is the EAD or the expected exposure amount once default occurs, which refers to credit commitments that have varying availability, such as revolving credit lines. The credit risk measure for a revolving line is usually expressed as a percentage of the amount that is drawn when default occurs. Deriving the EAD therefore requires an estimate for the amount of the credit line that will be drawn when default occurs.

The EL or amount of credit loss at risk from an individual obligor is defined by the credit exposure, but how the exposure is measured when extending a particular asset is dependent on a particular facility structure. For example, the credit exposure to a borrower on a plain vanilla fixed term loan is the risk of credit loss and default on the required fixed payments that are outstanding and due to the lender. If the loan is unsecured, the fixed principal and interest payments will be the basic features to measure and quantify the risk of credit loss. It is measured to reflect the facility's terms and conditions along with the scheduled amount that is owed at a given time and expected to be outstanding should default occur. However, when loans are secured, the credit exposure is measured according to the type of collateral and level of seniority that defines a facility repayment.

7.3.2 Calculating the Expected Loss

Calculating EL for a single stand-alone facility is relatively easy. Suppose you want to determine the expected loss on a $5,000,000 unsecured term loan to a machinery company that is internally rated to be a 5, which is equivalent to a BBB rating by the public rating agency. The internal credit rating is equivalent to a 0.20% probability of default, based on the bank's historical annual default rate. For the sake of simplicity, however, assume that the lender maps its internal credit ratings to that of the rating agency to give it an equivalent probability of 1.8%. Because it is a five-year term loan and is fully drawn, EAD is at 100% and LGD is at 50% according to the lender's own estimate. We see from Figure 7.5 that the EL on the facility is calculated at $45,000, which is the dollar expected loss amount for the BBB rated credit facility. The EL on the transaction represents the average dollar expected loss amount that the lender estimates to lose over the time period from similar types of loans, and is also the mean of all losses that could occur. Because the type of facility in our example is a term loan, we assume that it will be fully drawn if default occurs, which is why there is a 100% exposure. In contrast, if the facility was a revolving credit line, its utilization would vary throughout the term of the commitment and the EAD would have to be estimated. Suppose the lender determines that the EAD on a BBB rated facility is estimated at around 65% for the amount unused and that the average recovery

FIGURE 7.5

The "Credit Equation" Summarizing the Methodology of Calculating EL

PD		EAD		LGD		EL
Probability of Default	X	Exposure at Default	X	Loss Given Default	=	Expected Loss

Term Loan: USD 5 million to BBB rated company.

Five Year Term, Unsecured, No Amortization

Principal	PD		EAD		LGD		EL
USD 5 million	1.8%	X	100%	X	50%	=	USD 45,000
	S & P 5 years Cumulative Default Rate		USD 5MM- Term Loan Always Drawn		Bank's Estimate		

EAD & LGD loom large in the arithmetic

for a machinery company is estimated at 49%. The EL would therefore be $362.6K, as illustrated in Figure 7.6.

7.3.3 Characteristics of Expected Losses

Expected losses are those that lenders anticipate or expect to occur based on their historical credit default experience. They are the mean or average losses that are predicted to arise over a given time period and are considered to be a cost of doing business. A lender should account for expected losses in pricing as well as distinguish them, because they are not always the same as the loan loss reserves or charge-offs. The credit equation for deriving expected losses is based on the mean of the loss distribution for a fixed time period, which is usually one year. It is an approximate average loss for all of the different types of credit situations that can prevail throughout a one-year term. Loan loss reserves, however, are not always based on a fixed time period, and, in fact, may reflect the life of a facility. The time period can vary depending on the term to maturity for which actual losses are approximated to derive the net charge-offs. Although a typical time horizon is a one-year period, having several horizon periods is important, because the returns for credit products can vary based on their structure and the term to maturity. Another distinction is the regulatory requirements to derive the EL, which is known as the look-back-time period. Financial institutions that plan to adopt the IRB approach under the Basel II Accords are required to have historical data based on five to seven years to estimate losses. Alternatively, banks can adopt a variety of methodologies to derive their look-back-time periods for loan loss reserves. A third distinction is the use of commitment lines that expected losses encompass are excluded in loan loss reserves. Unfunded commitments including off-balance sheet obligations are converted into an equivalent

FIGURE 7.6

* When $EAD = L(\bar{E} + (1-\bar{E})ed)$

exposure amount and reflected in the EAD. A loan loss reserve excludes the unfunded commitments and must add such liabilities to the reserve amounts. Finally, because the concept of EL is intended to correspond to and account for losses that are not expected or unexpected losses, the loss estimates will often include future scenarios, while loan reserves are calculated based on actual historical experience. Economic losses can also be incorporated into the EL, unlike loan loss reserves, which must exclude certain direct and indirect costs. Fundamentally, loan loss reserves reflect a qualitative measure that EL seeks to improve upon by establishing a quantitative framework to measure the expected and unexpected losses.

7.4 UNEXPECTED LOSSES

Unexpected losses (UL) usually occur under stressful conditions and tend to have a significantly large impact on the institution's portfolio and overall profitability. Although the EL is the average or mean of a credit distribution function, the UL is the standard deviation of the distribution that measures the volatility or potential maximum exposure loss at a given confidence level (e.g., 95%, 99%). Unexpected losses also include the amount of capital that the organization will have as a cushion in the event that such extreme losses do occur. Lenders typically assess both unexpected and expected losses by using simulation modes such as Monte Carlo to evaluate the worst-case and stressed conditions under which an individual or portfolio loss might occur. Monte Carlo simulations are when a computer randomly chooses a value for each uncertain variable based on a probability distribution that is assumed for the variable. By assuming the variable we infer that one must be developed for each variable chosen. This process can be repeated an infinite amount of times by the computer (usually several thousand times).

Recall that the EL is

$$EL = PD \times EAD \times LGD.$$

Thus, the UL can be expressed as

$$UL = \sqrt{p - p^2} \times E \times S$$

The above expression indicates that the UL is the probability (p) that a credit loss could occur or could not occur under different scenarios that a borrower may face. To simply the expression, recall that E is stated as the actual loss that occurs for the EAD and S is the severity of the loss for LGD. When E and S are constant, the basic concern is the probability that default occurs or default does not occur, which is stated as p and $(1-p)$. This is no different than the original credit equation, but rather a simplifying assumption when the variables are fixed and can alternatively be expressed as

$$UL = \sqrt{PD \times (1 - PD)} \times EAD \times LGD.$$

The UL loss is then derived by taking the standard deviation of the EL, which is the average distance away from the mean of the credit loss distribution. The standard deviation is the positive square root of the variance or the degree of dispersion between the variance and the mean.* To measure the degree of dispersion away from the mean, the variance is used to derive a positive number by taking a probability weighted sum of the credit loss distribution multiplied by the squared differences. As the variance becomes larger, the mean will be more dispersed.

7.4.1   Calculating the UL

Suppose we wanted to determine the unexpected loss on a $3,000,000 BBB rated term loan facility. The UL would therefore be:

$$\sqrt{0.018 - 0.018^2} \times \$3,000 \times 0.40 = \$159,559.$$

The above calculation will generally vary depending on the particular credit product and facility structure. This is because the cash flows and features will differ among debt instruments, thus making their option-like qualities hold degrees of uncertainty for the individual loss estimates. Loans, for example, can be extended on either committed or uncommitted terms that may have uncertain drawdowns within preauthorized limits or specific prepayment options. Consideration must be given to the maturity dates on certain type of loans such as revolving lines of credit, which are usually structured with the option to call or terminate the line prior

---

*Recall from statistics that, because of mathematical conventions, the variance will always be positive in algebraic equations, so they can be added and subtracted in equations.

to its maturity date. The EAD of a revolving credit line is also impacted by how the facility is structured, such as a revolving term that would convert into a term loan. Collateralized Loan Obligations (CLOs) and other multiple lending products that are bundled into one credit facility are another example of uncertain cash flows that will affect the EAD. In addition there is the impact of credit mitigation features that may include, for example, letters of credit and guarantees on a transaction, which also drive the LGD. These types of transactions can be difficult to estimate when they hold legal and economic inter-relationships with third parties to guarantee the debt. Loan documentation must be carefully reviewed for covenant and collateral provisions to derive reasonable risk calculations, but also for assigning and selling transactions in the secondary markets.

Although the secondary market is easily available for selling syndicated corporate loans, the market for small- and middle-market loans is still evolving. Middle-market and smaller firms need to become more homogeneous in defining credit risk parameters for the different classes of credit assets that can be impacted by spreads and/or commitment fees. When E and S are uncertain and independent, the EL is essentially the same methodology that is derived from the product of each component. THE UL now includes the additional features of taking the variance of the probability that a loss will occur under different conditions to derive the following expression:

$$UL = \sqrt{(P - P^2)\bar{S}^2\bar{E}^2 + P \times (\sigma_S^2\ \bar{E}^2 + \sigma_E^2\ \bar{S}^2 + \sigma_S^2\ \sigma_E^2)}$$

If we knew that the S was 20% in the earlier example, then the UL would be computed to be

$$UL = \sqrt{(0.18 - 0.18^2)(0.4^2 3,000^2) + 0.18 \times (0.3^2 3,000^2)}$$

$$UL = \$1,310.24.$$

Although the credit exposure for a credit derivative can be quantified with the same approach, the risk of loss for structured credit products can be more detailed. As an example, the exposure on a credit default swap is based on the issuer's creditworthiness, although the derivative contract can be tied to a market variable such as a firm's equity price. The calculation would therefore have to be measured on a market-to-market basis according to the current replacement costs plus the future exposure that the derivative may have from market changes. Measuring the future exposure of a derivative is also based on the time remaining to maturity along with the expected volatility of the underlying asset. As the estimation of future exposures can be an independent and biased judgment, it is usually derived by simulating or credit modeling techniques.

7.5   CREDIT MIGRATION

The concept of credit migration is a modern credit application that is important for several reasons in that it is intended to manage the expected changes in borrowers' credit quality. A change in credit quality can affect how the borrower's debt is valued based on a rating upgrade or downgrade and relative to their exposure to default and credit-related events. This has been fundamental to the growth of the credit derivatives markets, which has promoted many of the advancements in credit migration. Active users of credit derivatives required a systematic approach to identify and monitor the changes that affected obligors' credit quality and ratings relative to the surrounding market events. Credit rating migration models have supported this need by providing a measurement tool to estimate the probability of a transition upward or downward on assets or borrowers over a given time. Because credit events can lead to moving borrowers from an initial rating category to another category, the resulting changes in credit quality and in transaction values can also affect the structural risks related to particular types of facilities in terms of repayment claims and covenant protection. In response to such events, lenders will incorporate downgrades and other provisions in the borrower's credit agreement as a means to limit or reduce their exposures from credit quality migration and related events. If a change in credit quality, for example, reduces the return on the debt asset, this could trigger an increase in the interest spread that a borrower is charged.

Credit rating migration models are summarized in transition matrices that indicate the likelihood of a transition rating change upward or downward over a specific time period that is usually one year. Transaction matrices are based on empirical observations of historical ratings and default data to derive a probability distribution that reflects each rating category. The chart in Table 7.1 illustrates a transition matrix for measuring the probability that an

TABLE 7-1

Using a Credit Migration Model

Initial Rating	Rating at Year-End (%)							
	AAA	AA	A	BBB	BB	B	CCC	D
AAA	90.81	8.33	0.68	0.06	0.12	0.00	0.00	0.00
AA	0.70	90.65	7.79	0.64	0.06	0.14	0.02	0.00
A	0.09	2.27	91.05	5.52	0.74	0.26	0.01	0.06
BBB	0.02	0.33	5.95	86.93	5.30	1.17	0.12	0.18
BB	0.03	0.14	0.67	7.73	80.53	8.84	1.00	1.06
B	0.00	0.11	0.24	0.43	6.48	83.46	4.07	5.20
CCC	0.22	0.0	0.22	1.30	2.38	11.24	64.86	19.79

Four sources of transition probability matrices: S&P, Moody, CreditMetrix, KMV.

issuer will have the same rating over a one-year period from the beginning of the period to the end of the period. For illustrative purposes, we will use a transition matrix that has been published by Standard & Poor's, which in this case has eight possible rating categories ranging from the highest credit quality of AAA to the lowest quality of CCC, including default. To understand how the matrix is read, refer to the vertical axis in the first row below the "Initial Rating" column, which shows the ratings at the beginning of the year. The horizontal axis reflects the "Rating at Year End" or at the end of the year. From these two points, the matrix measures the probability that an issuer will experience a net change in the row rating to the column status at the end of a specified period. The values that are diagonal in each row can be read as the probability that a borrower will have the same rating at the beginning and end of the year in percentages. If we refer to the model in Table 7.1, it can be read by concluding that of all of the issuers rated at the beginning of the year, that 90.81% were rated AAA at the end of the year, 8.33% were rated AA and 0.68% were rated A. This means that there is a 90.81% probability that the AAA rating will remain the same and a 0.70% probability that it will migrate to a AA rating by year end, as indicated in the second row. There is also a 0.09% probability that the same AAA rating will migrate to an A rating. Notice that the sum of each row is 100%, to reflect the fact that no matter what grade a rating category begins at, it will still have to end in one of the year-end rating categories regardless of whatever point at which it begins.

7.5.1 Measuring the Probability of Credit Migration

Suppose you want to measure the probability that a BBB rated bond or loan would remain at its' current rating or migrate to a better or worse grade over the one year period. If we take the estimates that have been derived in Table 7.1, we see in Table 7.2 that the probability of a BBB rated issuer remaining at its current rating one year later is 86.93%. At the same time, the probability of a default over the next year is estimated to be 0.18%, and the probability that the same obligor will migrate upwards from a BBB to become an AAA rated borrower is 0.02%. In reading the matrix, you will note that moving to the right reflects a downgrade and an upgrade is represented by movements to the left.

The major public rating agencies for bonds, syndicated loans, and most structured finance publish transition matrices. The data are based on historical information that covers the beginning and end of the year periods, although it is also published for 3-, 5-, and even up to 10-year periods. However, as we will discuss in Chapter 9 on the topic of Credit Rating Systems, many financial institutions will develop their own transition matrixes internally to give them a more accurate sample representation and data interpretation. This is because transition matrices provided by external agencies will usually tend to derive their estimates by using methodologies that are not inclusive of all of the factors that correspond with the composition of the financial institution's credit

TABLE 7-2

Measuring the Probability of Credit Migration

Initial Rating	Rating at Year-End (%)							
	AAA	AA	A	BBB	BB	B	CCC	D
BBB	0.02	0.33	5.95	86.93	5.30	1.17	0.12	0.18

Four sources of transition probability matrices: S & P, Moody, CreditMetrix, KMV.

portfolio. Many of these factors are derived in the definitions that are used to define the credit equation, which requires a consistent definition of how the loss components are derived.

Credit migration is also important for placing exposure limits according to the internal credit policies that define a financial institution's underwriting guidelines. If a bank has stated in its credit policy that the credit portfolio will only retain a certain limit of non-investment-grade loans, for example, an increase in these facilities can be monitored with the transition matrix. Regulatory capital requirements may also require underwriting and credit policy guidelines that limit loans and trading books to a specified percentage level. The consequence of failing to adhere to these guidelines could ultimately be a downgrade on the institution's public rating and willingness of investors to inject additional capital into overall operations.

7.6 ESTIMATING THE COMPONENTS OF THE CREDIT EQUATION

Because the parameters within the credit equation are tied to the credit process, the methodologies that are used to derive the metrics can have a pervasive impact on how transactions and portfolio credit risk is measured. The foundation to applying an appropriate methodology to estimate the credit equation is derived from the historical data that are usually contained in the credit application. Although most banks use sophisticated models to derive the metrics, as we have noted, the competing methodologies that prevail can result in different data estimates. Figure 7.4 reflects a common format that details how the credit process emulates the credit equation. The activities for originating new business begins with the credit philosophy and credit risk strategy that are embedded in the corporate credit culture. The credit risk strategy should be clearly reflected in the credit policy and procedures as it pertains to the types of services that are granted. Details on the organization's target markets should also be included, along with the portfolio composition mix, price and nonprice terms, limit structures, as well as approval authority and exception reporting. All of the activities in the credit process will basically be impacted by the measurement process and metrics that drive the lending operations. This begins with the PD, which is determined by evaluating creditworthiness from what has been detailed in the customer's credit applications and loan reviews. The probability of default or the likelihood that the borrower will not repay is generally a function of the bank's internal credit rating and reflects the borrower's creditworthiness. The probability of default is also used to determine the frequency distributions for portfolio default rates based on the credit decisions that have been made on historical credit applications. Compilation of LGD estimates is relative to the structural components of transactions such as those found in credit documentation. Estimating the severity or actual lost amount can also be derived from financial documentation detailing historical disbursements and repayment performances. In addition, LGD estimates are also relevant to those transactions that have defaulted and completed the workout process. Similarly, EAD is also a function of monitoring activities that measure the loss exposure amounts that a bank is owed when default does occur.

Estimating the credit equation metrics, however, can initially be a challenging task, particularly for lenders that have not retained sufficient historical data. There are several types of data that must be gathered and collected on the volume of credit defaults that have transpired relative to each type of credit risk by specific borrowers, issuers, or counterparties. The historical default information is then collected and integrated into the credit risk architecture so that risk information can be measured from a variety of technology platforms and multiple systems. Among the data requirements are all of the credit detail processes that we have outlined earlier in the chapter.

Many of the larger banks have now overcome this problem by estimating metrics equivalent to a minimum of five years for integration into their credit risk architectures. This process will also become part of the Basel II regulatory guidelines beginning in 2008. A closer look at the methodologies used in estimating expected losses will be discussed in the next section.

7.7 ESTIMATING PROBABILITY OF DEFAULT (PD)

To measure PD involves deriving a credit metric for which credit loss can be computed on the borrower's creditworthiness about the likelihood of default in the future. The PD is also referred to as the Expected Default Frequency (EDF), or the default rate, and represents the probability that a loan will default during a one-year time period. The EDF and default rate on a single loan, however, should not be confused with the terminology that refers to estimating the default probability for categories of portfolio borrowers. A PD on a single borrower is derived from a binomial probability distribution that is used to describe one of two mutually exclusive possible outcomes or, in our case, that the loan will default or it will not default. Mis-stating default risk can result in having all of the EL parameters inaccurately defined, which is again why this concept should not be confused with the credit quality of a group of borrowers. When referring to the likelihood of default, it implies the chance of default by an individual borrower or on the asset, relative to the frequency of historical defaults and how often they occur. Default rates are frequency measures that are used to quantify the minimum capital amounts that lenders need to retain on each credit facility against the loss of possible default. The ability to allocate capital is based on knowing the frequency of defaults that arises from constant incidences of defaults relative to a specific asset or group. This approach is an empirical methodology, because it is based on observing all possible distribution of default events that could occur for an entire population of each of the different classes of assets. That is, for every type of asset that a lender provides, a distribution function should be observed on all default possibilities and incidences that can transpire. As illustrated in Tables 7.3 and 7.4, default rates can be measured on either an exposure-weighted or incidence-weighted basis. The difference between these two

TABLE 7-3

Incidence-Weighted Default Measure

$$1 \text{ Year PD} = \frac{\text{Total number of obligor defaults in 2005}}{\text{Total number of all obligors at beginning of 2005}}$$

TABLE 7-4

Exposure-Weighted Default measure

$$1 \text{ Year PD} = \frac{\text{Monetary value of loan to obligors defaulting in 2005}}{\text{Monetary value of total loans at beginning of 2005}}$$

default rate measurements is that the incidence-weighted default rate is based on the number of portfolio borrowers that are estimated to default rather than on the exposure-weighted dollar amount. Although the borrower's credit rating will usually derive the PD, it should also be noted that because there is no standard definition of what constitutes a default, there can be different inputs into the credit rating system that quantify credit risk.

7.7.1 Estimating Default for Single Borrowers

The system applications that are typically used to distinguish borrowers' risks and derive the probability of default on individual borrowers can also vary across different credit portfolios. The most common applications that are used to estimate default risk are expert credit grading and credit default scoring models, or a combination of both can be combined into one approach. Expert judgment is a traditional credit application that is predominantly used for borrowers who have significant qualitative risk factors, such as large corporations. The application of "expert credit grading" is grounded in the subjectivity of how credit ratings are assigned by credit analysts that are considered to be experts in credit assessment and the prediction of defaults. When defaults for single borrowers are estimated with expert credit grading, borrowers are assigned to specific grading buckets to reflect the different categories of credit rating grades according to a series of defined credit qualities. The buckets can be categorized for specific credit qualities that may be relevant according to loan types, bonds, facility maturity, and so on. The buckets, for example, consist of high-, average-, or low-quality borrowers with high, average, or low default probability. An average default probability is then derived based on all of the borrowers within the respective rating categories.

Statistical credit scoring models form the second approach used to measure the default risk for individual borrowers. Although retail lenders have used these models since they were developed in the early 1960s by Fair & Isaac, the functions of the tasks that they perform have advanced over the years to now encompass a range of credit risk measurement techniques.* Since the 1980s, credit scoring models have been used by banks to evaluate borrowers' behavioral

---

*Fair & Isaac is a major credit bureau in both the United States and the United Kingdom that reports FICO scores to financial institutions on consumer financial data. The company is also known as Equifax.

characteristics relative to making credit decisions. A major benefit of using these models is that they have streamlined the credit process by providing a rigorous approach to screening credit applications while also reducing the time and costs of expert credit analysis. For specific product and credit lines, the models served as a prime indicator of creditworthiness according to how the facility was used. Secured real-estate lending, for example, would incorporate the features of a facility such as the collateral, loan-to-value, and debt service capacity into the scoring process, but unsecured credit-card lending relied more heavily on credit scoring for underwriting, pricing, and establishing line limits. Starting in the 1990s, credit scoring models began to gain acceptance in commercial and business sectors and have since come to be used in credit originations and to manage the specific credit risks for both individual and credit portfolio debt assets.

The basic concept behind these models is to calculate default risk from key financial risk factors by using data that are intended to separate good credit risks from bad ones. Borrowers are sorted into different risk classes based upon single or multiple variables to predict the likelihood of future default. A univatiate or single variable, for example, can be based on accounting ratios that are benchmarked against some norm for comparison. Depending on the lender's risk appetite, high-risk applicants will rank low and a numerical cut-off score will be determined for poor borrowers such as the exhibit in Figure 7.7. When multivariate assumptions are used, multiple data factors are combined and statistically weighted to render automated credit decisions.

Criticisms that prevail in credit scoring include that, because many of these models are accounting based, book value transparency cannot be guaranteed, as they are measured in discrete rather than in continuous intervals. Measuring default behavior on a continuous basis is important for recognizing changing market variables and conditions. Among the multivariate types of statistical scoring models that are commonly used to estimate default probabilities for individual borrowing transactions are discriminant analysis, linear probability, and logit models.

7.7.2 Discriminant Analysis

The discriminant analysis model attempts to make credit decisions and estimate default by combining five accounting ratios into a single index, which serve as predictive variables relevant to a

FIGURE 7.7

Credit Scoring Example

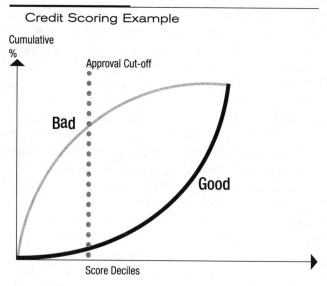

Source: Ernst & Young, September 15, 2005

borrower's financial data. The index score that is assigned to each borrower classifies them into a high or low default category. A familiar proponent of discrimant analysis as a default predictor is Edward Altman, who developed the Altman Linear Discriminant Model, which is also referred to as the Altman Z-score and is computed by taking a weighted sum of customer data*:

$$Z = 1.2X_1 + 1.4X_2 + 3.3X_3 + 0.6X_4 + 1.0X_5,$$

where $Z = 0$ if a firm becomes bankrupt and 1 if the firm does not, X_1 = working capital/total assets, X_2 = retained earnings/total assets, X_3 = EBIT/total assets, X_4 = market value of equity/book value of total liabilities, and X_5 = sales/total assets.

The model estimates a firm's probability of default by taking the average Z-value for a historical group of defaulted and non-defaulted loans as a measure for bankruptcy and credit approval. In theory, the higher the Z-score, the lower the default risk should

*Edward I. Altman has engaged in numerous works on distress debt and bankruptcy prediction while serving as the Max Heine Professor of Finance at New York University Stern School of Business and the Vice Director of its Salomon Center.

be. In a study performed by Altman, the average Z-values for defaulted and nondefaulted loans were found to be 1.61 and 2.01, respectively. The conclusion from this was that companies having Z-values less than 1.81 (the average Z-score value) were "very likely" to go bankrupt, but those with a score greater than 2.99 were unlikely to go bankrupt. For example, if Z is ≥ 2.99, then the borrower can be considered to be nonbankrupt and the credit facility can be approved. Alternately, if $Z \leq 2.99$, then the borrower is considered to be a candidate for bankruptcy and the facility should be declined. This can be seen in the practical approach whereby a borrower has the ratios $Z_1 = 0.2$, $Z_2 = 0$, $Z_3 = -0.2$, $Z_4 = 0.1$, and $Z_5 = 2$. If the lending decision is based on a cut-off Z-score of 1.81, according to the model's calculation, the loan should be declined, because $1.64 < 1.81$, as computed below:

$$Z = 1.2(0.2) + 1.4(0) + 3.3(-0.2) + 0.6(0.1) + 1.0(2) = 1.64.$$

Although lenders have used the model in both its present and modified forms, others have found weaknesses in this approach. One weakness lies in the fact that the model only considers default or no-default as a basis to predict default. A second lies in the fact that the weights that are used to estimate default are based on current conditions and do not include the possibility for future situations. A similar criticism prevails in the third weakness, in that the equation essentially ignores the business cycles and market conditions within which borrowers operate. The contention is that default probability should be measured during the different credit cycles and based on the underlying market factors. A fourth problem is that the model does not retain a database for defaulted loan reviews that can be used as a future benchmark reference.

7.7.3 Linear Probability and Logit Models

Another type of credit scoring application is the linear probability model, which attempts to measure default probability by classifying borrowers into different risk classes according to their historical repayment performance. The assumption here is that default is based on specific behavioral factors that coincide directly in proportion to the variables that affect them. The model applies a multivariate regression analysis (Zi) by taking certain default predictive factors similar to Altman's discrimant analysis. Prior repayment data are input into the model's equation to explain a borrower's former repayment performance and then used to estimate the likelihood of default in the future. A dependent variable is then multiplied with the observed independent variables to express the equation as

$$Zi = \beta \sum j \, Xij + \varepsilon i.$$

The estimated βj is then multiplied with the observed Xij to derive an expected value of Zi. This value can then be interpreted in a probability model according to the variables that influence the expected probability of default so that

$$E(Zi) = 1 - Pi.$$

Suppose the credit specialist determines from historical defaults that leverage, for example, is an influencing behavioral factor for repayment ability according to the variables that define the debt–equity (D/E) and sales–asset (S/A) ratios. In other words, by defining a value to each of the separate ratio variables in a linear equation, the repayment probability for a new loan can be estimated. The estimated probability is usually expressed as Zi, which is the expected value for the expected probability of default. To illustrate this by using leverage as a predictive behavioral characteristic for default, assume that a review of a borrower's credit application indicates 0.3 for D/E and 2.0 for S/A. The multivariate regression model for a new loan would then be extended into a linear equation to reflect the ratios so that the expected default probability would be:

$$Zi = 0.5(D/Ei) + 0.1 \, (S/Ai)$$
$$Zj = 0.5(0.3) + 0.1(2.0) = 0.35.$$

Because the estimated probability of default is outside the interval between 0 and 1, critics find the linear probability model to be statistically weak in that the Z cannot be a probability. Consequently, the weakness of linear probability was replaced by the logit model because of its ability to restrict the estimated range of default to lie between 0 and 1. Another criticism relates to particular types of models that are designed to produce a linear probability in default risk, which is unrealistic for default behavior. Because linear scoring models are based on limited assumptions of risk factors, it is difficult to derive a straight line or flat-maximum curving effect in predicting default, as unexpected variables can throw curves into measuring precisely.

The logit model constrains the cumulative probability of default on a loan to lie between 0 and 1 and assumes the probability of default to be logistically distributed in a similar fashion to the linear probability model. The regression model is then able to give estimates outside the interval. A major weakness to the logit model as a default predictor is that it assumes that the cumulative probability of default takes on a particular function form which reflects a logistic function. Cumulative probability refers to the fact that, over time, default generally will increase and therefore needs to be considered. At some point in time, the difference between the cumulative probability of default and a potentially variable default probability will be used to derive a marginal default probability.

An extension to the logit model, which is another credit scoring nonlinear alternative, is the probit model, which can also produce common values when multiplied by fixed factors. The probit model also contracts the projected probability of default to lie between 0 and 1, but differs from the logit model by assuming that the probability of default has a cumulative normal distribution rather than the logistic function.

7.8 TERM-STRUCTURE-BASED METHODS

Among the more recent models to estimate default risk are those that feature market-based techniques such as the term-structured or spread-based methods. Default probabilities are estimated by applying the risk premiums in corporate debt or loans to borrowers that have equivalent risk rating. By taking the spreads on risk-free discount Treasury bonds and comparing them to those on corporate bond issuers, the implication is that it can reveal the default probability for future payment. The probability of default is estimated according to the expected return of the facility, which is equal to the risk-free rate. Therefore, if you know the risk premium, the probability of default can be inferred and the expected returns after accounting for the probability of default is equal to the risk-free rate, so that

$$p(1+k) = 1+i.$$

Although this methodology is typically used to derive inferred probability from comparable bonds, it can also be generalized to loans or by adjusting the loan to varying default recovery rates.

7.9 OPTION MODELS

A more recent approach to estimating default probability has been the application of the options pricing model. Developed by Fisher Black and Myron Scholes in 1973 for pricing corporate securities, the model was subsequently applied to predict default after it was used by Robert Merton to price corporate debt in 1974.* The model is designed to evaluate credit risk by using stock market data to infer a firm's default based on the volatility of its asset price, which is related to the volatility of the firm's equity price. The assumption is that once the value of total outstanding assets falls below the nominal amount or value of a firm's outstanding debts, it will have insufficient funds to repay its debt obligations. The result will lead to a probability of default for the firm that is represented by

$$V = E + B(D)$$

where V = firm value, E = market value of equity, B = market value of debt, and D = face amount or value of debt. Because of the limited liability that a firm will have if assets are less than the firm's value, it in essence holds either a default or repayment option. The firm will either be able to repay the debt obligation and retain its assets along with any additional profits, or default on the debt and surrender its assets to creditors.

By taking economic and financial data that are based on related market developments, the model can predict market expectations about default predictability. It compares a firm's debt to a put option written on the obligor's assets, and the value of outstanding debt is the strike price or greater. For example, if a loan is extended to a firm, the bank will have a put option that is short on its assets, and the firm or shareholders will hold a long call option.

---

*Merton actually shared the 1997 Nobel Prize in Economics with Myron Scholes. Because of his death in 1995, Fisher Black did not receive the award but would have most likely shared in the prize.

FIGURE 7.8

Payoff to Stockholders

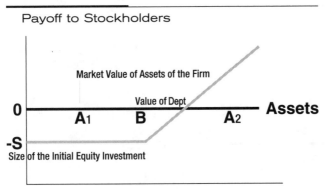

If repayment is made according to terms, the firm continues to make principal and interest payments and retains the upside of the option. However, if default does occur and the borrower is unable to repay, the stockholders, as the firm's owners and who have limited liability to creditors in the event of bankruptcy, will transfer their assets to the lenders and only lose their initial equity investment. Figure 7.8 illustrates the shareholders' payoff function, in which B is the value of the loan and A is the market value of the firm's assets, which represents the initial equity investment. The lenders can only expect to receive the required loan payment at B, which is repaid if A > B. If the firm's assets fall below B, default will occur and the assets are then transferred to the lenders. The payoff to the lenders in Figure 7.9 is the amount of the loan that was extended to the firm that is represented by B, which is similar to writing a put option on the assets at B, or the value of the debt at the exercise price. It is the minimum of B or A. If the firm defaults, the stockholders would transfer the assets at A_1 to the lenders, but if it repays the loan, the value of the firm's assets at A_2 would be retained along with the difference of A2−B, because debt is repaid at OB.

The usefulness of the options pricing model in measuring credit risk is that it is based on both historical and current financial data, which are used to incorporate ongoing firm-related developments with market expectations relevant to the likelihood of a firm's default. Because the model is forward looking, it is an improvement on traditional applications that were originally conceived, such as the historical bond default probabilities or historical recovery rates and bond mortality rates, to predict default. A weakness of the

FIGURE 7.9

Payoff to Debt Holders

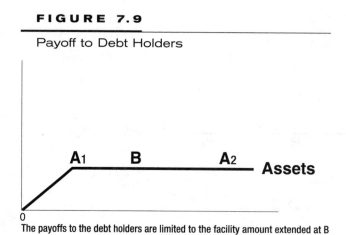

The payoffs to the debt holders are limited to the facility amount extended at B

model is that it assumes that, unlike bonds, loans (particularly for middle-market and small commercial lenders) are not traded on the open market nor are all firms continuously traded. This makes the model difficult to use for many credit borrowers. Another concern is how volatility is measured on the underlying assets, which can affect the calculation.

7.10 ESTIMATING LOSS GIVEN DEFAULT (LGD)

Loss given default is a modern credit risk phenomenon that measures the severity of a credit loss relative to the amount that can be recovered. Estimates for LGD are also based on mitigating the exposure from structural elements that act to reduce the overall exposure loss amount. For example, the type of collateral that is held against the loss of default along with third-party guarantees to support the credit obligation can affect the LGD calculation. Another factor affecting LGD is the priority of claims or the debt seniority level to recover the loss. For example, syndicated loans will usually give lenders first priority in bankruptcy claims, which should be considered in measuring the amount lost or estimated recovery value. Estimates of LGD are usually made for a point in time based on the lender's average historical loss experience according to the debt type and seniority structure. The difficulty in estimating this metric is that various definitions of default can prevail for which a loss may not be incurred. For example, some lenders might define default as the inability to repay a debt

obligation, but another may include defaults that occur on a nonaccruing status. This is often seen in instances when a borrower is
60 days late, for example, on a respective credit obligation and
subsequently becomes current by the 90th day. Although this may
technically be a default, the lender has still recovered on the obligation. Another concern also prevails in estimating the recovery
amount for borrowers who enter into bankruptcy. Because it is difficult to predict the amount that can be recovered on a defaulted
facility, using historical data may not always be accurate in estimating the replacement value post-default. This is attributed to the
time that it typically takes for the courts to settle bankruptcy
claims, which is usually longer than a year.* Estimating the severity of the loss therefore requires consideration of the various scenarios under which defaults may occur and a borrower's condition
after default. The amount that may eventually be recovered on a
defaulted obligation is equivalent to the recovery exposure or discount rate, which is usually contingent on any collateral and its
corresponding current market value. One approach to estimate
LGD is based on the recovery rate:

$$1 - \text{recovery rate} + \text{administrative costs.}$$

Although the above methodology works for loans and bonds, an
alternative approach is used in credit facilities that are not liquid:

$$\text{LGD} = \frac{\text{predefault value} - \text{postdefault value}}{\text{predefault value}}.$$

Under classical credit with the use of the one-dimensional credit
rating scale, LGD was combined into the PD and calculated as a
single credit risk measure. The combined rating represented the PD
and the portion of the facility that was likely to be lost given the
event of default. Because this calculation did not give a precise estimation of the fractional amount expected to be lost once default

---

*The typical time for lenders to recover on defaulted funds when companies emerge from
bankruptcy ranges between 18 months and 2 years. Based on the market valuation of the
debt during this time, the net present value of the cash flows will be different from the
time of loan origination. Given the time it takes before recovery is actually realized, including the various recovery costs for interest collected, legal costs, and other expenses, the
actual recovery amount will be quite different from the market valuation of the debt.

occurs, it impacts how loss distributions are constructed and measured. A clearer definition is obtained when LGD is identified as the recovery rate $(1-RR)$ and percentage amount the lender estimates to receive on a defaulted credit facility.

Estimating the recovery amount for a borrower who enters into bankruptcy may not be practical before the bankruptcy court has completed a review of the case, thereby making LGD an irrelevant matter at the time of default. Lenders must therefore consider these types of scenarios as part of their loss data when estimating recovery amounts. Regulatory guidelines under the Basel Accords state that "banks should not simply measure the loss recorded in accounting records, but include the discount effects, funding costs and direct and indirect costs associated with collecting on instruments to determine loss. The Basel II Accord, however, defines a default to occur when one or more of the following conditions take place:

- It is determined the obligor is unlikely to pay its debt obligation on principal, interest, fees in full.
- A credit loss is associated with any obligation of the obligor, such as charge-offs, specific provisions, interest or fees.
- The obligor is more than 90 days past due on any credit obligation.
- The obligor has filed for bankruptcy on similar protection from creditors.

Under these guidelines, default may consist of the borrower being unable to repay the obligation, whereas, at other banks, it can represent a nonaccruing status. These guidelines have made the matter of default a bit more precise, although it still may be irrelevant at the time of default or before going into workout.

Because of the relationship between the recovery rate and PD, default rates are related to any variation in recovery. If a borrower defaults, the recovery rate typically will be dependent on the collateral and seniority, which is also dependent on the economy and market conditions. If the economy is in decline, recovery values are expected to be low due to a low market value for the collateral and a high probability of default. Table 7.5 shows the recovery rates that Moodys' obtained for different classes of assets based on seniority. They found that the highest recovery rate is tied to the senior secured class because it has the highest priority of payment on defaults, and the junior subordinated obligors had the lowest

TABLE 7-5

Recovery Rates

Class	Mean (%)	Standard Deviation (%)
Senior secured	52.31	25.15
Senior unsecured	48.84	25.01
Senior subordinated	39.46	25.59
Subordinated	33.71	20.78
Junior subordinated	19.69	13.85

Source: Moody's Investor Services Recovery Rates, 2000

recovery rate. Recovery rates have also been found to be correlated with their industries, rating classes, and credit product types. A study by Altman and Kishore on the behavior of recovery rates by industry, seniority, and amount was conducted by using 700 defaulted bonds issuers during the period 1978–1995. They determined that the average recovery rate was $41.70, with the public utility sectors having the highest recovery rates and the lodging and health industry (specifically hospitals and nursing facilities) having the lowest recovery rate of $26.49.

7.11 ESTIMATING EXPOSURE AT DEFAULT (EAD)

The EAD is an internal estimate on the outstanding amount that is lost or at risk to be lost when default occurs. It is usually reflected by E and dependent upon four factors, that includes the potential exposure, facility structure, use of the commitment and the use of a mark-to-market (MTM) calculation. It does not represent the current exposure amount when the facility is extended, and its estimation is dependent on the type of credit product that is extended. For a loan facility, the EAD is based on the nominal amount or estimated outstanding amount for a committed but partially undrawn credit line. For bonds, it is also the nominal amount, but credit derivatives requires that EAD is estimated as the positive market value. Therefore, the EAD or exposure amount is dependent on how a credit facility or commitment will be used, the facility structure, as well as the mark-to-market value and the potential exposure that could be at risk.

Because the value of EAD is dependent on the amount the borrower has already repaid when default takes place, it is the potential exposure that could be at risk on a revolving line of credit, for example, given the limit and drawdown amounts prior to default. Measuring the EAD or outstanding equivalent amount at the time of default is also dependent on the type of credit risk process and facility structure that the lender has in place. This means that, if a strong credit infrastructure is in place, lenders are better able to monitor a borrower's credit condition and limit drawdowns before default occurs. For example, as most borrowers approach default, there is a tendency to fully draw down on a line of credit. Having the appropriate facility monitoring mechanisms for covenants, collateral, and other conditions as a borrower nears default will guide the lender to cut the line before it is fully drawn.

Estimating EAD requires an evaluation of historical data and the accompanying structural features relevant to the facilities. As an example, the type of borrowers that have lines of credit and their corresponding internal credit ratings can indicate much about the credit assessment process. Given the borrower's credit rating a year prior to default, the credit specialist can review the monitoring process to evaluate how these borrowers used their credit lines before default occurred. They should consider whether the credit rating declined by two or more grades before default and how the migration of the line relates to its use.

7.12 THE ROLE OF MODELS IN THE CREDIT PROCESS

The implementation of credit risk models is contingent on how a bank may define credit losses and the horizon period in which such losses are measured. Models are typically constructed in one of two categories: default mode model or mark-to-market. Default mode models are designed to only estimate the likelihood that a borrower will default and not any changes in the credit quality. If default occurs, the credit loss will usually be estimated to be the present value of the recovery amount less the administration or workout costs. At some banks, however, default may consist of the borrower being unable to repay the obligation, but at other banks, it can represent a nonaccruing status. A problem in this methodology is that the actual recovery amount or cash flows from a defaulted borrower often cannot be identified before the workout is complete. Consequently, LGD may be irrelevant at the time of default. Another limitation of default mode models is the timing horizon over which the credit risk is measured. Because loans can be extended for periods greater than the one-year time horizon that is generally captured by the default modes, the model may ignore credit losses greater than a year, which is typically less than the maturity of the debt. The primary reason that lenders use a one-year time horizon is attributed to the available credit quality data and the liquidity derived from the secondary loan and credit derivative markets. At the same time, many banks are designing their own proprietary credit risk models as part of rating systems and making provisions for up to 5- and even 10-year time periods. Another approach has been for lenders to adjust their internal credit ratings to reflect the time horizon. For example, a longer-term loan would receive a lower credit rating than a shorter-term credit facility.

Aside from calculating the probability or likelihood of default, default models are designed to determine and quantify the amount of risk cash flows that lenders will not receive should the credit event occur. However, because models are nothing more than predictors of default, the more accurately that a model is designed, the better can credit risk exposure be predicted and mitigated. Consequently, the models are subject to data shortcomings and input weaknesses. For example, the available market data on loan books are not as extensive for small and middle-market corporate borrowers as for large corporate borrowers. In response to this, middle-market lenders are constructing their own models by calibrating internal credit ratings to historical frequencies of rating migrations. Default models recognize credit loss only when the obligor defaults, and not when the credit quality declines. When an obligor defaults, the lender suffers a loss equal to the exposure amount less the sum to be recovered, adjusted for the recovery costs and time. This is LGD, and is estimated by the exposure amount times $1 - RR$.

In contrast, a multistate or mark-to-market model estimates the probability of default as well as a change in the facility's economic value due to default or credit downgrade. Although originally developed and used by bank trading desks, the MTM models have rapidly expanded to now include banking loan books to capture changes in both the default as well as economic value. For this reason they are considered multistate, because default is recognized as a deteriorating credit quality that leads to default as well as from a downgrading or credit rating migration. The value of the loan is based on the market-determined structure of credit grades for the respective loan grade. In addition, the discount rate used is tied to the market reflection of a deteriorating credit quality or higher credit spreads. When using a multistate model, the lender must evaluate whether a company will default, remain BBB rated, migrate up to A or downward to C. A BBB rated company for example, under the default mode model, would only lose value on a defaulted loan in the event of default equivalent to the LGD. However, under the MTM paradigm, credit losses would be realized in the event of default, as well as in the event that the borrower was downgraded or if the prevailing market interest rates were to rise. For these reasons, default models are becoming less popular compared with mark-to-market models, which provide greater information on both the time horizon as well as the borrower's credit quality. The default mode model would not recognize these factors until the obligor had defaulted. This was demonstrated in the case of Worldcom and Enron, both of whom had credit quality changes several times prior to their default. Advocates of default models, however, argue that the capability to correlate credit risk portfolios limits along with pricing of securitization and capital calculation represents a form of multistate usage provided by default models. This process of calibrating to market variables such as the equity price, market capitalization, or bond credit spreads, is now being undertaken for middle-market firms by mining and collecting select historical data. The selected data is based on a variety of variables that may affect an obligor's behavior or default predictability, such as the amount of debt capacity to service a borrower's financial obligations or interest coverage ratios. Once the variables are identified, then relationships are assumed or postulated among them relative to how they impact events of default and default behavior. As discussed above, this represents an expert system type of model, upon which Moody's KMV model is based. As lenders did not traditionally need to maintain the relevant data to create default models, over the past five years they have been engaged in collecting historical information in an effort to either create their own credit risk models or to integrate them into their systems and credit portfolio management process. They are also being used for regulatory capital requirements and other financial institution purposes.

7.13 CONCLUSIONS

Credit risk measurement is integrated into the credit process in order to limit the amount of credit risk exposure outstanding as well as to mitigate the exposure amount with credit risk mitigants and earn an adequate compensation on the total amount of extended credit. The framework to measure the exposure on individual facilities is based on the credit equation that quantifies expected and unexpected losses. Expected losses are usually accounted for in the price of the transaction, and unexpected losses occur under unexpected or stressful conditions. For large corporate borrowers individual models are used, but small- to middle-market borrowers will more often use a form of credit scoring to determine the credit equation. The models that are used can be default or mark-to-market, although the latter has become more popular among lenders.

Expected and unexpected losses also have to be determined for credit migration, which is the probability of credit events occurring from a rating upgrade or downgrade. Changes in credit quality for borrowers can reduce the returns on the facilities, which may also trigger an increase in the amount that is charged to extend the transaction.

CHAPTER DISCUSSION QUESTIONS

1. What are the main elements of default probability?
2. Distinguish between probability of default, loss given default, and exposure at default?
3. How is credit risk mitigated in measuring credit facilities?
4. What is the difference between default and mark-to-market models?
5. Calculate the expected and unexpected loss for the BBB-rated company based on the information provided in Table 7.6.

TABLE 7-6

Rating at Start of Year

Rating at end of Year	AAA	AA	A	BBB	BB	B	CCC	Default
AAA	9,366	66	7	3	3	0	16	0
AAA	583	9,172	225	25	7	10	0	0
AAA	40	694	9,176	483	44	33	31	0
BBB	8	49	519	8,926	667	46	93	0
BBB	3	6	49	444	8,331	576	200	0
BBB	0	9	20	81	747	8,418	1,074	0
CCC	0	2	1	16	105	387	6,395	0
Default	0	1	4	22	98	530	2,194	10,000

Source: Adapted from "Corporate Defaults: Will things get worse before they get better?" Leo Brand, Reza Bahar, Standard & Poor's Credit Week, January 31, 2001.

Probability of default (PD)	0.22%
Risk rating	BBB
Commitment amount	$10,000,000
Outstanding amount	$5,000,000
Maturity	1 year
Collateral	Unsecured
Draw-down percentage (unused draw down at default)	40%
Average additional use of normally unused line	65%
EAD	$79
Standard deviation of EAD	$14
LGD (based on risk rating, maturity, and type)	30%
Standard deviation of LGD	19%

BIBLIOGRAPHY

Altman, E. I. "Financial Ratios Discriminant Analysis and the Prediction of Corporate Bankruptcy," *Journal of Finance*, 1968, 589–609.

Altman, E. I. and Saunders, A., "Credit Risk Measurement: Developments Over the Last 20 Years," *Journal of Banking and Finance*, 1998; 21, 1721–1742.

Altman, Edward, Caouette, John, and Narayanan, Paul, *Managing Credit Risk, The Next Great Financial Challenge*, Canada: John Wiley & Sons, 1998.

Black, Fischer and Scholes, Myron, "The Pricing of Options and Corporate Liabilities," *Journal of Political Economy*, May–June, 1973.

Davis, Peter and Williams, Darrin, "*Credit Risk Measurement*: Avoiding Unintended Results," *RMA Journal*, Oct. 2004.

Duffie, Darrell and Singleton, Kenneth, J., *Credit Risk, Pricing, Measurement and Management*, Princeton, NJ: Princeton University Press, 2003.

Gupton, G., Finger, C. and Bhatia, M. "CreditMetrics," Technical document, JP Morgan, 1997.

KMV Corporation, "Uses and Abuses of Bond Default Rates," San Francisco, CA: KMV, 1998.

Marrison, Chris, *The Fundamentals of Risk Measurement*, New York: McGraw-Hill, 2002.

Merton, Robert C., "A Model Mind, Robert C. Merton on Putting Theory into Practice", *CFA Magazine*, July–Aug. 2004.

Mester, L.J. "What is the Point of Credit Scoring?" *Federal Reserve Bank of Philadelphia Business Review*, September/October 1997, pp. 3–16.

Credit Portfolio Management

8.1 INTRODUCTION

In this chapter we will discuss the basic concepts behind credit portfolio management and highlight the distinctive factors that drive the management of a portfolio of credit assets compared to a single asset. We will also discuss how the application and techniques of modern portfolio theory are being applied in credit risk management and discuss the aspects that must be evaluated in portfolio credit risk. To build on our introduction to credit risk modeling, which was initially presented in Chapter 7, we will conclude with a synopsis on the various models that are being used in managing credit portfolios to maximize the optimum use of a lender's capital.

8.2 OBJECTIVES OF CREDIT PORTFOLIO MANAGEMENT

Over the last decade, portfolio credit risk management has become a utility function that banks use to implement their business strategies. This change in perspective is attributed to the greater appreciation that credit specialists have gained for how debt portfolios can deteriorate earnings and shareholders' value. Fundamental to this is the mindset around capital and the need for quantifiable credit risk information to support management decisions about the economics of credit in originating and holding transactions. Without determining an appropriate price and the economic capital requirements to service transactions, organizations can err in selecting profitable transactions at above market prices or in selling them at prices that are below market values. This is also why the risk components on individual transactions need to be measured and analyzed to assess how each debt asset will affect the overall credit portfolio performance. Along with managing the foregoing dimensions of credit risk exposures there is a need to evaluate how individual transactions contribute to other assets in the credit portfolio. Rather than retain unprofitable transactions, the impact of any changes that existing assets have on the portfolio must also be assessed and measured as part of ongoing monitoring so as to meet portfolio return requirements.

The application of improving portfolio returns and reducing capital requirements is similar to an asset management function in that credit facilities must also be categorized according to respective asset classes. Typically, a top-down approach is used that begins with clearly defined goals by management regarding the desired credit portfolio performance for each business unit. Once this is decided upon, the credit portfolio manager will then shape the portfolio in a manner that meets the expressed strategic goals. New loans will be identified and acquired according to how they will improve the risk-adjusted returns for each of the organization's individual business units. Figure 8.1 illustrates a credit portfolio risk management model that proactively manages exposures for profitability. Credit relationships are maintained by account officers, who originate and structure facilities for credit department approval. The functions of business development and the credit department remain separate to remove any dual role responsibilities between presenting and evaluating transactions and also to assign clearly defined roles to credit specialists for assessing and risk-rating facilities. A separate function also exists for the credit portfolio manager to optimize portfolio returns by using a variety of techniques. First there is the concern to realize optimum portfolio risk-adjusted returns by having transactions appropriately priced. This is the primary reason why portfolio transactions are retained as well as why pricing should be evaluated by marking all facilities to market. Transactions that are not mark-to-market (MtM) should have comparable market-based prices in order to evaluate the merits of their portfolio contribution. Aside from holding a loan to maturity, portfolio managers can decide that the credit portfolio needs to be rebalanced for optimal returns by choosing to sell an asset or to securitize a group of assets. Another option is to identify new assets to add to the credit portfolio based on the dynamics

FIGURE 8.1

A Credit Portfolio Risk Management Model

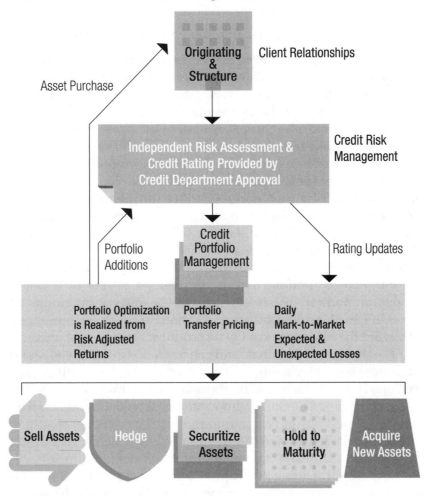

of the risk profile and according to the effects of changing the portfolio mix. Because selecting and adding new transactions to portfolios can result in increased exposures, portfolio managers may also request a credit department analysis to identify the risks at the transaction and portfolio levels. Such an assessment can also indicate that, although a particular transaction offers a high return, the risks are such that the portfolio manager may need to have credit protection to hedge against default by purchasing a credit derivative. These are the options that drive the functions behind having a proactive credit portfolio model and that are also influenced by the estimated expected and unexpected losses.

8.2.1   What is Portfolio Credit Risk

Chapter 2 initially introduced the concept of portfolio credit risk management as one of two of the basic components of business credit risk (with transaction risk being the other component). Portfolio credit risk is the aggregate credit risk exposure that is derived from multiple groups or classes of assets rather than a single asset. Unlike transaction credit risk, which arises each time a new facility is approved and disbursed, portfolio credit risk is comprised of intrinsic and concentration risk. To briefly review these concepts, you may also recall that intrinsic risk is derived from factors that are unique to specific borrowers and industries. When the nature of these factors affects many borrowers to which lenders have a high degree of exposure, it will create a concentration of similar types of risks throughout a portfolio. The concentration of portfolio risk is represented by the total dollar amount proportion that is extended to borrowers or groups of borrowers in the same industry, location, as well as from those borrowing the same types of credit products. An example of banks with a high degree of intrinsic and concentration risks can be found in the large lender write-offs that occurred during the credit decline in 2001. The consequences of the macroeconomic events in the telecommunications industry, for example, served to reinforce why financial institutions have come to recognize the impact that high exposure limits have on individual portfolio segments. As a result of the high volumes of telecommunications defaults during this time, expansion lending for capital infrastructure programs was brought to a screeching halt for most firms throughout the sector. Most importantly, in the midst of a global economic slowdown, telecommunications lenders found themselves exposed to a concentration of telecom borrowers known for having significant capital expenditures as a result of the industry in which it operates. Lenders who had invested heavily in this sector were suddenly exposed to significant defaults that subsequently have become notable for both their size and frequency. Tables 8.1 and 8.2 illustrate that among the ten largest corporate bond defaulters in 2002, 8 out of 10 of the defaulted issuers on $67.28BN were in the telecommunications industry and represented 24.6% of the

TABLE 8-1

Defaults Notable for Size in 2002*

Company	US$ Billions
WoldCom, Inc.	23.24
NTL Communication Corp.	8.48
Adelphia Communications Corporation	6.94
Telewest	5.20
United Pan-Europe Communication N.V.	5.13
Conseco, Inc.	5.09
Global Crossing Holdings Ltd.	3.80
Marconi Corp.	3.27
Intermedia Communications Corporation	3.12
Williams Communications Group, Inc.	3.00
Total	67.28

*Ten largest corporate bond defaults in 2002.
Source: Moody's

TABLE 8-2

Subsector Distribution of Weakest Issuers (December 4, 2002)

Subsector	Distribution (%)
Telecommunication	24.6
Media & entertainment	17.5
High technology	8.8
Capital goods	7.0
Retail/restaurants	7.0
Automotive	5.3
Health-care	5.3
Oil & gas exploration & production	5.3
Utility	5.3
Consumer products	3.5
Finance co.	3.5
Forest products & building materials	1.8
Homebuilders/real estate co.	2.8
Insurance	1.8
Metals, mining & steel	1.8

Source: Standard & Poor's Global Fixed Income Research

FIGURE 8.2

Net Income of Telecom Services Firm

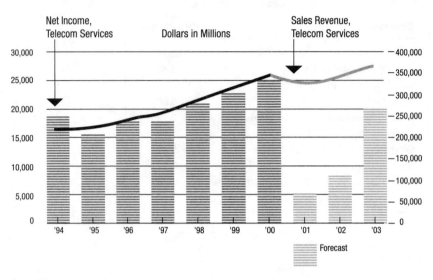

Source: Economy.com

weakest issuers. The reasons attributed to this wave of defaults by high profile companies like WorldCom and Global Crossing, to name a few, are important to note for their impact on bank credit portfolios. Along with competitive pressures that placed a downward spiral on industry pricing was the heavy indebtedness of borrowers to upgrade their equipment at a time of changing technology. Although the industry had exhibited a steady growth of net income during the period 1996–2000, Figure 8.2 highlights how the company defaults were accompanied by a decline in profits beginning in 2001. Major multinational lenders, including Citigroup, JPMorgan Chase, and Bank of America, were among the lead syndicated lenders, with approximately $365BN in debt exposure to the telecom industry.[1] The concentration of credit portfolio risk held by these banks to the sector was also accompanied by a degree of industry correlation defaults relative to their level of industry exposure. In other words, the extent to which the telecom assets' defaults occurred at the same time was based on correlating factors that caused the defaults to move together. Financial institutions that had either direct or indirect exposure to one or more borrowers in the telecommunications sector or subsector were therefore affected by telecom industry correlation defaults. JPMorgan Chase, for example, reported in 2002 a series of high-profile losses on its $117 billion commercial loan portfolio that were largely attributed to bankruptcies by telecom customers and included a $2.2 billion facility to Global Crossing.[2]

The effect of concentration risk is why lenders diversify their exposure limits across the number of borrowers and to the various types of debt facilities that they hold in their portfolios. When exposure concentration limits are placed on particular sectors, financial institutions are able to better defend against the volatility that accompanies high portfolio concentrations. Establishing limits on the amount of credit extended to a specific borrower or industry, region, country, and so on and diversifying the portfolio composition, can reduce the risk of credit losses and contribute to higher marginal returns. This is the heart of portfolio credit risk management—to mitigate the inherent credit risk in debt transactions by constructing portfolios with a diverse mix or group of facilities that are appropriately allocated to optimize the overall portfolio credit returns. To see this concept more clearly, one should be familiar with the fundamentals of modern portfolio theory, which is discussed in the following section.

8.3 THE FUNDAMENTALS OF MODERN PORTFOLIO THEORY (MPT)

The concept of modern portfolio theory (MPT) is not new to the financial world, as the relevancy of its application was originally introduced by Dr Harry Markowitz in the early 1950s.* Although initially presented as a concept that has since become commonly used in the management of equity securities, Markowitz theorized that the returns on a diverse group of risky assets are more consistent than the returns on single assets. Markowitz succinctly summarized how he derived his MPT in the following exerpt:

> I was a Ph.D candidate at the University of Chicago, and I had to pick a dissertation topic. I picked up a book by John Burr Williams,

---

*In 1990, Markowitz along with Merton Miller and William Sharp, won the Noble Prize in economics for his work on MPT. He shared the prize with Miller and Sharpe for their works on the capital assets pricing model (CAPM), which further advanced the MPT theory.

The Theory of of Investment Value, which says that the value of a stock should be the expected present value of its future dividends. But I thought that if I was interested only in the expected value of a security, then the value of the portfolio would only be the expected present value of that security—and that wouldn't work, because you wouldn't want to put all of your eggs in one basket. People choose their portfolios based on risk and return. So I simply asked the question, "What would be the return based on a weighted sum of those expected values?" This all happened in one afternoon, while I was reading this book and I did what all economists do: I drew a graph showing the minimum risk for the maximum return—and that was "the efficient frontier."[3]

Based on the mathematical model that he developed, which is now known as the Markowitz model, Markowitz demonstrated how optimal portfolio returns can be realized when the risk in a portfolio is reduced through diversification. The principle behind MPT is to evaluate the risk components of a single asset against those of other portfolio assets to measure its marginal increase in portfolio risk.

In simple terms, the range of returns on a single security over a certain time period can be summarized in a probability distribution function. If we assume as in Figure 8.3 that the returns on a single security are based on a normal distribution, we can then measure the location of where the range of returns will lie for the security by the mean (μ) and standard deviation (σ). For a normal distribution, the mean represents the average expected return and the standard deviation is the distance of the security's return from the mean. Given that the width of σ measures how far the average expected

FIGURE 8.3

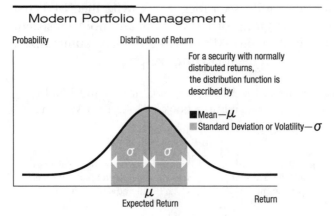

Modern Portfolio Management

FIGURE 8.4

Modern Portfolio Management

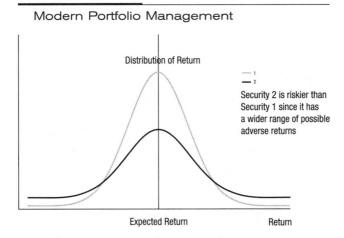

The equation can be used to summarize the risk and return of two securities, where x_1 is the proportion of security 1 in the portfolio, x_2 is the proportion of security 2 in the portfolio, $E[R_1]$ is the expected return for security 1, and $E[R_2]$ is the expected return for security 2. This means that the returns for security 1 are linear to the returns on security 2 because they lie on a straight line mathematically. For every possible value of R, there is also a group of possible randomly distributed R values that are normally distributed and for which their expected values lie on a straight line. The relationship between each security and how they move together is the result of the correlation between them, which must be measured when assets or new loans are added to a portfolio.

return will vary from the mean in a normal distribution. Figure 8.4 illustrates that the more volatility that a given expected return has, the wider the range of possible returns that can be expected. When this concept of risk and return is applied to multiple assets, the probability distributions are added together for all of the assets in the portfolio. The sum result for a portfolio of assets will be a weighted average of the proportion of the assets, as illustrated by the expression.

$$E[R_p] = x_1 E[R_1] + x_2 E[R_2]$$

8.3.1 Measuring Asset Correlation

What distinguishes the risk of a single asset from a portfolio of assets is the degree of correlation between them and how the returns will be impacted when adding one asset with another. The variance from having more than one possible return when a single asset is added with another can be illustrated by using the example of two securities that we will call Asset 1 and Asset 2. If Asset 1 has a tendency to move in the opposite direction to Asset 2 then these two assets are said to have "negative correlation," and they can be effective in cancelling out each other's volatility. Figure 8.4 illustrates that Asset 2 has a wider range of adverse returns than Asset 1 because Asset 2 has more volatility based on the distribution of the returns. Adding Asset 2 to the portfolio will not improve the risk/return on the portfolio if both assets have a high degree of correlation to each other. The portfolio will therefore have additional risk from a perfectly correlated asset than it would have if a less correlated asset were added. An example of this would be a loan to a swimsuit manufacturer, which would have a high degree of correlation to a facility extended to a sunscreen product manufacturer. As both of these manufacturers will most likely be impacted by similar market and industry conditions, a negatively correlated asset would provide a cushion to the lender when earnings are in decline. If both assets over the long term trended upwards or moved in tandem with each other, their combined returns would be equal to the average of the two assets, but with substantially reduced volatility.

To measure the correlation of two assets, which can range from -1 (perfectly negatively correlated) to $+1$ (perfectly positively correlated), we need to determine whether there is a positive or negative covariance between them. The covariance measures the degree that returns on two assets move together or in tandem with each other. The smaller the covariance between two assets, the less related they are to each other and the lower the standard deviation will be on their combined portfolio effect. Alternatively, if the assets are more related to each other they will have a larger covariance, which means that the standard deviation will also be higher. To derive the covariance between two assets we can use the summation formulas:

$$E[R_p] = x_1 E[R_1] + x_2 E[R_2]$$
$$\sigma p^2 = x_1^2 \sigma_1^2 + x_2^2 \sigma_2 + 2x_1 x_2 \, \text{Cov}_{1,2}$$
$$\text{Cov}(1,2) = \sigma_{1,2} = p_{1,2} \sigma_1 \sigma_2$$

where $p_{1,2}$ = correlation

FIGURE 8.5

Low Return Correlation

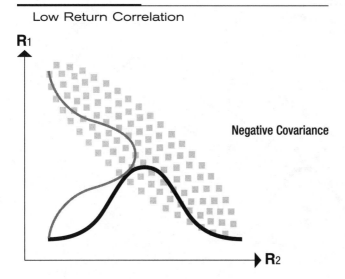

This expression represents how a portfolio's variance is dependent on the variance and covariance of the two assets. Although the variance represents the square of the standard deviation, the covariance is the product of the two variables or, in the case of our discussion, the product of the two assets and their degree of correlation.

As illustrated in Figure 8.5, a negative covariance reflects that the security has a low return correlation, which means that when Asset 1 has high returns, then the returns on Security 2 will typically have low returns or vary inversely. In our example we see that Asset 2 has a negative correlation if it moves in the opposite direction to Asset 1, which can result in cancelling out the volatility from Asset 1. If the assets move together as illustrated in Figure 8.6, they will have a positive covariance and a high-return correlation. When asset returns move together in this manner, the high returns on Asset 1 will be accompanied by high returns on Asset 2. As long as the correlation is less than +1, the assets will behave differently from each other and cancel out some of the volatility. If the assets both trend upwards over the longer term, a combination of them will have a return equal to the average of the two assets' returns but with substantially reduced volatility.

In an example such as the one that we have given above, the optimum portfolio would be to have two securities with a negative covariance, in which the assets would be very out of sync with each

FIGURE 8.6

High Return Correlation

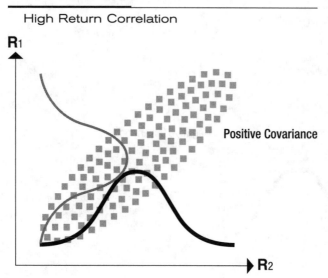

other. For example, Asset 1 will perform exceptionally well and yield sufficiently high returns to offset any low returns that the poor performance on Asset 2 may have. A negative correlation such as this between tangible assets, however, is more often than not rare, as asset prices tend to correspond to "macro" factors like economic growth, interest rates, oil prices, and so on. Portfolio managers will attempt to reduce their risk in these situations by diversifying and using assets that have a low positive correlation. It is through diversification that the return correlation between two assets with the same risk and return profiles can increase the portfolio's expected return while reducing its risk. As additional assets are added to the portfolio, those that have low correlations can enhance portfolio returns while reducing risk up to a point where additional returns comes with greater risk. Each combination of Assets 1 and 2 along with an additional asset will reduce the level of risk for each level of return. Therefore, if we have an infinite number of assets in a portfolio that are represented by n, the portfolio risk is the total of the variance and the covariance. The point of MPT is that the risk contribution of an individual security is a function of the security's weight in the portfolio and its correlation with the other portfolio securities. Assets do not need to be

FIGURE 8.7

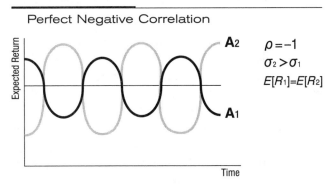

Perfect Negative Correlation

$\rho = -1$
$\sigma_2 > \sigma_1$
$E[R_1] = E[R_2]$

negatively correlated to have some volatility smoothing as illustrated in Figures 8.7 to 8.9. When correlation as a statistical measurement is defined by the relationship between Assets 1 and 2, we can see that Figure 8.7 reflects a perfectly negative correlation of −1 in which Asset 2 rises and Asset 1 declines, and a perfectly positive correlation of +1 is exhibited in Figure 8.8 to demonstrate that both assets are moving in the same direction. If there was no relationship between the assets, they would have zero correlation, as exhibited in Figure 8.9. If a portfolio is adequately diversified, then the assets can yield maximum returns for all possible risk levels as well as provide minimum risk for all possible levels of expected returns. The reduction of risk from diversification is what Markowitz describes as a portfolio that lies on the efficient frontier.

FIGURE 8.8

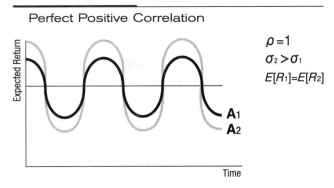

Perfect Positive Correlation

$\rho = 1$
$\sigma_2 > \sigma_1$
$E[R_1] = E[R_2]$

8.4 ESTABLISHING AN EFFICIENT FRONTIER

The "efficient frontier" is the name given to the line that joins all portfolios that have efficiently achieved a maximum return for all possible levels of risk with the minimum risk for all possible expected rates of return. Portfolio managers want to construct and maintain portfolios that are on the efficient frontier with a risk–return trade-off that has minimum risk and maximum return. Because of the relationship between risk and return, the optimum goal is to realize higher returns as the risk of loss from a single asset becomes significantly reduced from diversification. Markowitz concluded that an optimum portfolio could be achieved similar to the one in Figure 8.10, by considering all combinations of the risk vs. return for a group of assets. This is based on a portfolio that has been diversified into a variety of asset classes whereby any point actually on the curve, or close to it, should be an efficient portfolio, but any point below the curve will be an inefficient portfolio. This is the first condition to derive an efficient frontier, to provide minimum risk for all possible expected returns. The second condition is to achieve the maximum return for all possible levels of risk. These two conditions for deriving an efficient frontier are typically found in the region that lies on an upwardly sloped curve in the graph.

Finding an efficient frontier is not possible without knowing in advance how a particular asset or group of assets will perform and what the correlation between them will be. This is also why portfolio assets need to be frequently rebalanced in response to continuously changing market conditions. Despite the desire to realize

FIGURE 8.9

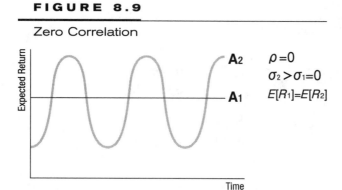

Zero Correlation

$\rho = 0$
$\sigma_2 > \sigma_1 = 0$
$E[R_1] = E[R_2]$

FIGURE 8.10

The Efficient Frontier

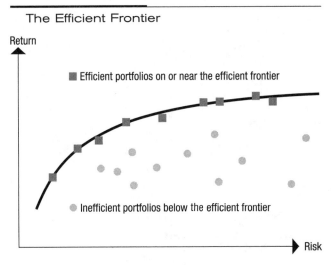

higher returns with lower risk, the efficient frontier illustrates the limits to how a particular group of assets will perform. When assets are added to a portfolio, they will change the shape of the efficient frontier by changing the asset returns and their correlation with the rest of the portfolio. This is, in fact, a normal transition, as risk profiles always change over time and must be adjusted to bring the portfolio back into alignment with the risk/return objectives. A diverse portfolio that is regularly rebalanced to find the most efficient frontier will thus be at any point that lies up along the top, exterior region of the curve. Any point of the curve that lies in the lower, interior portion would instead be an inefficient portfolio.

Although the above principles of MPT and the efficient frontier originated from Markowitz's work with a portfolio of equity securities, a similar framework for using this approach has now evolved in credit portfolio management. Applying this technique to a credit portfolio, however, does pose some particular distinctions for debt products that are dissimilar to an equity portfolio, which are discussed in the next section.

8.5 DISTINGUISHING CREDIT RISK IN DEBT PORTFOLIOS

A primary distinction in applying MPT theory to a portfolio of debt instruments rather than to one of equity securities is an emphasis

FIGURE 8.11

Credit Risk Loss Distribution

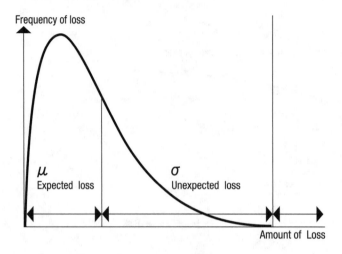

on defaulted facilities and their expected recovery values in credit portfolio credit risk. Unlike equity securities, which are characterized by a normal probability distribution function that is symmetrical, Figure 8.11 shows that the credit returns on a loan portfolio are asymmetric and that the shape of the distribution for a credit default is not normal. The distribution functions for credit risk tend to be highly skewed rather than symmetric, as it would be when the probability distribution is normal. This reflects the limited potential to earn significantly high returns on credit transactions, despite the unlimited exposure amount that could potentially be lost. Another distinction of credit portfolio risk lies in how the credit loss distributions and expected returns are defined, measured, and evaluated. The distribution functions that measure credit losses will vary depending on the credit products and their structures. In general, the credit loss exposures for different debt instruments are very uneven and have lumpy distribution functions to reflect how the frequencies are not balanced around the mean. It also indicates the high loss severity and lower probability of losses that arise when extending credit. Typically, the emphasis in analyzing credit portfolios is to determine the joint probabilities of defaults or credit events occurring, and quantifying the loss should such an event happen. In other words, what are the expected and unexpected losses for a group of individual credit facilities in the portfolio's risk, and what will be the risk contribution as new transactions are added. The answers to these questions are dependent upon the portfolio's loss distribution relative to the frequency of defaults. If the loans are simply on a stand-alone basis and without the effects of correlation, a binomial distribution is applied to determine whether default does or does not occur. The volatility that individual loans apply to a portfolio arises from continuously random default frequencies occurring. This changes when we introduce correlation, which brings about joint default probability, as the default by one borrower can lead to other borrowers having similar credit risks that result in joint defaults. If the borrowers have a high correlation, then the probability of joint defaults will also be high, and the credit portfolio will have a high or positive covariance.

Another distinction is that bank credit portfolios are inclusive of business and commercial credit, in addition to many subportfolios too. Credit portfolios, for example, can have subportfolios, which is common for the small- and middle-market borrowers, which may include loans and residential mortgages. Many of these subportfolios have a large number of relatively equal-sized exposures that are accompanied by high default rates and low default correlations among the different subportfolios. The relevancy of the above distinctions is that they are all linked to the credit process to derive the hierarchal levels of credit portfolio management, which is illustrated in Figures 8.12 and 8.13. Managing the credit portfolio is built around the credit policy on each individual transaction. Beginning with the measurement of a transaction that is based on the credit equation, Figure 8.12, details how each of the parameters can be defined in the credit policy. All of the transaction attributes that make up each of the portfolios and subportfolios should also be dictated by the lender's credit policy and guidelines relative to how the exposure limits are measured and managed. Figure 8.13 further exhibits the three levels a lender must manage, beginning with the borrower's creditworthiness and followed by the facility's impact as a transaction as well as how each segregated exposure will integrate into the portfolio.

8.5.1 Defining Measurement Parameters in Portfolios

A credit portfolio is exposed to a group of risks rather than an individual stand-alone loss and therefore the expected and unexpected losses are estimated according to a distribution of default

FIGURE 8.12

Portfolio Credit Risk Measurements Linked to the Credit
Policy

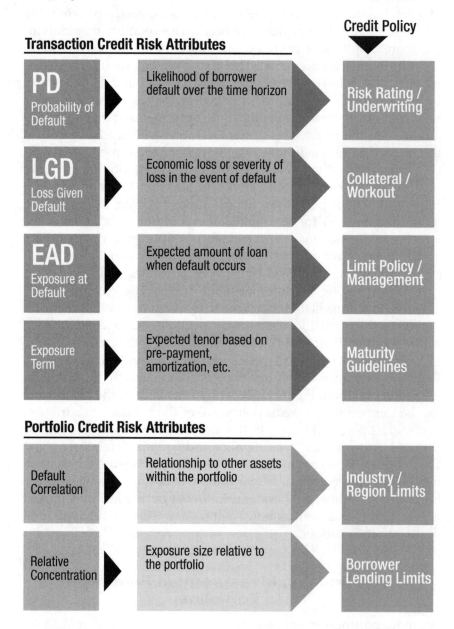

FIGURE 8.13

Credit Portfolio Management Links to the Credit Process on Three Levels

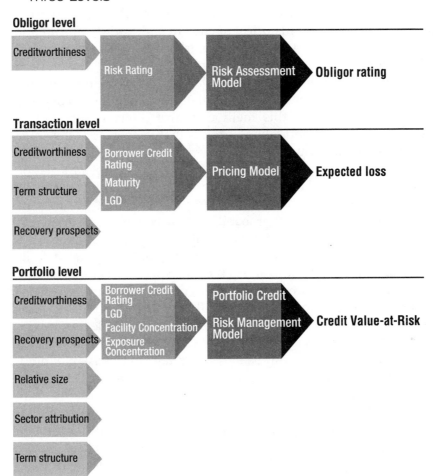

frequencies for the group. Because of the effects of correlation and the different types of credit products, this is not a straightforward process and is why a variety of credit risk models and modeling applications have advanced into the market. In general, however, there are three approaches that are used to derive default frequencies, which including equity market information, ratings transitions, and default models. Equity market based data are derived from the bond markets or credit–default swap data for name-specific issuers. Because of the liquidity of credit derivative products, equity market information is particularly useful, because it provides a broad coverage of the various funding strategies and compensates for weaknesses in how default data are derived in transition ratings and credit spread approaches. Transition matrixes are usually based on historical agency default rating information, credit spreads, as well as on equity market data. This approach will also incorporate current market data into the credit default parameter for borrowers that have similar credit and industry characteristics and also offer an acceptable benchmark for large corporate borrowers. Although this method allows direct observation of default rates, a limitation, however, is that it does not offer much for the small- and middle-market borrowers, as well as that unrelated credit issues may be included in equity price information. The effects of unrelated credit issues may also be captured in the evaluation of correlation, particularly as it pertains to marginal and cumulative default probability data contained in transition matrixes. Cumulative defaults specify the aggregate probability default observations over previous years, but marginal defaults provide loss observations in each of the specific years, given that defaults have not occurred in those periods. For these reasons, default categories for borrowers will be limited across industries, regions, or rating classes, as well as at more granular levels. Having limited historical and cross-sectional data to estimate across a broad systematic base can be a disadvantage in precisely defining portfolio credit risk components along with the inability to separate liquidity and default risk.

Third-party default models are another systematic tool to monitor credit portfolio concentration that arises from additional exposure to one or a group of related borrowers. These models attempt to capture default behavior for portfolios of credit exposures by estimating the probability of default from both historical data as well as statistical observation. Loss estimates will usually not exceed by more than a certain percent of default occasions and are also a form of value-at-risk with a 99.5% confidence level. Because of the various types of model approaches that can be used in determining how default is defined, the measurement factors that drive these models must be consistent. Figure 8.14 details the components that a comprehensive portfolio credit risk model includes. First, a credit risk model must be able to capture the **default risk** for expected and unexpected losses, beginning with an individual borrower's probability of default established from

FIGURE 8.14

Components of Credit Portfolio Measurement

A comprehensive Credit Risk Model Framework has
several key components

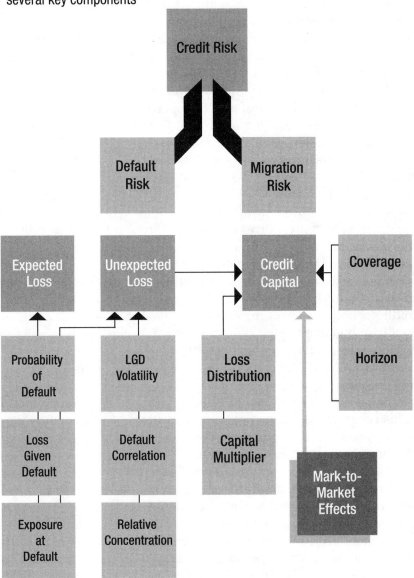

historical data and through statistical observations. Default risk should also measure **credit migration** for any changes in a borrower's credit quality to determine how it will impact the aggregate portfolio. Another factor that must be captured is the **severity or loss given default** for the amount that is estimated to be the **exposure at default** or the recovered and collected amount in the event of default. The unexpected losses must also capture the degree of **correlation** between transactions and their respective risk sources and **volatility**. In addition to determining the primary factors that affect a portfolio's risk-adjusted profitability, managing the credit portfolio also entails identifying the specific credit exposures that yield the highest risk-adjusted returns. The risk contribution that a new transaction will have on portfolio risk as well as any **concentration** risks are important to understand because firms that are affected by similar market, economic, or industry conditions can have default dependencies that lead to joint defaults by borrowers. The ability to improve portfolio profitability will be attributed to identifying the main sources of credit risk concentration and diversification. Each new facility that is added to an existing portfolio should be accompanied by a credit risk assessment relative to the other portfolio transactions. New facilities that are highly correlated with existing portfolio transactions will contribute to additional credit portfolio risk and may need to be substituted with a higher quality or higher compensating transaction. Default correlations are driven in the credit process by how the credit policy defines portfolio industry limits along with borrowing lending limits for concentration risk attributes.

Joint defaults will typically occur from macroeconomic and industry-specific consequences. As we indicated earlier in the chapter, correlation between borrowers arises from similar sources and consequences that can be inherent in business operations. Macroeconomic risk sources can arise from market factors such as rising oil prices, interest rates, or higher commodity prices, all of which can bring systematic financial shocks that may extend across regions. Defaults are also dependent on industry shocks such as the effects that terrorism had on the airline industry beginning in 2002. When there is general economic stability, credit losses will tend to be low, along with volatility across asset classes. However, when the economy is in decline or recession, credit losses will rise along with asset volatility. In addition there are industry-specific risk sources such as a rise in the price of raw materials that can also bring a financial shock to a portfolio of borrowers. Any of these events can increase the degree of concentration in borrowers and markets, a development that further has the potential to be systematic and create vulnerable deteriorating conditions throughout the banking systems. Finally, because credit risk is measured from the probability distribution of economic loss due to credit events, the models must be able to identify the expected and unexpected credit losses. The credit portfolio manager wants to determine the measures of capital profitability along with the capital amount that will be needed for the institution's credit portfolio rating. Understanding the risk–return profile of the financial lender's credit portfolio should also be captured in the model.

The merits of consistency that a model may have in capturing the above factors have continued to be a subject that is up for debate. In the next section we will discuss some of the alternative portfolio credit risk models that lenders are using, and discuss their strengths and shortcomings.

8.6 ALTERNATIVE PORTFOLIO CREDIT RISK MODELS

Credit Portfolio risk models attempt to compensate for the inability to observe default risk on an ongoing basis, by applying a set of theories that attempt to predict default behaviour based on a set of values. The approach that is taken to design a model in effect determines what the credit risk model predicts. Embedded in all of the models that have become accepted by the financial industry to calculate portfolio credit losses are values that represent a body of financial data. These values are expressed in mathematical equations and are based on assumptions from which judgments are inferred. From these data, credit portfolio managers will analyze a portfolio's performance under varying likely and even hypothetical "worst-case" scenarios and will also engage in ongoing evaluation of portfolio performance from a regulatory perspective.

Several model approaches are used to define how credit loss is estimated as well as to capture the respective portfolio measures. All of the model approaches that we will be discussing throughout the remainder of the chapter attempt to capture default risk and estimates of the portfolio's expected and unexpected losses along with economic capital. The primary distinction, between the models lies in how they capture and measure the correlation effects for credit defaults. In fact, herein lies the challenge behind modern credit risk. This is because measuring portfolio credit exposure entails a range of necessary complex calculations in order to quantify direct correlation between two firms. Because of the many variables that determine firm-specific default, there is no exact equation to determine the default correlation that one company may have with another. The only way to precisely measure this would be to repeatedly observe over time companies within the portfolio that would either default or not default, although the time factor in doing so would be much too consuming.

Several portfolio credit risk models have come to represent the industry accepted standards that are used to calculate portfolio credit losses. First we will discuss the structural model approach that is derived from Merton's asset value model. The other approaches that we will cover are the actuarial and econometric approaches.

8.6.1 Structural Models

Structural models rely on market information to estimate default risk by predicting default based on the value of the firm. Default is triggered when a firm's debt obligations become greater than the actual value of its assets. In other words, the probability of default is related to the proportion of the firm's debt and equity in the capital structure. If a firm's stock market and equity values indicate that its assets are below the face value of its debt, the assumption and inference would be that the firm is bankrupt and default will occur. Structural models are typically used for illiquid credit products, and although credit spreads can be easily correlated to the equity markets, they typically do not incorporate rating migrations. One of the most widely used structural models for commercial credit portfolios is the Merton default model, because it supports the ability to simulate an asset's correlation into the credit risk correlation for a loan portfolio. An example of the Merton model is the KMV model, which is a subsidiary of the public rating agency, Moody's Investor Services. The KMV model has been constructed from an extensive database that provides the probability of default for each obligor, or the expected default frequency (EDF) as it is known. The EDF gives a statistical measure in standard deviations for the probability that a firm will default based on the distance to default between the market value of the firm's assets

FIGURE 8.15

Credit Risk: The KMV Model

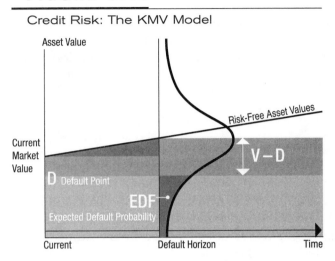

and the default point according to the par value of its debt. The theory behind the model includes an estimation of the firm's market value and the volatility of its assets. This is required to calculate the distance to default, which is an index measure of default risk, as illustrated in Figure 8.15. It is the region underneath the probability distribution and below the default point, which is also considered to equate to the liabilities of the firm. The distance to default is subsequently converted into the actual probability of default by using the default database.

Although the KMV model is in fact a form of the options pricing model that is proprietary to Moody's, the theory behind this version of the options formula can be summarized using the Black–Scholes options formula,

$$E = VN(d_1) - De^{-rT}N(d_2)$$

where E = market value of equity, V = firm value of the assets, σv = volatility of asset values or the percentage standard deviation, r = risk-free borrowing rate, D = Debt at par/Default Point, T = time of maturity, and N = cumulative normal distribution function valued at d_1 and $d_2 = f(\sigma V)$. Rather than use N, KMV calibrates it to a database that analyzes historical default probabilities and loss distributions related to default and migration risks to derive the expected default frequency. The equation results in two known variables for E and σ (market value of equity and the equity volatility), and the two unknown variables are V and σ (firm value of assets and its asset volatility). Because we have the two unknown variables, the relationship between equity volatility and the volatility of the firm's asset values provides the additional condition needed to solve for asset value (V) to give the expression

$$\Delta = \frac{\Delta E}{\Delta V} = \frac{E\sigma_E}{V\sigma_V}.$$

With the two unknown variables, the forward distribution for the value of the firm's assets can then be applied through a repeat process to derive the distance to default (DD). DD is the difference between the market value of the firm's assets and the default point (par value of debt), expressed in standard deviations. By taking the observed values, DD or the standard deviation is assumed to be normally distributed and defined as

$$DD = \frac{A - \mu}{\sigma a}.$$

As an example, if we take a firm that has $100MM in assets with a default boundary of μ that is 80 and asset volatility of $10MM, the distance to default can be calculated as

$$DD = \frac{100 - \mu}{10} = 2,$$

to determine that there are 2 standard deviations between the mean of the distribution and the point of default.

KMV has developed an empirical database of relationships between DD values and associated likelihood of default (EDF) to capture the EDF for individual borrowers, as illustrated by the EDF for Philips Services Corporation in Figure 8.16. The translation is necessary because the default probability distribution is not normally distributed, as the actual distribution has fat tails. In addition to the EDF, KMV also has a Portfolio Manager model that applies the concept of modern portfolio theory and the efficient frontier. Once accessed into the Portfolio Manager module, the program can then perform a variety of functions, including stress-testing the probability of portfolio losses, and measure the risk-returns on individual as well as all portfolio credit exposures.

Proponents of KMV find that the model is more precise in accurately estimating default probabilities as well as in anticipating

FIGURE 8.16

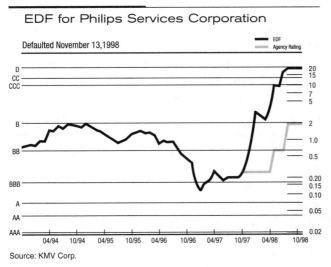

EDF for Philips Services Corporation

Defaulted November 13,1998

Source: KMV Corp.

changes in the EDF much earlier than the agencies have down-graded borrowers. Many banks that use the KMV model to determine default risk will map it to the agency's rating classes, because it provides current market data. The weakness in this approach is that EDFs tend to be for a one-year time period, but rating agencies tend to rate borrowers through the cycles for long-term borrowing needs.

8.6.2 CreditMetrics

Another structural model that is slightly different from KMV is CreditMetrics, which uses the credit rating migration approach to calculate credit risk across individual portfolios and subport-folios. Originally developed in 1997 by J. P. MorganChase and co-sponsored by KMV Corporation and five leading money center banks, including Bank of America, BZW, Deutsche Bank, Morgan Grenfell, Swiss Bank Corporation, and UBS, CreditMetrics calculates portfolio losses over a specific one-year time horizon as a result of an upgrade, downgrade, or default. The model incorporates a market-risk-based approach with analytic applications equivalent to CreditVaR to compute credit risk exposures for different types of loans, bonds, and credit derivative instruments. Transition matrices are used to determine asset returns according to the probability of rating migration for individual obligors. The matrices provide all possible portfolio combinations of asset ratings for each asset in a portfolio. To determine the valuation of a nondefault credit event, such as an upgrade or downgrade, the model uses a bond valuation approach based on forward zero curves for each rating category to calculate the value of all the portfolio assets under each rating assumption. We can illustrate this with an example taken directly from CreditMetrics in Table 8.3 for all of the possible year-end values for a two-asset portfolio. The matrix has calculated the estimated year-end values for two-assets, one rated BBB and the other rated A; for both we want to determine their values if they migrate up to AAA by the end of the year.[4] Under this scenario, the year-end value for the BBB instrument, which is exhibited horizontally, has been computed at $109.37 if it upgrades to AAA and at $106.59 for the A bond to upgrade to AAA. This means that, for all of the combined rating migration values that each bond can have during a one-year time period, the portfolio has computed 64 possible different values for each asset to derive a total portfolio value of $215.96. As the value of each asset is known for each rating category, the portfolio value of each rating combination is simply the total of each of the 64 combinations of ratings. The distribution of values for all possible rating migration changes is based on eight different values for each asset, ranging from $102.26 for the default of both assets to the total portfolio value of $215.96 if both assets are upgraded. Once the 64 portfolio values are derived, the model will compute the portfolio risk measures for the two assets with the mean and standard deviation, to measure the volatility in any credit quality changes.

For a portfolio of assets, the primary objective is to derive the risk measures that consist of the expected return and volatility or risk around the expected value along with the joint probability that the assets will move or migrate together. This requires the estimation of the correlations between migrations. Using the asset value matrix and the joint probability matrix, where p_i = joint migration likelihood and m_i = expected portfolio values, the mean and standard deviation for the two assets are given by

$$\text{Mean: } \mu_{Total} = \sum_{i=1}^{S=64} p_i \mu_i = 213.63$$

$$\text{Variance: } \sigma_{Total}^2 = \sum_{i=1}^{S=64} p_i \mu_i^2 - \mu_{Total}^2 = 11.22 \quad \sigma_\rho = 3.35.$$

TABLE 8-3

Example from CreditMetrics

		Year End Value/A							
		AAA	AA	A	BBB	BB	B	CCC	Default
		106.59	106.49	106.30	105.64	103.15	101.39	88.71	51.13
AAA	109.37	215.96	215.86	215.68	215.01	212.52	210.76	198.08	160.50
AA	109.19	215.78	215.68	215.49	214.83	212.34	210.58	197.90	160.32
A	108.66	215.25	215.15	214.97	214.30	211.81	210.05	197.37	159.79
BBB	107.55	214.14	214.04	213.85	213.19	210.70	208.94	196.26	158.68
BB	102.02	208.61	208.52	208.33	207.67	205.17	203.42	190.74	153.15
B	98.10	204.69	204.60	204.41	203.75	201.25	199.49	186.82	149.23
CCC	83.64	190.23	190.13	189.94	189.28	186.79	185.03	172.35	134.77
Default	51.13	157.72	157.62	157.43	156.77	154.28	152.52	139.84	102.26

Source: Credit Metrics

The mean or expected value of the portfolio is a weighted average of the default probabilities for all of the possible migrations for the BBB/A pair of ratings, summarized as

$$\text{Mean} = p_1 * V_1 + p_2 * V_2 + \ldots + p_{64} * V_{64}$$

where p_1 = probability of being in State 1 and, V_1 = value of State 1.

In addition to the standard deviation that the software uses to determine the volatility of the expected value, the software program also uses the percentile measure. Because the standard deviation does not always accurately measure volatility for distributions of asymmetrical debt products, the percentile will measure a migration probability within 1%. The corresponding probabilities that are used can be obtained from historical probability matrixes of rating agencies. Specifically, CreditMetrics actually derives its transition probabilities from Moody's KMV, although they can also be obtained from S&P. Some financial institutions also use the transition probabilities from their internal proprietary models.

Because structural models base default risk on a firm's value, CreditMetrics in turn associates default risk with an obligor's credit rating, which also serves as the model input parameters. Once the assets become less than the outstanding liabilities, the model's assumption is that the borrower's credit rating will reflect the firm's asset value and provide a default threshold for defaults, credit upgrades, or downgrades. Specifically, each obligor is assumed to have a specific set of migration thresholds related to its asset returns (or the firm's value) and credit quality. The model assumes that firm's asset returns are normally distributed by using the X–Z transformation formula to denote how many standard deviations the various asset returns are away from the mean. Asset returns have a cumulative normal distribution that is denoted by $\Phi(Z)$, which can be mapped to migration probabilities as represented schematically in Figure 8.17. Transition threshold values are determined for each obligor to correspond to the probability they will assume a certain credit rating in the area. Figure 8.18 summarizes the model's threshold values according to the transition probabilities for various credit events to occur. Based on the asset return thresholds, which range from

$$Z_{\text{Def}} \ Z_{\text{CCC}}, Z_{\text{BBB}}, Z_{\text{AAA}},$$

FIGURE 8.17

Threshold Value Model

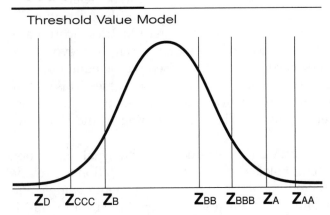

Z_D Z_{CCC} Z_B $\qquad$ Z_{BB} Z_{BBB} Z_A Z_{AA}

default will occur if $R < Z_{Def}$. A downgrade to CCC will occur if $Z_{Def} < R < CCC$, and so on. For any two obligors, the model can also determine the covariance matrix and the correlation coefficient between them. Based on the correlation of the asset values between two borrowers, a joint distribution of probable ratings can then be derived over a horizon period. Suppose we have a correlation coefficient of 30% which is represented by p, we see that the joint distribution for

FIGURE 8.18

Joint Migration Likelihoods for a Two-Asset Portfolio

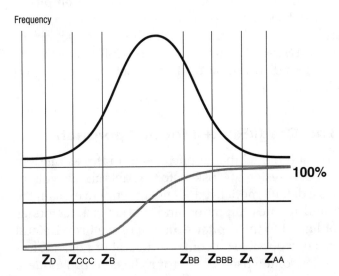

Frequency

100%

Z_D Z_{CCC} Z_B $\qquad$ Z_{BB} Z_{BBB} Z_A Z_{AA}

the probable ratings of the BBB/A borrowers can be determined by having the asset values or p, which is the basis for the calculation. To develop the correlations and volatilities, CreditMetrics incorporates country and industry indices of economic activity to develop the measurement of assets co-movements, based on the equity correlations that are used to correspond with firm asset values. This is done by mapping the portfolio borrowers to their respective industries and deriving their equity correlations according to the respective weights.

Under the CreditMetrics approach, a financial institution can consolidate credit risk across the entire organization to provide the standard VaR credit analysis with an assessment of single and multiple assets along with their respective credit exposure. VaR is calculated for the exposure of different portfolio instruments, including the credit returns volatility that may arise from a credit event as well as the correlations between assets on a portfolio basis.

8.6.3 Actuarial Models

Actuarial models represent a statistical methodology that is derived from the analysis of event risk used in the insurance industry. Natural disaster events such as earthquakes, storms, and floods are managed by estimating their combined potential portfolio effects with simulated scenarios to forecast future potential losses. Actuarial models predict default by using gamma or beta distributions as well as rating matrices that are calibrated to empirical default distributions. This same approach is now used as a credit portfolio management application, with the introduction of CreditRisk+ by Credit Suisse Financial Products (CSFP), which estimates a portfolio's loss distribution or default risk by focusing on historical credit losses.

8.6.4 The CreditRisk+ Model Approach

CreditRisk+ is a default model that applies default rates as random variables, and remodels systematic risk factors as default rate volatilities. Although it is a default model, it does not attempt to explain the cause of default and ignores migration and market risk factors as default risk is not linked to the capital structure of the firm. Default models provide for two possible outcomes—default or no default—and belong to the class of intensity-based (or reduced form) models.

For a large number of obligors, the loss distribution of a loan portfolio for a given time period can be described as a Poisson distribution function based on the number of defaults. The model also assumes that the mean default rate is stochastic in that it is derived by chance. The Poisson distribution is used because of the limited parameter requirements, and is defined by the average number of occurrences of events, for example, default denoted by n, with the probability of the n instances of default to be given by

$$\text{Prob } (n \text{ defaults}) = \frac{\bar{n}^n e^{-\bar{n}}}{n!}.$$

The model framework and assumptions used in the actuarial model are that a portfolio is divided into a group of homogeneous sectors in which obligors share common risk factors. The model allocates borrowers to different sectors of risk according to their mean default rate and default volatility rate. The obligors can be categorized into one or more of the exposure band sectors as given by Table 8.5.

Exposures and expected losses are standardized in terms of exposure units (L) so that

$$\varepsilon_{i,j} = \frac{\lambda_{i,j}}{L} \quad \text{(Standardized expected loss of obligor } i \text{ in band } j\text{)}$$

$$\nu_{i,j} = \frac{L_{i,j}}{L} \quad \text{(Standardized exposure of obligor } i \text{ in band } j\text{)}$$

$$\tilde{\nu}_{i,j} = \text{Rounded } (\nu_{i,j})$$

The exposures and expected losses of all obligors can then be aggregated within each exposure band:

$$\tilde{\nu}_j = \sum_{i=1}^{A} \tilde{\nu}_{i,j}, \quad j=1,\ldots,m.$$

The expected number of defaults in each exposure band then becomes

$$\mu_j = \frac{\varepsilon_i}{\tilde{\nu}_j} = \frac{\sum_{i=1}^{A} \varepsilon_{i,j}}{\tilde{\nu}_j}$$

TABLE 8.5

Obligors		$i = 1,..., A$
Credit bands		$j = 1,..., m$
Prob (default)	P_i	for obligor i
Net exposure	$L_{i,j}$	for obligor i in band j
Expected loss	$l_{i,j}$	for obligor i in band j
	$l_{i,j}$	$= L_{i,j} \times P_i$
Exposure unit	L	Expressed in terms of specific currency (e.g., $100,000)

CreditRisk+ assumes that the mean probability has a Gamma distribution function. By using the Gamma distribution, the portfolio will take on similar characteristics as those of credit risk losses by using algorithms to derive various analytic results so that the expected number of defaults for the portfolio can be expressed as a function of the probabilities of default events.

The model also allows the user to assign counterparties to country/industry sectors by linking default rates with macroeconomic factors. Individual and country/industry default rates are obtained from internal/external transition matrices or internal credit analysis. Although the model's software does not estimate default correlations, it is presumed that default correlations and joint probabilities will be developed through simulations such as Monte Carlo. The statistical simulation models will estimate the combined joint distributions of default probabilities for individual borrowers according to the effects of sector-specific risk factors on default rates, for example, the unemployment rate, growth rate of GDP, the level of long-term interest rates, foreign exchange rates, government expenditure, and the aggregate savings rate. Correlations between default rates for different obligors are considered to arise from the covariance structure of the underlying macroeconomic variables. The model's output provides risk analysis tools that feed directly into regular VaR and economic capital models. In addition there are various management reports that it provides, including details on Portfolio Aggregate Exposure, Expected Loss, Standard Deviation, the Loss Distributions, and Risk Contributions.

8.6.5 Econometric Models

Another approach to credit risk modeling is the econometric-based application, which is also known as the reduced-form model. Econometric models predict default by linking macroeconomic factors (e.g., unemployment, interest rates, GNP) to rating transition matrices. Default risk therefore varies depending on the economic circumstances of the environment. Monte Carlo simulations are then used to predict the loss distributions for default based on potential assumptions about the credit environment. Most times a logit model will be used that adapts the logistic equation to a series of explanatory variables. A common econometric model is Credit Portfolio View, which was developed by McKinsey. Since it was introduced to the market in 1997, the model has applied macroeconomic variables to assign default states probabilities to borrowers in certain countries and industries, by using Monte Carlo simulations to calculate the loss distributions. Factors that may also be used to define credit events are unemployment rate, foreign exchange, gross domestic product, and so on. One criticism of the model is that it is limited to credit portfolios, because correlations among borrowers do not encompass variables beyond those at a macro level. Another weakness is that the model is limited to speculative graded credit facilities under the assumption that weak-credit-quality borrowers tend to react more strongly to systematic economic risk. Consequently, it is limited in evaluating investment-graded borrowers that may encounter deteriorating default probabilities.

8.7 CONCLUSIONS

Credit Portfolio Management originates with a top-down approach that begins with the type of returns sought to be realized. Because lenders seek to leverage their returns, they have transitioned to using techniques that originated under modern portfolio theory. Although credit risks in debt portfolios have distinguishing features, the risks in a portfolio must be measured relative to how each individual transaction will impact the portfolio. The primary models that are used to monitor individual transactions on the portfolio include the structural, actuarial, and econometric approaches.

CHAPTER DISCUSSION QUESTIONS

1. Discuss how lenders are undertaking active Credit Portfolio Management and describe their approach to credit risk analysis.
2. Distinguish between Moody's KMV Portfolio Manager, CreditMetrics, CreditRisk+, and the CreditPortfolioView model approaches.
3. Discuss the impact that individual transactions can have on a credit portfolio and explain how a facility can contribute to portfolio credit exposure.
4. How does the mix of a credit portfolio impact on concentration exposure and diversification?
5. What impact does credit portfolio management have on economic capital?
6. How do loan portfolio risks differ from the risks of a single transaction?
7. How does covariance or correlation contribute to the reduction of risk?
8. A lender has two loans for $1,000,000 each. One loan has an expected return of 15% and a standard deviation of 20%, and the other loan has an expected return of 10% and a standard deviation of 15%. It is determined that the covariance between the two loans is 2%, so what is the expected return and standard deviation of the portfolio?

BIBLIOGRAPHY

Bennett, Paul, "Applying Portfolio Theory to Global Bank Lending," *Journal of Banking and Finance* 8, 1984, pp. 153–169.

Black, Fischer and Scholes, Myron, "The Pricing of Options and Corporate Liabilities," *Journal of Political Economy*, May–June, 1973.

Credit Suisse Financial Products, "CSFP: CreditRisk+ Technical Manual; A Credit Risk Management Framework," Technical documentation, 1997, Credit Suisse First, Boston, pp. 16–21.

Credit Risk Modeling Design and Application, New York; Glenlake Publishing Company, Ltd, 1998, Elizabeth Mays.

Crosbie, Peter, J., "Modeling Default Risk," Manuscript, KMV Corporation, Jan. 1999.

Crouch, Michel, Galai, Dan and Mark, Robert, "A comparative analysis of current credit risk models," *Journal of Banking and Finance* 24, 2000, pp. 60–117.

Dwyer D., Kocazie A. and Stein Roger, "The Moody's KMV EDF™ RiskCalc™ Next-Generation Technology for Predicting Private Firm Credit Risk," Moody's KMV Company, 2004.

Federal Reserve, "Credit Risk Models at Major U.S. Banking Institutions: Current State of the Art and Implications for Assessments of Capital Adequacy," Federal Reserve System Task Force on Internal Credit Risk Models, May 1998.

Kealhofer, Stephen, "Portfolio Management of Default Risk," KMV Corporation, Feb. 1998.

Mays, Elizabeth, *Credit Risk Modeling: Design and Application*, New York: Glenlake Publishing Company, Ltd., 1998.

Merton, R., "On the Pricing of Corporate Debt: The Risk Structure of Interest Rates," *Journal of Finance*, 29, 1974, pp. 449–470.

Morgan J.P., "Credit Metrics" Technical document, New York, 1997.

Ritter, Lawrence and Silber, William, *Principles of Money, Banking and Financial Markets*, New York: Harper Collins, 1974, pp. 447–456.

Wilson, Thomas, "Credit Portfolio Risk (I, II)," *Risk Magazine*, Sept./Oct. 1997, pp. 111–117 & 56–61.

Wilson, Thomas, "Portfolio Credit Risk," *FRBNY Economic Policy Review*, Oct. 1998, S. 71–82.

Credit Rating Systems

9.1 INTRODUCTION

In this chapter we will discuss the pivotal role that credit rating systems have come to play in managing credit risk for lenders. Under modern credit risk management, rating systems have developed to provide two basic components that are essential to the credit process and risk management practices. The first component is to assign the credit risk grades by ranking transactions according to the perceived credit risk and the second is to group credits to distinguish among possible outcomes by quantifying the default risk and loss estimates. First we will present how the credit rating systems are used to integrate a range of credit functions and how they provide a conceptual framework to guide loan originations and throughout the credit process. This will be followed by presenting an overview on the key features of the credit risk architecture, which determines the specific functions that credit rating systems have in a lending environment. Next we will explain the differences between internal and external ratings and how they are used by various users. Because all transactions, whether good or bad, have some level of default risk, the assumption is that the degrees of risk can only be identified through credit grades that distinguish the different default frequencies. This is why the application of differentiating the levels of risk through credit grades or scales is necessary and requires that rating systems are validated, a topic that will conclude the chapter.

9.2 THE ROLE OF CREDIT RATING SYSTEMS

In most of the major money center banks, credit rating systems have become the cornerstone to managing a range of credit functions that serve to also provide a road map for management decision making. In addition to providing a conceptual framework to guide loan originations, the applications of credit rating systems have evolved over the years to serve as a foundation for multiple credit and risk management practices. Aside from providing the key risk indicators to assess creditworthiness, credit rating systems also serve as the link to measure default probability according to assigned rating grades or categories. The link is made by using the credit rating system to categorize credit risk into varying risk rating scales that define risk according to the organization's credit philosophy and processes. This has, in effect, resulted in transforming credit rating systems into a systematic process in which the day-to-day practice of credit decision making has become customized through formal risk ratings or grading scales.

Several reasons have contributed to this trend of greater reliance on risk rating systems as the primary source for credit risk identification and monitoring. A primary reason is that, as a measurement of asset quality, credit rating systems have improved the precision and effectiveness of managing credit risk exposure and made the process more efficient and less time consuming. Secondly, they provide a conceptual credit risk framework for transactions and facility structures by summarizing risks and measurable outcomes of credit default loss. Third, as a portfolio monitoring tool, risk rating systems can also be used to meet regulatory requirements such as by monitoring exposure concentration limits, allocating loan loss reserves, and managing capital requirements.

Unlike classical credit practices in which accounting and rating systems were not configured to capture and measure risk exposures, credit rating systems today are designed to create a value chain to information that can be easily identified for portfolio optimization. The concept of value chain optimization has advanced under modern credit and finance as a key aspect for a financial entity's future competitive positioning. Credit grades are used to identify the degrees of default risk that are inherent in all transactions in order to meet the established hurdle rate in risk-adjusted pricing. By differentiating the levels of risk through credit grades and scales, loan spreads are then based on the corresponding rated default loss probabilities and volatilities. Risk-adjusted decision making becomes emphasized across business lines and throughout the organization into a centralized credit portfolio management function.

As the focus of banks has moved from revenue and cost management to effective risk control, the need for information to support credit decisions has become of paramount importance. Historically, credit risk decisions were derived from limited available information, which was largely subjective and limited to specific individual business units. Banking and trading units did not have information available to them that was relevant to all aspects of the credit process, which often resulted in an inability to make credit decisions from a strategically profitable risk-adjusted focus. As credit risk management has advanced to capital optimization, the credit rating system is the basis from which risk measurement analytics are used to consistently evaluate transactions across all asset classes and portfolios.

The quality of credit decision making has also improved as a result of rating systems that are developed to provide a single source of data for all applications in the Risk Management, Finance, and Regulatory Reporting sectors. As illustrated in Figure 9.1, the most sophisticated rating systems are configured to integrate individual risk variables by using alternative analytic technologies capable of linking a range of data capabilities that include predicting default probability and pricing in loan originations, management reporting, portfolio monitoring, and allocating economic capital. Loan and trading desks can attain effective online access to information that is not restricted to a particular business unit. Risk grading scales are effected to report on specific changes in the borrower's credit conditions such as a rating migration. The systems are also designed and supported by integrating rating classifications according to defined risk buckets so that account officers can rely on credit rating systems to monitor the limits of customer and counterparty credit exposures. Credit rating system reports will often summarize the portfolio's aggregated exposure according to all of the rating classes and limits. For lenders with systems designed to compute economic capital, the rating categories are the basis for computing the required amount according to the exposure, term of the facility, and portfolio concentration. Generally, the higher credit grades will indicate a greater degree of transaction risk and require a higher capital allocation. This will impact the credit granting decision and price of extending the credit product. Similar management decisions may also be made by linking the reserve amounts from the credit rating classifications to derive and report on reserve allocations.

FIGURE 9.1

Credit Risk Management System

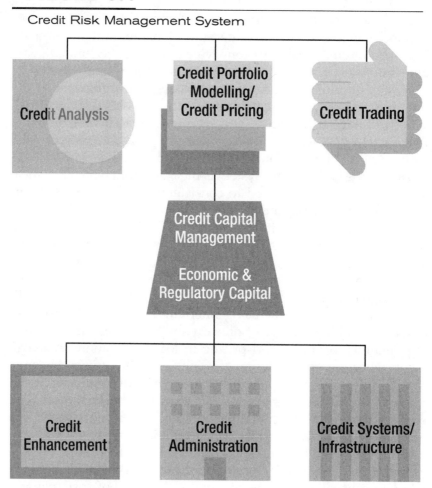

Although credit rating systems can be configured according to the sophistication and size of an organization's activities, there are key differentiations in the components and information systems approaches that lenders may use. A primary factor that contributes to the variation in types of credit rating approaches among different lenders is an organization's credit culture. If the credit culture and experience is more relationship-oriented, there will be a tendency for greater reliance on the subjectivity of individual transactions that result in respective adjustments to credit ratings. Alternatively, an organization may stress the quantitative aspects of transactions as opposed to the qualitative risk factors that they view to be difficult to measure. Lenders will also have different philosophies and make different judgments regarding the degrees of risks that are inherent in each transaction as well as how to quantify the potential loss exposures. All of these factors will contribute to the risk management approaches that are used by organizations and how risk is measured from credit rating information. A key element, however, in the forces that drive how credit rating systems are operated and applied to a bank's credit risk management practices is the credit risk architecture.

9.3 CREDIT RISK ARCHITECTURES

Because of the advances in information technology and portfolio credit risk management practices, credit rating systems are designed to leverage a range of data capabilities that begins with loan origination. This practice has become part of what is known as the enterprise risk management framework, in which risk architectures are built into technology platforms that incorporate performance and strategy applications, such as the example in Figure 9.2. By capturing a mass of data across all of the business and operating departments, the credit risk architecture acts as the "engine room" for all of the conceptual methodologies that are required to evaluate risk. This concept of utilizing credit rating systems in risk decision making has led banks to make significant investments in information technology, which requires integrated systems architecture to incorporate complex analysis and modeling techniques. The risk architecture components to assess loss characteristics consist of expert judgment, analytic risk models, or a combination of both. These application techniques define the basis for summarizing risk measures from the different credit grades or rating scales that identify the varying degrees of risk, and also distinguish how transactions are risk rated.

9.3.1 Expert Judgment

Expert judgment in rating credit transactions is a key classical credit application. Although internal rating systems will compute and calculate most of the primary analytical detail in assessing and measuring risk, credit specialists should nonetheless be familiar with them and the criteria for how transactions are evaluated and risk rated. Theoretically, the ratings are arrived at by gathering the

FIGURE 9.2

Credit Risk Management Architecture

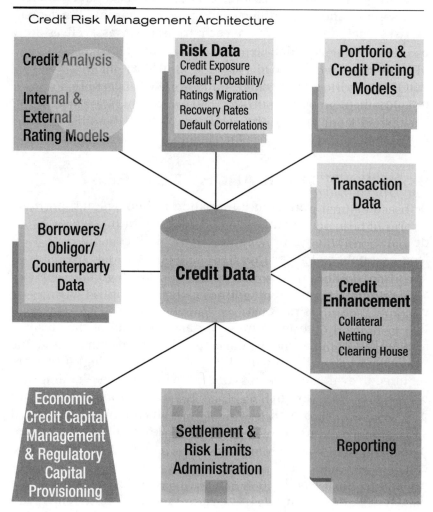

borrower's financial and nonfinancial information and allocating a grade equivalent to the bank's rating standards and criteria, which are subsequently weighted to derive a final grade. Rather than accepting the rating as a simple spreadsheet that has calculated the indicators from the input data, credit specialists look beyond the face value of reported financial data, because it is usually not a firm's true economic condition but only an approximation. An independent credit analysis is performed by a credit specialist, who is considered to be highly skilled in rating transactions because of having an extensive level of knowledge regarding particular borrowers or industry segments. The credit specialist will weigh all of the short- and long-term factors that may influence a borrower's credit quality throughout the duration of the credit facility. Typically, credit risk models will assign a rating that usually requires financial adjustments to be made to reflect what is in the analyst or rater's view, a more realistic estimate of the borrower's actual credit condition. The reason behind making the adjustments, in the opinion of the credit organization, is that default cannot be determined by solely relying on the corresponding model weights, because the factors that affect it are much too complicated and therefore require independent judgment and knowledge. For example, management performance under difficult circumstances can affect credit quality and the estimated level of risk exposure derived from a quantitative model may not be accurate. The statistical models that are used to assign a rating to the quality of management will therefore normally require adjustments to reflect the analyst's view of more realistic estimates. Without such adjustments, the rating would not be entirely accurate and could lead to weaker underwriting standards.

It is assumed that when expert credit specialists make adjustments to credit ratings that they are relative to the circumstances of a particular transaction according to the established guidelines of the rating criteria. An important criterion when using expert judgment is that when grades are changed from what the system quantifies, the lender's credit policy is expected to be the basis for how the grade is derived. This is a key factor in the use of expert judgment when assigning credit ratings, in that the guidelines to which ratings are adapted is based on human judgment. Advocates of this application believe that without such adjustments, ratings will not be entirely accurate and, as a result, underwriting standards on a transaction may be weakened. In contrast, critics contend that because two experts for the same facility can perceive different risks, expert judgment is too subjective and holds degrees of bias. The debate centers on whether credit risk can be accurately measured to quantify default given the trend to estimate risk when assigning ratings only based on a model approach. This has led to the second technique for summarizing credit risk transactions through the application of credit risk models.

9.3.2　Rating with Models

The use of credit rating models is derived from a combination of numeric inputs relative to varying borrower factors and characteristics. Theoretically, ratings are derived after equivalent risk grades are computed for a borrower's financial and nonfinancial data according to the statistical model inputs and risk analysis compatible with a particular lender's operations. These models are configured according to the variables and assumptions that credit specialists perceive as the likelihood of default to which they apply mathematical equations that define default risk. The mathematical equations are then applied to compute the borrower's risk according to a credit grade that is equivalent to a rating category. Many of the common types of statistical credit risk models that are used to assess risk consist of those that were discussed in Chapters 7 and 8. These models correspond to particular data input in the form of scoring models, regression models, logit, or discriminant models as well as structural and econometric models.

9.3.3　Key Features in Credit Risk Architecture Infrastructures

Credit rating systems that provide all of the key risk management functions require that credit risk architectures have the appropriate technological framework to capture all of the practices, processes, and controls for managing credit losses. Although business models will vary at individual banks, a credit portfolio management function must be supported by an appropriate credit risk architecture that links all of the technological platforms with the designated portfolio credit risk model. The design and execution of the portfolio management process will also differ along different product and business lines. Because debt instruments have different structures and degrees of credit risk, the calculation techniques along with the measurement characteristics and parameters will not be the same for each of the asset portfolios and subportfolio classes. This is determined by whether lenders use a one-dimensional or two-dimensional risk rating system. In a one-dimensional rating system similar to the illustration in Table 9.1, the assigned facility rating represents an approximate probability of default based on the borrower's general creditworthiness. A criticism in using one-dimensional credit rating systems is that they do not encompass all of the credit risk parameters to compute the measurement

TABLE 9-1

One-Dimensional Rating System

	Risk Grade						
	I	II	III	IV	V	VI	VII
Industry			X				
Business				X			
Management				X			
Financial			X				
Facility structure	X						
Security		X					
Combined			X				

characteristics for the PD, LGD, EAD, EL, and UL. Loss parameters are only provided for the PD and UL, but will often exclude variables to quantify the severity and recovery amounts. This is one reason why two-dimensional rating systems were advanced and designed to separately assess default risk by the borrower and LGD for the severity of loss in the event of default. Specific loss measures that are applied to the rating grades do not have exposures that can measure and capture all of the loss parameters separately. For example, a facility that is collateralized and structured in such a way as to mitigate the lender's credit risk exposure may compute a lower expected loss than what it should actually be. Another weakness of one-dimensional rating systems is that, because they tend to have a limited number of risk grades, credit specialists may not be able to accurately measure a facility's loss exposure. Many medium or small lenders that have limited product lines, however, continue to use a one-dimensional rating system. Although they lack the ability to apply sophisticated multiple rating grades, the credit organizations instead often rely more on controlling and maintaining the credit relationships.

At most of the major money center banks and even many regional banks, two-dimensional rating systems are used because, in doing so, consistent measurements can be applied to each of their specific banking and trading books. The systems are designed to compare the risk exposures with loans and other credit exposures and also to measure debt facilities independently of

TABLE 9-2

Two-Dimensional Rating System

	Risk Grade						
	I	II	III	IV	V	VI	VII
Client Rating							
Industry			X				
Business				X			
Management				X			
Financial			X				
Client Grade			X				
Facility Rating							
Facility Structure	X						
Collateral		X					
LGD Grade		X					

borrowers for both current and future replacement values.* The credit risk architects at these institutions rely on operating designs that provide both an obligor and facility rating, to calculate and measure credit risk exposure for the expected loss criteria on a specific facility transaction. A two-dimensional internal rating system such as the one in Table 9.2, is designed to capture both the borrower's probability of default along with the expected facility loss. The borrower's rating represents an assessment of the probability or likelihood of default, and the facility rating assesses transaction-specific factors related to the possible loss on a particular facility. Borrower ratings are also featured to be mapped to default probability buckets and facility ratings determine the loss parameters in the event of default. Two-dimensional rating systems can be aligned more effectively to different credit risk architecture and credit portfolio model systems, because they provide more information about transactions and their impact on portfolios. Having

---

*For credit derivative and trading products, exposure is an estimate of how much a counterparty might owe over the life of a transaction (or portfolio of transactions). It is comprised of current mark-to-market of the transaction (immediate cost to replace the contract) plus the potential exposure of a transaction over time given any changes in market rates that could increase the current mark-to-market in the future. Compared to obligor exposure, the magnitude of potential exposure component is uncertain and can only be estimated by simulation at a certain confidence level.

this capability is particularly important for credit derivative product transactions, many of which are not rated, and this is the reason why investors will use the public rating agencies to acknowledge banks, internal rating systems. The standard rule of thumb is that if a bank's credit ratings are satisfactory or better, it indicates to the investor that the institution has an effective internal risk rating system to measure, monitor, and appropriately manage credit transactions. Caution should be exercised, however, in how ratings are derived, because the different model assumptions and functions can also lead to different portfolio results.

For banks that use multidimensional systems to measure individual loss characteristics, a consistent application should be followed in how they define the parameter values, particularly as it relates to the different asset classes across the many portfolios as well as across different regions and industries. This is essential for accurate credit exposure measurement and so that new exposures can be rated for their risk/return. There are many different unique obligor and facility characteristics that may make measuring a facility quite tricky, along with the typical borrower characteristics such as the industry sector, geographical location, and corporate structure. Transaction-specific characteristics such as the facility amount and nature of any collateral taken along with the seniority and loan covenants are among a few of these characteristics.

Credit risk system architectures should consistently clarify how internal risk ratings are assigned according to the quantification of default and loss estimates. The objective is to have an internal rating system that can apply multiple calculation methodologies for each asset class of small, middle-market, and large corporate borrowers to produce an assigned rating that indicates the risk of borrower default and transaction-specific factors for all asset classes. The distribution of exposures should therefore be across all grades with no significant concentrations in any one grade. Effective risk architectures should also develop a management framework that places limits on portfolio loss volatility appropriate for the institution's capital structure and risk appetite.

Depending on the sophistication of the credit risk architecture, the credit rating system will capture facility transaction data that are spread over a number of years to identify corresponding or similar transactions. Information on prior defaults and recovery rates along with loss statistics is needed to identify and apply to related relevant cash flows. Loss parameters such as the LGD and EAD rather than only the EL can be computed over time, to provide credit specialists the benefit of evaluating and refining all of the loss estimates by comparing them to the internal loss experience. For example, internal credit ratings can assign facility ratings to one of several LGD grades based on the likely recovery rates associated with various types of collateral, guarantees, or other facility structures.

9.3.4 Assessing Creditworthiness

Beside the effectiveness that credit rating systems have displayed for measuring, they are also being used as the first step in loan originations and with the borrower's credit assessment. Under modern credit risk management, the credit process has become structured towards internal risk rating systems that use a bottom-up approach, which begins with loan origination. This has made the credit rating systems operate as part of the day-to-day credit risk decision-making process. Although this process of customizing credit attributed to greater frequency of credit facility monitoring, the credit culture at many banks continues to rely on a combination of expert judgment and credit modeling because of the uniqueness in different transaction structures. Although we have already discussed the reasons why each approach is used, it should be noted that the upcoming Basel II Accords will tend to impact those banks that use the advance IRB Approach. Given that the larger banks will be integrating their credit rating systems into daily operations and decision making, the implication in not doing so can be a lack of confidence placed in the credit rating models and systems.

Because of the complexity in measuring certain credit products, banks will attempt to deploy multiple risk rating systems for various business lines in which each system used operates with different rating scales. The purpose in doing so is to emphasize a greater degree of discrimination between defaulting and non-defaulting borrowers. However, given that rating systems have to be calibrated to default probability values for consistency and accuracy, any deviations from the estimated variables could lead to inaccurate regulatory capital allocations. Calibration is a process of model validation that lenders undertake on the assumptions that are used to derive default rates and loss estimates. It is a review that credit rating systems are performing accurate default

calculations and a justification for the assumptions that are being
used to quantify and distinguish the degrees of risk. In the wider
context, it is also a test of the lender's internal systems and controls
and an indicator for the degree that a firm relies on the credit rating
system in daily decision making. Calibrating a diversified credit
portfolio comprised of various types of credit assets can be difficult,
as it requires that a link is made between the lender's internal rating scale and cumulative default probabilities. Default probabilities
are assigned to the rating model output in a grade or acceptable
scale value for the term of debt assets with the longest maturity in
the portfolio. Because default rates can be subject to extreme volatility, any deviations from the model estimates can result in inaccurate
forecasts and calculations. If the estimated default probability is too
high compared with what the model computes, a higher amount of
economic capital will have to be allocated along with a higher price
to the borrower. A lower default rate will lead to lower economic
capital and lower credit pricing. The effectiveness of calibrating is
therefore dependent on the amount of reliable internal data that are
available to statistically derive accurate default rates. Data accuracy
is important to estimate the different credit products, which are
composed of varying maturities, industry sectors, and types of
obligors. More importantly, the production of reliable risk estimates
should also be for the full length of the different credit cycles on
which portfolio borrowers operate. Without having sufficient historical data there may be limited detail for statistically deriving
accurate default rates.

9.4 CREDIT RATINGS

Credit ratings act as a guide to the risk of a credit and the probability that lenders will be repaid for the risk that they have
extended. They are used to support the credit assessment and to
determine the basis for which the lender will evaluate borrowers.
The most common types of credit ratings that lenders use are
internal and external ratings, such as those provided by the public rating agencies. Lenders will also use external ratings for large
public companies to evaluate the credit quality of a corporate borrower's securities and compare how its public debt has been
assessed. Because a company's credit rating can be impacted by
the type of rating system from which it is derived, many lenders
have developed their own proprietary internal credit rating

systems. Internal ratings are based on historical customer information relative to the credit relationship that a borrower has with
the financial service entity, although for regulatory reasons, the
larger banks will map their internal ratings to those of the major
public rating agencies. Internal ratings that are used by commercial banks and credit suppliers are designed to numerically
summarize the risk of loss or default by a borrower who is unable
to pay an existing debt obligation. Despite the common objectives
for evaluating a borrower's repayment ability, the methodologies
that are used in internal and external ratings will differ in several
aspects. The differences between the types of ratings will be
discussed in the next section.

9.4.1 Proprietary Internal Credit Ratings

There are several major differences that distinguish the credit
rating of banks from those of the public rating agencies. A major
difference is that credit suppliers are exposed to the risk of default
on borrowed funds whereas the rating agencies are not providers
of debt capital. Another difference is that most of the credit ratings
that are provided by the rating agencies have, until a few years ago,
emphasized ratings on capital market debt issuances. Their ratings
methodology has therefore primarily been focused on long-term
bond issuers, a fact that was recently noted when Moody's,
Standard & Poor's, and Fitch announced changes to their risk grading methodology on corporate loans.* For this reason, the credit
parameters for banks must be inclusive of the different types of
funding products that they service, along with the specific characteristics and transactions of their borrowers. Unlike those of the rating agencies, another difference in bank credit risk ratings is that
the risk ratings at banks are based on confidential information,
some of which may not be disposed for public availability. Bank
credit ratings are used in the loan origination process to support
the underwriting guidelines upon which credit decisions are made

---

*Although the risk grading changes will primarily affect the leveraged or below-
investment-grade loans, it is designed to better measure the EAD for the recovery amount
in the event of default. The decision to implement this change was based on the attempt to
reflect that loan holders usually recover a higher value than bondholders in bankruptcy.
The agencies thus decided that the ratings for these borrowers will result in triggering
rating upgrades and hopefully contribute to cost savings for these corporate borrowers
from a decline in their funding costs.

FIGURE 9.3

Internal Ratings Process

The Issuer - Obligor Rating

Financial Risk Assessment

- ■ **Financial Statements**
- ■ **Cash Flow**
- ■ **Profitability**

Business, Industry and Management
Country Risk

The Issue - Facility Rating

Structure
Subordination
Third-Party Support
Collateralization
Term

and to calculate most of the primary analytical detail in credit analysis. Figure 9.3 details a bank's credit risk rating process relative to the risk assessment and risk measurement process. This process is an extension to the format for the risk evaluation technique that was discussed in Chapters 5 and 6.

Banks need internal credit rating systems that continuously provide updated information to reflect a "point-in-time-grading scale" consistent with particular time horizons. A "point-in-time" credit risk rating is more consistent with a borrower's business or industry economic cycle under the present circumstances. As the borrower's circumstances and economic conditions change on a year over year basis, so also will point-in-time ratings change to reflect the respective time period from which a borrower has transitioned. This tends to provide a more precise estimation of each individual borrower's probability of default in order to derive equivalent exposures for the maximum loss amounts over the life of credit facilities and portfolio transactions. Given that lenders and credit providers also want to remove low credit quality and weak performing assets off the balance sheet, they are therefore interested in current circumstances and events for making credit portfolio management decisions. For this reason, credit transactions need to be risk rated on an ongoing basis to assess for the worst-case scenarios as part of the monitoring process. In addition, credit transactions have to be accounted for in the current phase of the credit cycle as part of the risk horizon time period. Although the typical time period is usually one year, because of the longer maturity terms on credit facilities, lenders will also use longer risk horizons of up to five, or even more years.

Credit ratings by public rating agencies, alternatively, tend to be forward-looking in evaluating the likelihood that a borrower will default on long-term future obligations. The default rates provided by credit rating agencies reflect an average default frequency for obligors in each rating category according to their industry and geographical regions. Although banks require a more precise measurement criterion that is consistent with particular time horizons to accurately rate all asset classes, external ratings only link the probability of default across a broad range of risk buckets. Consequently, public ratings compute "average" defaults that are based on "through-the-cycle" grading, which may not be relevant for an individual lender's credit portfolio risk. Through-the-cycle ratings usually assess the borrower's conditions according to the worst cases that are anticipated and how severe a respective downside event will be. Consequently, a limitation that many lenders will find in using them is that they are only current at the time that ratings assessments take place and may not always necessarily be effective in detecting declining credit quality. This is primarily attributed to the fact that through-the-cycle ratings do not consider a borrower's probability of default on a year-over-year basis, but rather they assign borrowers to groups that are considered to have a common default frequency with other borrowers. Although point-in-time ratings will yield greater volatility as conditions continue to frequently change, some banks have also sought to combine rating system components that provide both point-in-time and through-the-cycle applications. The problem in this approach is that it clashes with a consistent credit philosophy and credit risk strategy across an organization's credit portfolio.

9.4.2 Number of Credit Grades

Bank rating system architectures will often require more definitive credit grades than what external ratings may provide. The number of risk grade levels that are required by lenders is dependent on the individual lender's business and portfolio composition. In general, banks that have a high volume of large corporate lenders tend to require an increased number of risk grades and distinctive levels of risk definitions. This is because having a large number and degree of grading scales will enable the lender to better refine the degrees of risk levels. Loss estimates can be better measured to differentiate default risk in assets ranging from relatively low risk levels to relatively high risk levels for a lender that has many portfolios of obligors and counterparties. Lenders who have fewer and smaller grades are limited in that they do not have a meaningful exposure distribution across their graded categories. This will lead to having a high exposure concentration in particular sectors and result in higher regulatory capital allocations. Banks therefore need to have a meaningful distribution of exposure across grades so that each grade does not exceed a specified gross percentage of credit exposure. Even the use of $+/-$ distinctions similar to the rating agencies can provide more detailed information on the proportion of assets that are concentrated in particular risk categories.

Most banks, over the past several years, but especially those among the major money centers, have invested in significant upgrades to their credit risk architectures in which credit gradations are known to range between up to 15 through 20 grades. The upgraded architect systems are designed to provide relatively finely graded rating scales in order to more appropriately price credit risk and compute economic capital requirements. This was confirmed in a 2002 survey sponsored by the International Association of Credit Portfolio Managers (IACPM) in conjunction with the International Association of Swaps and Derivatives Association (ISDA) and the Risk Management Association (RMA). Of the 71 large financial institutions primarily located in North America and Europe to whom the survey was distributed, 41 respondents, representing 66% of those surveyed, indicated that the number of facility ratings used by them ranged from a low of 4 to a high of 25, with a median of 10 and an average of 10.6.

In general, lenders will use numerical credit grades, but the public rating agencies tend to use letter grades for the rating scale that comprises the 22 graded categories that are illustrated in Tables 9.3 and 9.4. A primary distinction in the credit rating symbols used by Standard & Poor's and Fitch for investment- and

TABLE 9-3

Credit Rating Symbols: Investment Grade

Moody's	S&P and Fitch	Comment
Aaa	AAA	Prime. Maximum safety
Aa1	AA+	High grade. High quality
Aa2	AA	
Aa3	AA−	
A1	A+	Upper medium grade
A2	A	
A3	A	
Baa1	BBB+	Lower medium grade
Baa2	BBB	
Baa3	BBB−	

non-investment-grade borrowers is that both S&P and Fitch Ratings use a "+" or "−" in their ratings to denote relative status within major rating categories. The suffix for A+ is better than A, which in turn is better than A−, even though they are not added to AAA rated entities or to categories below CCC. In contrast, Moody's modifies its ratings categories (Aa or Caa) by adding numerical suffixes such as 1, 2, 3 to indicate relative credit quality,

TABLE 9-4

Credit Rating Symbols: Non-Investment Grade

Ba1	BB+	Non-investment grade
Ba2	BB	Speculative
Ba3	BB−	
B1	B+	Highly speculative
B2	B	
B3	B−	
Caa1	CCC+	Substantial risk
Caa2	CCC	
Caa3	CCC−	
Ca	CC	
C	C	
D (Default)	D (Default)	

TABLE 9-5

Internal Ratings Process

Risk Rating	Risk Level	Agency Rating	
1	Low	AAA/Aaa	
2	Low	AA/Aa	
3	Low	A+/A+	Investment Grade
4	Medium	A/A,BBB/aa	
5	Medium	BB/Ba	
6	Medium	B+/B+	
7	High	B/B	Less than
8	High	CCC/Caa	Investmet Grade
9	High	CC/Ca	
10	High	C/C	
11	Default		

with 1 being the strongest. Despite these distinctions, a BBB+ rating by S&P and Fitch Ratings is similar to a Baa1 rating by Moody's.* Alternatively, banks will map their facility risk ratings, to correspond with external ratings, similar to the example in Table 9.5.

9.4.3 Reliable Data Quality

Because a credit portfolio approach to managing risk emphasizes sophisticated measurement models and tools that consist of various different analytic applications, without having reliable data quality to estimate credit loss, the model inputs will result in the computation of inaccurate estimates. This is another reason why clarity and consistency in how default is measured is therefore essential to the credit risk measurement process. Establishing internal credit ratings requires for lenders to gather reliable data on the performance of prior credit transactions together with historical loss information. Based on the information that is gathered and collected, the institution identifies rating categories to separate the

---

*Note that Moody's only expanded its lowest rating Caa to Caa1,2,3 in June of 1997. Its reasons were because of the expansion of the high-yield bond market. Moody's currently rates $30,000 billion of debt, of which $21.5 billion falls into the Caa category.

credits into buckets that will subsequently be used to estimate the default probabilities. The ratings are derived by assigning the individual credit transactions to different credit classifications according to the statistical rules that apply to the assigned credit categories.

Institutions that have attempted to rely on published industry sector data, including surveys, have usually found the results to be unreliable. This is because the particular data did not reflect historical loss amounts for particular incidences of default and therefore could not capture the portfolio's sensitivity for the loss parameters. Many banks have been challenged by the effort required to obtain accurate and reliable historical data on loss amounts for default incidences. Traditionally, they would only retain historical data on defaults and rates of losses, at best, for a one-year period. Maintaining statistical data over a five- to ten-year period on rates of loss after a default, has proven to be something that was historically not retained. The lack of such detail therefore made calculating credit risk difficult.

Given that a considerable amount of effort must be expended to collect all of the data to map internal ratings to default probability, smaller banks are more challenged in designing internal rating system. This is typically because a smaller bank may lack the required financial resources including the ability to gather and collect the required data. Smaller banks that do not have sufficient data to estimate loss parameters will use external ratings data to map their internal ratings. Banks that have decentralized their credit approval processes may also find it difficult to gather and collect all of the required data. Gathering essential information about rates of loss after a default event should be a focus for all banks in the future, specifically as it relates to the evolution of the default process. For example, a loan exposure at the moment of default can become equity during workout and subsequently earn a profit for the lender while in workout. During this time, the borrower has restructured and begun to recover, thereby now making the LGD a profit.

9.4.4 Mapping Internal Ratings to External Ratings

Lenders that do not have sufficient data to estimate their own loss estimates will map their internal ratings to those of the public rating agencies. Mapping is essentially a tool that is used to categorize risks to a rating scale that is equivalent to one of a third-party benchmark. In other words, the lender translates the scale of measurement to the benchmarked scale of measurement. Many lenders that have developed their own internal proprietary risk rating systems will also map to assigned default rates of the public rating agencies. This gives the ability to develop a consistent methodology for gathering historical and future updated probabilities of defaults across various classes so that they can build up a database for their expected losses on exposures. Transition matrices that are derived from internal ratings are also mapped to compare with the data that are produced by the agencies. The transition matrices are a critical input into the CVaR, to assess the credit risk of loan and bond portfolios. Similar to those of the credit rating agencies, they reflect the likelihood that a credit rating will decline over a particular period of time. Because they are derived from internal information of borrowers that are obligated to the lender according to their industry rankings and countries, they are considered to be more accurate when compared to external rating matrices, which tend to provide averages for a broad class of obligors and industries. This is because the rating agencies, as we discussed earlier in the chapter, do not always update the borrowers' conditions throughout the year and may lack information to fully reflect the true default probability.

9.5 EXTERNAL CREDIT RATINGS

Similar to internal ratings, external credit ratings are also intended to provide information and credit risk indicators to creditors and investors about the future creditworthiness of an obligor. Users of external ratings obtain opinions about companies' fundamental credit strengths according to different classifications of credit risk that are summarized in an ordinal ranking of risk measurement. The grading symbols that are used in external ratings are essentially the independent judgment of rating agency credit specialists. In general, a hybrid system is used in external ratings that consists of expert judgment, supplemented by credit risk models. Lenders will also use external ratings to calculate their PDs by mapping the agency's PDs to that of the bank's internal rating scale. Default risk is measured by grouping the pool of obligors in each rating category into corresponding bucket rating scales to derive their probability of default or an average default rate. The major external credit rating providers are Moody's and Standard & Poor's in the United States and the France based Fitch Ratings, all of which have a long history in rating large public corporations. These agencies, not surprisingly, have come to gain universal acceptance in part because of the breadth of companies that they cover and the easy accessibility by users to their ratings coverage. More importantly, the regulatory licences that they hold have given both Moody's and Standard & Poor's a dominant market position over the 130 other credit-rating agency providers.

An advantage that public rating agencies possess is their high level of skilled capital in the form of industry analysts or specialists, who continuously monitor and rate the credit quality of corporate bond and security issuers. Rating agency credit specialists have an extensive level of knowledge of the circumstances and factors that influence a borrower's credit quality. Consequently, they are considered to be uniquely qualified in providing independent analyses on the short- and long-term credit risks of the companies that they follow. Because the cost of retaining similar human capital in the banking industry has become so expensive, most lenders today have discontinued retaining specialized industry sector credit specialists in favor of relying on the knowledge base in public rating agencies. In fact, many credit specialists employed by the public rating agencies are also former bankers who have transitioned their skills from banking because the industry has reduced the number of credit analysts that emphasize industry specialization.

9.5.1 Functions of External Ratings

The services that external rating agencies provide have expanded over the years along with the significant role that they provide to the global financial community. Although they are most recognized for their ratings on corporate bond issuers, they are nonetheless also an important resource for regulators, banks, as well as a host of fiduciary agents. Mutual funds and pension fund trustees, for example, are mandated to purchase bonds that only have high ratings from approved licensed credit rating agencies. In addition to rating and monitoring securities, the financial industry disintermediation and modern credit risk practices have also expanded the services of external rating providers. New credit products for many classes of borrowers have created a market for external ratings on bonds, commercial paper, sovereign debt, syndicated loans, structured products, credit derivatives, and mutual funds. Advances in portfolio management have also increased the reliance on external ratings not only by banks, but by asset managers and other money advisers, who may not have their own in-house internal rating systems. Broker-dealers rely on external ratings to evaluate counterparty trading partners along with other regulated financial market participants to obtain quantitative data. Users depend on external ratings because they are perceived to be without the bias found in internal ratings, as well as being transparent and opaque. Critics, however, have questioned the effectiveness of the foregoing attributes and begun to re-examine the role of external rating agencies.

9.5.2 External Ratings Methodology

The major public rating agencies are direct in both verbal and written communications, stating that their ratings are only an opinion, which may not be the views of the entire market. They also issue disclaimers relative to any notions on what their credit ratings measure based on their opinions. The probability of default on a rating is an attempt to measure the risk of credit loss and not a measurement of market risk or price appreciation. Understanding that ratings are not designed to reflect the swings and declines of firm's business or supply–demand cycles is important, because they rate "through-the-cycle" and are slower to make adjustments on short-term credit quality events than the debt or equity markets.

Although the rating agencies have never detailed the theoretical assumptions constructed in their rating models, they do emphasize qualitative and quantitative factors relative to their credit ratings. Table 9.6, highlights a summary approach of the criteria that Moody's considers to evaluate corporate borrowers. First, Moody's indicates that their ratings are not based on a defined set of financial ratios or rigid computer models and they apply an **emphasis on the qualitative**. Secondly, as a rule of thumb, they are looking through the next economic cycle or longer, because ratings are intended to provide an analytical **focus on the long-term** risks. External ratings analyze and measure the

TABLE 9-6

The Ratings Approach

Financial Risk Assessment

- Emphasis on the qualitative
- Focus on the long term
- Global consistency
- Level and predictability of cash flow
- Reasonably adverse scenarios
- Seeing through local accounting practices
- Sector-Specific Analysis

Source: Moody's.

fundamental factors that will drive each issuer's long-term ability to meet debt payments. These factors may include a change in management strategy or regulatory trends, such as, for example, the current market emphasis on the Basel II Accords that will be discussed in the next chapter. Third, the external ratings approach incorporates several checks and balances that are designed to promote the universal comparability of rating opinions to derive **global consistency** in rating particular borrowers. Fourth, the issuer's capacity to respond favorably to uncertainty is also a key in having assessments made on the **level and predictability of cash flows** for future cash generation in relation to its commitments to repay debt holders. The fifth approach in Moody's ratings is that they aim to measure the issuer's ability to meet debt obligations against **reasonably adverse scenarios** that are particular to the issuer's specific circumstances. They deliberately do not incorporate a single assumption and instead attempt to apply internally consistent economic forecasts. Sixth, the agency focuses on **seeing through local accounting practices** to understand both the economic reality of the underlying transactions and on how differences in accounting conventions may—or may not—influence true economic values. In the analysis of assets, for example, the concern is with the relative ability to generate cash, not with the value stated on the balance sheet. Finally, Moody's rates with a **sector-specific analysis** given that the specific risk factors likely to be weighed in a given rating will vary considerably by sector. These factors are considered under a range of stress situations and conditions.

9.5.3 Rating the Credit Quality by External Agencies versus the Lenders

Because the rating agencies serve as middlemen between debtors and creditors as well as the investing public, criticism has prevailed about how they lag behind the markets as near-term events do not always necessarily affect medium- or long-term credits. Confidence in the credit rating process has also been low among financial professionals at many of the issuing firms. A survey by the Association for Financial Professionals (AFP) in December 2004, found that 34% of corporate practitioners believed the ratings on their debt to be inaccurate, compared to 29% in 2002, and 41% responded that ratings did not reflect changes in creditworthiness in a timely fashion. The study further revealed that, along with downgraded companies, 36% of upgraded companies stated that their ratings were inaccurate.

This ongoing debate about the role of the predominant rating agencies has been relentless since both Standard & Poor's and Moody's came into the spotlight under post-Enron pressure. Among the questions that began to surface was how the agencies evaluated corporate governance, accounting quality, and disclosure requirements. Critics argued not so much that the agencies had failed to detect Enron's imminent bankruptcy, but more that there was a delay in identifying the decline in credit quality for several major issuers. Defaults on several other major companies also occurred around the same time, causing significant financial losses to investors. For example, Enron was still rated by the agencies as low-investment-grade quality on November 21, 2001. A decline in the company's credit quality did not become acknowledged until November 27, 2001, when it was downgraded to BBB− from BBB by Standard & Poor's. The following day, on November 28, 2001, it was again downgraded to B−, but was in bankruptcy by December 12, 2001. Similarly, Argentina was placed on credit watch by Standard & Poor's on November 1, 2000, and downgraded 14 days later to BB− where it remained for over a year until it was downgraded to Ca on December 20, 2001, the same month that it defaulted. Similar concerns have also been raised in Europe, where the agencies for the present time have warded off any attempts for them to become subject to regulatory scrutiny.

In the United States, immediate questions began to surface on whether the public rating agencies had effectively used their exception from Regulation FD to ask management the tough questions that might have particularly brought some of the accounting shenanigans at Enron to light.* When initially called before Congress, the agencies reported that market feedback had indicated that there was no reason to change. Members of the Senate Government Affairs Committee reacted by noting that with 90% of revenues derived from assigning ratings (meaning that the issuers are their primary constituency), they were shocked to hear such self-serving conclusions.† The questions have continued as legislators recently labeled both agencies as a "rating agency duopoly" that holds the keys to the financial markets.[1] Members of the U.S. Congress have attributed this position to the U.S. regulators' ongoing refusal to sell more regulatory licences to competitive rating agencies. Complaints have also prevailed about whether the rating agencies should be more transparent regarding how they reach their rating conclusions. These issues of transparency were based on responses from investors and creditors who acknowledged that although they do want long-term views, they also want shorter review periods in light of any changing company or market circumstances. The general perception was that the designated credit rating symbols in Tables 9.3 and 9.4 did not sufficiently serve to distinguish the credit rating grades according to an obligor's short-term risk levels. Another demand expressed was the trend to place a greater emphasis on borrowers' liquidity positions, particularly as they relate to companies' near-term sources of cash and credit under stressful conditions. These concerns were in addition to pressure that the agencies also faced from the European Parliament regarding their "conflicts of interest," which was considered to be further advocated by the requirement of the Basel II Accords for banks to use external credit ratings as part of their measurement process. More recently, the U.S. House of Representatives approved a bill that would alter the regulatory landscape for all credit rating agencies by approving the "Credit Rating Agency Duopoly Relief Act" of 2006. The bill is currently pending passage by the U.S. Senate and, depending on whether it passes, the

---

*Reg. FD is a reqirement by the SEC that was designed to create greater accountability between the investing public and institutional investors. The rule was implemented as an attempt to prevent public companies from making selective disclosure to market professionals and certain shareholders, as an attempt by regulators to require firms to release crucial nonpublic information and bring the greater accountability.
†Senate hearings on Rating Agencies—members of the Senate Government Affairs Committee investigating the rating agencies role in the Enron scandal.

Securities and Exchange Commission will lose the ability to designate credit rating agencies as "nationally recognized rating agencies" or NRSROs. Rather than restrict the issuance of ratings to the three primary agencies that now control over 80% of the market, the bill would allow a credit rating company that meets certain standards and has over three years of experience to register with the SEC as a statistical rating agency.[2]

In response to the criticisms, Standard & Poor's initiated the distribution of Credit Outlooks, which was designed to identify the potential credit direction of a short- or long-term rating by focusing on any changes in the issuer's fundamental or economic business conditions. It focuses on identifiable events and short-term trends that could lead ratings to be placed under special surveillance or critical monitoring. Although an outlook is not necessarily a precursor of a ratings change or future credit watch conditions, it was designed to provide users with an early-warning sign by offering insight into how a company is performing. If the outlook rating is positive or negative, the rating may be raise or lowered, if it is stable, a rating is not likely to change, and if the outlook is developing, the rating can either be raised or lowered. Some common events that could lead to a positive, negative, or developing designation are mergers, recapitalizations, voter referendums, regulatory actions, or anticipated operating developments. A problem in using these applications as a guide for warning signs is that lenders may not always distinguish the relevancy and may view these indicators in such a manner that finds companies falling off the credit cliff due to rating triggers. In other words, credit deterioration can become compounded by provisions such as rating triggers or financial covenants that place pressure on a company's liquidity or its business to a material extent.

9.6 RATING OFF THE CREDIT CLIFF

Rating triggers provide creditors and counterparties with optional rights in the event that a borrower's credit rating declines to a certain level. These rights vary from clauses in the credit agreements that require the pledging of assets to pricing grid changes tied to rating downgrades or upgrades. Lenders will issue debt instruments with ratings-based triggers to protect against credit deterioration. Borrowers have also come to accept these mechanisms because, without them, they would have to pay a higher cost of debt. Rating triggers also serve to protect investors, although it has been found that they can lead to liquidity problems for companies rather than simply providing a means of protection. Early repayment acceleration clauses can be included in loan agreements that can subsequently result in higher cost of debt for companies along with the need for new capital financing. These factors can contribute to "credit cliff situations" that result in dire circumstances for a firm. In other words, rating changes can put material pressure on a company's liquidity as well as the operations of its business. For example, a company that is downgraded for its credit performance will not only have an increase in its cost of capital, but the problems that it is experiencing can become exacerbated by the lack of financial resources. In a December, 2001, position paper that was published by Moody's regarding proposed changes in ratings methodology, the argument was made that rating triggers can have unexpected and sometimes highly disruptive consequences for both lenders and borrowers alike.[3] It was found that rating triggers and other protective covenants contribute to developing credit cliffs, and the acceleration of the cost of capital as a result of credit deterioration. More importantly, companies that have more than one triggering clause can find themselves experiencing an accumulation of negative consequences. This position was supported in a May 15, 2002, survey taken by Standard & Poor's on more than one thousand U.S. and European investment-grade debt issuers. The survey revealed that less than 3%, or 23 companies, showed serious vulnerability to rating triggers or other contingent calls on liquidity, which could turn a moderate decline in credit quality into a liquidity crisis. About half of the companies responding had exposure to some sort of contingent liability, but only a small number of companies faced proximity to a so-called "credit cliff," indicating that credit deterioration could be compounded by rating trigger provisions in financial covenants that could put pressure on companies' liquidity to a material extent.

Some common credit cliffs can also include credit obligations that require government support dependency. In the early 2000s, the California utilities thought there was only a remote possibility of the state not supporting the utilities, although this proved not to be the case. The holding company of Pacific Gas and Electric, PG & E Corporation, eroded when the rating triggers in its commercial paper back stop lines led banks to terminate their funding obligations, which subsequently resulted in downgrading to junk status.

When the banks failed to fund the lines, the company defaulted, leaving the funding sources for the commercial paper as claimants in bankruptcy. In addition there were the cross defaults on the firm's senior note obligations that also occurred as a result of the rating triggers, in which both the parent and holding company were unable to meet critical debt obligations. A similar case was that of Southern California Edison, whose debt agreements did not have direct rating triggers but were contained in third-party agreements. SEC's contracts with third-party energy providers required the company to collateralize ongoing power purchase agreements. When unusually high energy prices in 2000, along with a regulatory rate restriction, left the company without available borrowing power, it was barred from getting financial relief in order to restructure its debt outside of bankruptcy due to rating triggers. The company was required to maintain, under the rating trigger, specified credit ratings that could be collateralized by a letter of credit or other specified credit mitigant. Without available borrowing capacity, the company was forced into a liquidity crisis that ultimately led to the State of California having to replace SCEs original agreement.*

9.7 VALIDATING CREDIT RATING SYSTEMS

Credit rating systems have to be reviewed to certify that the entire internal processes for which they operate are uniform for ongoing rating and monitoring functions. The review of an internal credit rating system is formally defined as the validation of the system. The purpose of validation is twofold. First, lenders that plan to use their internal rating systems to determine economic capital charges are required by regulatory authorities to validate their internal ratings. Two, financial institutions need to test the suitability and reliability of the quantitative and qualitative rating system criteria to evaluate their methodologies and processes. They also need to establish a benchmark performance against external credit ratings. The chart in Figure 9.4 presents an overview of the functions that are required to adequately validate a rating system. Although these functions highlight the basic regulatory requirements under the

---

*In January 2001, the state of California replaced SEC's business by procuring wholesale gas business, which enabled the firm to avoid having to collateralize future power sources and seek regulatory relief.

FIGURE 9.4

Validation Chart

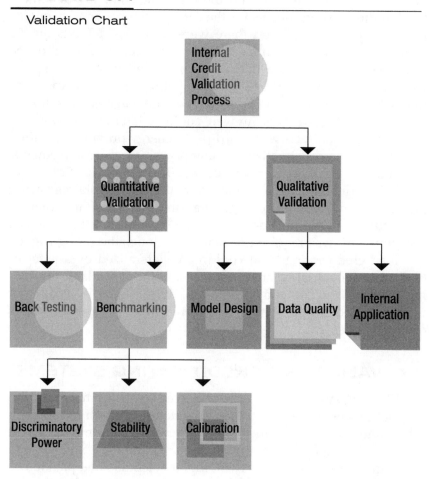

two IRB approaches for Basel II, they also serve as a basis that lenders can use for the standardized approach, with the exception of the LGD and EAD risk parameters.

9.7.1 Quantitative and Qualitative Validation

Quantitative and qualitative validation of credit rating systems is dependent on whether the rating system is expert judgment or model based. Because model-based systems rely on statistical methodologies, they are designed to capture the various risk factors that were discussed earlier in this chapter. Rating grades should reflect the borrower characteristics, asset size, and exposure amount, all of which are derived from internal default information. Ratings that are derived from expert judgment are usually validated by having well-documented credit rating procedures. For quantitative validation the criteria to assess the quality of the rating system are measured by back testing or benchmarking the credit portfolios. Ratings must be back tested to ensure that the probability of default estimates that are established with specific rating grades are based on historical experience and empirical evidence. Back testing consists of the various types of statistical methodologies that are used to evaluate how effective the system estimates the default probabilities. Many of the major money center banks have engaged in collecting and back testing internal data for several years. Although there is no specific time frame that can be prescribed for the amount of time needed to amass the required back-testing data, on average, at least 3 to 5 years of data are needed to gain a sense of confidence in the data. Some have been able to gather sufficient data to associate their PDs for each obligor's rating and then back tested the default frequencies based on the actual default performance of entities in a particular grade to the rate of defaults that are predicted by the bank's rating. A common back-testing application that is used is the binomial distribution, which has been derived from market risk back testing. This test is based on the hypothetical assumption that the actual number of defaults that correspond to all of the rating grade PDs are correct after one year, or they are not correct. Any major differences between the estimated PD of the rating grades and the default rates would result in having to reject the hypothesis. This would also result in the quality of calibration being unreliable. The binomial distribution, however, assumes that defaults are independent and does not consider the effects of correlation to cyclical circumstances.

Quantitative validation is intended to validate the system's discriminatory abilities along with its stability and calibration quality. Strong discriminatory power is present when defaults among high-rated borrowers are at a minimum default percentage. Weak discriminatory power exists when defaults are high among highly rated borrowers and result in a large default percentage. Discriminatory power is important to the quality of calibration and the mapping process. If the loss parameters display only a slight deviation from the actual estimated PDs, the system is fairly well calibrated. For multilevel rating systems that include the facility risk rating, the system should be calibrated to all of the risk parameters. Credit rating systems will also need to be validated for the qualitative factors. When a combination of both methodologies is used, a model-based system will require having sufficient historical default information. Qualitative validation evaluates the data quality relative to the model design that is used to test the data and the internal applications from which the data are derived. Lenders without sufficient data will usually rely on external rating agencies. External ratings serve as a benchmark that can be compared to the deviated estimates. When deviations are identified, they should be investigated and resolved. As discussed earlier, benchmarking is dependent on the type of methodology used.

An effective credit rating system should also be capable of acting as an "early-warning indicator" to identify borrowers before they default and who subsequently do default. This process reflects the measure of a system's discriminatory power for after a transaction has been booked to the credit portfolio and known as "ex ante." Currently, no rating system has been proven to be this precise, although there are several market systems that act as "early-warning indicators." What the organization does want at least is to have a system that can discriminate the relative degrees of risk so that the system will be compatible with the default estimates.

9.8 CONCLUSIONS

Credit rating systems are at the heart of credit risk management in that they provide a road map to the entire credit process. Depending on the type of credit risk architecture that a lender has, the credit rating system can be used in the enterprise risk management process whereby it is incorporated into technology platforms that capture a mass of data across various business and operating departments. The application techniques also undertake the credit risk grading process in which the assessment and measurement process is driven by the model system that is used. Credit rating systems can be either one- or two-dimensional depending upon the architecture's infrastructure.

Although most lenders prefer to use their own internal proprietary rating systems, lenders that may lack the required infrastructural components will alternatively map their ratings to those of the external credit rating agencies. The users of external ratings, however, must be concerned with how ratings are derived and prefer to rate at a "point-in-time" rather than "through-the-cycle," which does not encompass all scenarios and operating cycles related to particular borrowers.

Credit rating systems must also be back tested to validate their ongoing rating and monitoring functions. Validation is required for both the quantitative and qualitative aspects of the credit rating systems to test the suitability of the manner in which the lender is risk assessing and measuring the particular facility transactions.

CHAPTER DISCUSSION QUESTIONS

1. Distinguish between expert judgment and credit risk models. When is each used and what is the advantage in using each of these applications.

2. What are the key features that lenders need in their credit risk architectures? What are the major functions that these features provide for a lender?

3. Why would a lender use an external credit rating rather than rely on the institution's proprietary internal rating system?

4. Describe a rating trigger and its advantages and disadvantages?

5. Discuss the pros and cons of back testing and benchmarking the credit portfolio to external ratings?

6. What is the role of the internal rating system under modern credit risk management?

7. When using the internal rating system to measure transactions, what applications do multidimensional systems perform that one-dimensional rating systems do not? Distinguish between the types of credit providers that will operate each type of internal rating systems?

8. Reliant Resources, Inc., was incorporated in August 2000 to provide electricity and energy services to wholesale and retail customers in the United States and Western Europe. In 2002, the company was downgraded by Moody's and Standard & Poor's to Ba3/BBB with the following commentary from Moody's:

New York, July 31, 2002—Moody's downgraded the issuer rating and bank loan ratings assigned to Reliant Resources, Inc. (RRI) to

Ba3 from Baa3 and assigned a senior implied rating of Ba3 to RRI. Given ties to the RRI rating, Moody's also lowered the issuer rating assigned to Reliant Energy Capital Europe to Ba3 and placed the Baa3 assigned to Reliant-Energy Mid-Atlantic (REMA) on review for potential downgrade. Moody's lowered to Ba3 the rating assigned to Orion Power Holdings and lowered the rating assigned to Reliant Benelux to Baa2. All ratings remain on review for possible downgrade. The RRI downgrade reflects Moody's view that RRI's cash flow from operations is unpredictable relative to its debt load and its financial flexibility is limited. The company needs to refinance approximately $2.9 bn of bridge bank debt maturing in February, 2003 and $800 million of the $1.6 bn corporate revolver which matures six months later. We note that both the RRI and the Orion Power Holdings ratings had assumed the refinancing of the secured bank debt at Orion Midwest and Orion New York, and this has not occurred. Moody's said that the near term outlook for RRI's wholesale business is poor, driven by depressed wholesale prices both here and in Europe, constrained capacity markets, and poor credit conditions in the energy trading sector, all of which will pressure margins and challenge RRI's ability to generate stable cash flow from operations. We note that RRI's retail business lends a measure of diversity to the company's earnings.

In addition, Standard & Poor's placed the company on CreditWatch and published in the RatingsDirect the following rationale for this action:

Rationale

Reliant Resources Inc.'s ratings are on CreditWatch with negative implications, reflecting the concern that a lack of market confidence or the risk that another rating agency would lower Reliant's ratings to noninvestment grade could create liquidity issues as counterparties demand increased collateral to maintain trading relationships. To a lesser degree, Standard & Poor's is concerned that management was until recently unaware of "wash" power transactions, the simultaneous sale and repurchase of electricity, usually at the same price, which are used to increase reported trading volumes. Standard & Poor's will review Reliant's trading control systems and the steps that management is taking to ensure sustained and proper compliance. Reliant decided to cancel a $500 million debt issuance on May 10, 2002, due to the disclosure of its involvement in wash transactions. This action precipitated a rapid and severe loss of market value. Still, Reliant has until February 2003 to refinance a $2.9 billion bridge financing used to acquire Orion Energy Inc.

The ratings on Reliant and its subsidiaries Reliant Energy Mid-Atlantic Power Holdings LLC, Reliant Energy Capital (Europe) Inc., and Reliant Energy Power Generation Benelux N.V. reflect high acquisition-related interest costs and the inherited cost structure of the acquired Orion Power Holdings. The business prospects of the combined entity, coupled with management's generally conservative business and financial strategy, should enable the company to maintain measures of debtholder protection that are appropriate for the 'BBB' rating. Specifically, debt at less than 50% of total capital and cash interest coverage of about 4 times ($\times$).

With the acquisition of Orion, Reliant owns nearly 17,000 MW of operating generating capacity in the U.S., and nearly 4,000 MW under construction or in advanced development. In 2004, Reliant has an option to buy the 80% of nonpublic holding of the company's 14,000 MW of generating capacity in Texas, which would give Reliant a more balanced diversity. Reliant expects about 35% of pretax earnings to come from the Texas market, about 20% from the Mid-Atlantic wholesale market, around 15% from New York, and about 15% from the Western region, including California. About one-half of Reliant's wholesale (nontrading) gross margin for 2002 and 2003 are hedged. Reliant also serves the Texas retail market, which provides a higher margin than sales to wholesale customers. Retail sales are expected to account for at least 25% of consolidated income (before eliminations) over the next several years. In response to the significant investor concern arising from this disclosure, Reliant has stated that it will reduce its mark-to-market trading activity, which currently accounts for 8% of earnings before interest and taxes.

Reliant's potential exposure to additional collateral calls in the event of a downgrade is viewed by Standard & Poor's as high, with key exposures of about $900 million (variable) under its margining agreements—note that a portion of this amount must be triggered by multiple events. Reliant has $1.3 billion in bank line liquidity to cover this scenario. To Standard & Poor's knowledge, there have not been any calls for additional collateral postings resulting from the withdrawal of the $500 million financing.

Review the background and financial summary statements for the company and decide whether they indicate the company's proximity to a liquidity crunch? Can you ascertain whether the company was about to fall off the credit cliff?

Annual Income Statement (Millions of $s)	Dec 01	Dec 00
Sales	36,546	18,722
Cost of sales	35,050	18,284
Gross operating profit	1,496	438
Selling, general & admin. expense	487	—
Other taxes	—	—
EBITDA	1,009	438
Depreciation & amortization	247	—
EBIT	762	438
Other income, net	128	(147)
Total income available for interest expense	889	291
Interest expense	63	—
Minority interest	—	—
Pre-tax income	826	291
Income taxes	272	88
Special income/charges	—	—
Net income from cont. operations	554	203
Net income from discont. opers.	—	—
Net income from total operations	554	203
Normalized income	554	203
Extraordinary income	—	7
Income from cum. eff. of acct. chg.	3	—
Income from tax loss carryforward	—	—
Other gains (losses)	—	—
Total net income	**558**	**210**

Annual Balance Sheet (Millions of $s)	Dec 01	Dec 00
Assets		
Current Assets		
Cash and equivalents	119	90
Receivables	1,597	1,811
Inventories	174	99
Other current assets	2,856	5,068
Total current assets	4,745	7,069
Non-Current Assets		
Property, plant & equipment, gross	4,602	4,049
Accum. depreciation & depletion	—	NA
Property, plant & equipment, net	4,602	4,049
Intangibles	848	1,007
Other non-current assets	2,059	1,350
Total non-current assets	7,508	6,407
Total assets	**12,254**	**13,475**

(*Continued*)

Annual Balance Sheet (Millions of $s)	Dec 01	Dec 00
Liabilities & Shareholder's Equity		
Current Liabilities		
Accounts payable	1,002	3,405
Short-term debt	321	127
Other current liabilities	2,264	4,949
Total current liabilities	**3,587**	**8,480**
Non-Current Liabilites		
Long-term debt	868	892
Deferred income taxes	—	31
Other non-current liabilities	1,695	1,740
Minority interest	—	—
Total non-current liabilities	2,563	2,663
Total liabilities	**6,150**	**11,143**
Shareholder's Equity		
Preferred stock equity	—	—
Common stock equity	6,104	2,332
Total equity	6,104	2,332
Total liabilities & Stock Equity	**12,254**	**13,475**
Total common shares outstanding	288.8 Mil	240.0 Mil
Preferred shares	0	0
Treasury shares	11.0 Mil	0

Annual Cash Flow (Millions of $s)	Dec 01
Cash Flow from Operating Activities	
Net income (loss)	558
Depreciation and amortization	247
Deferred income taxes	22
Operating (gains) losses	(233)
Extraordinary (gains) losses	—
Change in Working Capital	
(Increase) Decr. in receivables	676
(Increase) Decr. in inventories	(59)
(Increase) Decr. in other curr. assets	(213)
(Decrease) Incr. in payables	(1,084)
(Decrease) Incr. in other curr. liabs.	(39)
Other non-cash items	—
Net cash from cont. operations	(127)
Net cash from discont. operations	—
Net cash from operating activities	**(127)**

(Continued)

Annual Cash Flow (Millions of $s)	Dec 01
Cash flow from investing activities	
Cash Flow Provided by:	
Sale of property, plant, equipment	—
Sale of Short-Term investments	—
Cash Used by:	
Purchase of property, plant, equipmt.	(840)
Purchase of short-term investments	—
Other investing changes net	2
Net cash from investing activities	**(838)**
Cash Flow from Financing Activities	
Cash flow provided by:	
Issuance of debt	217
Issuance of capital stock	1,696
Cash Used for:	
Repayment of debt	(736)
Repurchase of capital stock	(190)
Payment of cash dividends	—
Other financing charges, net	12
Net cash from financing activities	**1,000**
Effect of exchange rate changes	(6)
Net change in cash & cash equivalents	29
Cash at beginning of period	90
Free cash flow	(967)

Ratios		
ROE	9.1%	9.0%
ROA	4.0%	2.6%
ROS or profit margin	1.5%	1.1%
Gross margin	4.1%	2.3%
EBIT margin	2.1%	2.3%
EBITDA margin	2.8%	2.3%
Days AP outstanding	10.44	67.97
Days AR outstanding	15.95	35.31
Days inventory in stock	1.81	1.99
Debt/equity	0.19	0.44
Debt/EBITDA	1.18	2.33

Quarterly Income Statement	Jun 02	Mar 02	Dec 01	Sep 01	Jun 01
Sales	8,561	7,042	6,689	10,304	9,681
Cost of sales	7,955	6,698	6,309	9,893	9,339

(Continued)

Quarterly Income Statement	Jun 02	Mar 02	Dec 01	Sep 01	Jun 01
Gross operating profit	606	344	381	412	342
Selling, general & admin. expense	167	107	86	122	97
Other Taxes	—	—	—	—	—
EBITDA	439	237	295	290	245
Depreciation & amortization	106	71	67	72	43
EBIT	333	166	228	218	201
Other income, net	18	12	8	22	79
Total income avail. for interest exp.	351	179	235	240	281
Interest expense	67	39	11	8	20
Minority interest	—	—	—	—	—
Pre-tax income	284	140	224	231	261
Income taxes	105	43	57	98	86
Special income/charges	—	—	—	—	—
Net income from cont. operations	179	97	167	133	176
Net income from discont. opers.	—	—	—	—	—
Net income from total operations	179	97	167	133	176
Normalized income	179	97	167	133	176
Extraordinary income	—	—	—	—	—
Income from cum. eff. of acct. chg.	—	—	—	—	—
Income from tax loss carryforward	—	—	—	—	—
Other gains (losses)	—	—	—	—	—
Total net income	**179**	**97**	**167**	**133**	**176**
Assets					
Current Assets					
Cash and equivalents	460	257	119	272	85
Receivables	2,519	2,264	1,597	2,377	3,434
Inventories	115	224	174	153	165
Other current assets	2,819	2,581	2,856	4,039	4,997
Total current assets	5,912	5,326	4,745	6,841	8,681
Non-current assets					
Property, plant & equipment, gross	9,304	9,005	4,602	4,805	4,475
Accum. depreciation & depletion	434	335	—	244	202
Property, plant & equipment, net	8,870	8,670	4,602	4,561	4,273
Intangibles	2,384	2,620	848	935	916
Other non-current assets	2,466	2,157	2,059	2,637	2,488
Total non-current assets	13,719	13,447	7,508	8,132	7,676
Total assets	**19,631**	**18,773**	**12,254**	**14,973**	**16,357**

(*Continued*)

Quarterly Balance Sheet	Jun 02	Mar 02	Dec 01	Sep 01	Jun 01
Liabilities & Shareholder's Equity					
Current liabilities					
Accounts payable	1,605	1,311	1,002	1,117	1,922
Short-term debt	5,848	5,537	321	213	176
Other current liabilities	2,375	2,304	2,264	4,338	4,929
Total current liabilities	9,827	9,151	3,587	5,669	7,027
Non-Current Liabilites					
Long-term debt	1,131	1,126	868	962	908
Deferred income taxes	—	—	—	72	164
Other non-current liabilities	2,136	2,176	1,695	1,956	1,859
Minority interest	—	—	—	—	—
Total non-current liabilities	3,267	3,302	2,563	2,990	2,931
Total liabilities	**13,094**	**12,453**	**6,150**	**8,659**	**9,957**
Shareholder's Equity					
Preferred stock equity	—	—	—	—	—
Common stock equity	6,537	6,320	6,104	6,314	6,400
Total equity	6,537	6,320	6,104	6,314	6,400
Total liabilities & stock equity	**19,631**	**18,773**	**12,254**	**14,973**	**16,357**
Total common shares outstanding	299.8 Mil	299.8 Mil	288.8 Mil	299.0 Mil	299.8 Mil
Preferred shares	0	0	0	0	0
Treasury shares	10.1 Mil	10.4 Mil	11.0 Mil	0	0

Quarterly SCF (Millions of $s, Cum. for FY)	Jun 02	Mar 02	Dec 01	Sep 01	Jun 01
Cash flow from operating activities					
Net income (loss)	275	97	558	390	257
Depreciation and amortization	177	71	247	179	108
Deferred income taxes	95	41	22	(94)	27
Operating (gains) losses	(110)	(65)	(233)	(35)	(34)
Extraordinary (gains) losses	—	—	—	—	—
Change in working capital					
(Increase) decr. in receivables	(753)	(262)	676	444	(149)
(Increase) decr. in inventories	(80)	12	(59)	(53)	(66)
(Increase) decr. in other curr. assets	72	350	(213)	169	363
(Decrease) incr. in payables	467	200	(1,084)	(980)	(179)
(Decrease) Incr. in other curr. liabs.	(35)	(27)	(39)	149	52

(Continued)

Quarterly SCF (Millions of $s, Cum. for FY)	Jun 02	Mar 02	Dec 01	Sep 01	Jun 01
Other non-cash items	4	(11)	—	93	(51)
Net cash from cont. operations	114	405	(127)	262	328
Net cash from discont. operations	—	—	—	—	—
Net cash from operating activities	**114**	**405**	**(127)**	**262**	**328**
Cash Flow from Investing Activities					
Cash Flow Provided by:					
Sale of property, plant, equipment	—	—	—	—	—
Sale of short-term investments	—	—	—	—	—
Cash Used by:					
Purchase of property, plant, equipmt.	(3,279)	(3,128)	(840)	(720)	(500)
Purchase of short-term investments	—	—	—	—	—
Other investing changes net	(2)	1	2	11	11
Net cash from investing activities	**(3,281)**	**(3,127)**	**(838)**	**(709)**	**(489)**
Cash flow from financing activities					
Cash Flow Provided by:					
Issuance of debt	3,727	2,926	217	185	149
Issuance of capital stock	—	—	1,696	1,698	1,698
Cash used for:					
Repayment of debt	(228)	(75)	(736)	(1,237)	(1,694)
Repurchase of capital stock	—	—	(190)	(20)	—
Payment of cash dividends	—	—	—	—	—
Other financing charges, net	8	10	12	9	9
Net cash from financing activities	**3,507**	**2,861**	**1,000**	**635**	**162**
Effect of exchange rate changes	2	(1)	(6)	(6)	(5)
Net change in cash & cash equivalents	341	138	29	182	(5)
Cash at beginning of period	119	119	90	90	90
Free cash flow	(3,165)	(2,722)	(967)	(458)	(172)
Ratios					
ROE	2.7%	1.5%	2.7%	2.1%	
ROA	1.2%	0.7%	1.4%	0.8%	
ROS or profit margin	2.1%	1.4%	2.5%	1.3%	

(*Continued*)

Quarterly SCF (Millions of $s, Cum. for FY)	Jun 02	Mar 02	Dec 01	Sep 01	Jun 01
Gross margin	7.1%	4.9%	5.7%	4.0%	
EBIT margin	3.9%	2.4%	3.4%	2.1%	
EBITDA margin	5.1%	3.4%	4.4%	2.8%	
Days AP outstanding	18.41	17.86	14.50	10.31	
Days AR outstanding	26.85	29.34	21.79	21.05	
Days inventory in stock	1.32	3.05	2.52	1.41	
Debt/Equity	1.07	1.05	0.19	0.19	
Debt/EBITDA	15.89	28.08	4.03	4.05	

BIBLIOGRAPHY

"Achieving Excellence in Credit Risk Management; Risk Solutions-Custom Credit Risk Services from Standard & Poor's," 2003, The McGraw-Hill Companies, 2003.

Basel Accord, "The Internal Ratings Based Approach," Supporting Document to the New Basel Capital Accord, Jan. 2001, Point 226.

Cantor, Richard and Packer, Frank, "Multiple Ratings and Credit Standards: differences of opinion in the Credit Rating Industry," Federal Reserve Bank of New York, 1995.

Grant, Jeremy, "Pressure mounts over ratings agency duopoly," *Financial Times*, July 11, 2006.

Krakoviak, Joe, "Survey—Banking Industry Borrowing Lessons From Manufacturing for Substantial Cost and Growth Benefits," June 13, 2006, www.RiskCenter.com.

McCafferty, Joseph, "Credit Ratings Get Poor Ratings," *CFO Magazine*, Dec. 14, 2004.

Moody's, "Global Credit Research Rating Action," Moody's Investor Services, March 22, 2002.

NB Summary approach taken from Moody's framework. Moody's, "The Unintended Consequences of Ratings Triggers," Moody's Investor Services, Dec. 2001.

O'Neill, Leo, (S&P) to SEC, "We are not the Watchdogs." Credit Watch—A CFO Interview, *CFO Magazine*, Jan. 1, 2003.

Ratings Direct; Standard & Poor's; Reliant Resources Inc., May 14, 2002.

RiskCenter Staff, "AFS Recommends Potential Reforms to Credit Rating Agency Oversight," New York, Aug. 15, 2006, www.RiskCenter.com.

Tett, G., "Rating Agencies change Loan Gradings," *Financial Times*, May 17, 2006.

www.marketguide.com

www.reliantresources.com

The Economics of Credit

10.1 INTRODUCTION

In this chapter we will discuss how the modern credit risk approach has changed the economics of credit in order to achieve more profitable earnings and in an effort to maintain global stability in the financial markets. To better understand the framework for maximizing the profits of credit, we will first review how lenders have decomposed the profitability of extending credit in order to be adequately compensated and maximize their profits. This is in part due to the increasing complexity of credit risks contained in funding products among the different types of borrowers, in conjunction with the related funding risks in lenders' balance sheet structures. As a consequence, profitability has moved away from measuring the difference between funding and lending rates to now measure the performance of the credit facility by realizing a hurdle rate of return on the bank's capital. For these reasons we will subsequently focus on the role that capital adequacy plays in a bank's capital requirements and introduce the concept of economic capital. The chapter will conclude with an overview and discussion of the Basel Accords and how it has impacted credit risk management as well as the financial markets in general.

10.2 PRICING CREDIT TRANSACTIONS

Lenders earn profits by underwriting and distributing credit facilities according to their performance. Because pricing is an essential ingredient to overall loan profitability, the objective is to originate incremental assets that will improve portfolio returns and retain those credits as long as their risk/return maximizes earnings and increases shareholders' value. Although this premise has been advocated by classical credit practitioners, who historically used a marginal cost pricing approach, it fell short nonetheless in meeting the objective, as pricing was not risk-adjusted for facilities retained on the balance sheet to maturity. Marginal cost pricing serves to incrementally increase facility pricing so that lenders are compensated for the additional costs of extending each credit transaction. For example, suppose a credit request is made for a term loan that will be used for working capital purposes from a long-standing aircraft manufacturing customer. If the lender already has a relatively high exposure to this industry sector, under marginal cost pricing the transaction will be priced according to the portfolio's risk. This means that pricing may not be attractive to the customer because of an ailing industry sector, which will result in having to charge a higher interest rate to adequately compensate for the additional portfolio risk exposure. Under this scenario, the customers' profitability is tied to the price sensitivity of the overall portfolio returns. Given that facilities have to be appropriately priced to compensate lenders as well as to provide acceptable returns to investors and creditors, herein lies the problem with marginal cost pricing. As the cost of funds to extend credit is typically obtained from varying funding supplier sources, the marginal or additional costs that must be charged to the borrowers may not be acceptable for the overall risks to lenders. Generally, lenders will attempt to reduce their funding costs by replacing them with cheaper sources to derive a marginal cost in establishing a pricing rate. However, if a sufficient price is not charged for the transaction in lieu of losing new business, overall portfolio returns can subsequently be impacted, especially when defaults rise and credit spreads become wider and more volatile. In contrast, when loans are priced too highly, all of the relevant risks need to be identified in order to adequately allocate their costs, otherwise volatile credit spreads can also diminish a portfolio's overall performance.

Another commonly used mechanism in pricing credit facilities is the cost plus approach in which a transaction's risks are priced to reflect comparable market valuations on similar debt instruments in addition to other fees and service costs. Pricing is therefore derived from base rates that serve as indexes for the lender's cost of funds. The cost of funds for financial institutions is also known as the transfer price or the interest rate charged for the lender to source the funds from its borrowing sources. Although the facility starting price is derived from the credit quality of the borrower, the amount of profit above this is the point at which the matched funding costs are greater than the costs to service the transaction.

For deposit-taking institutions, a primary cost is the interest-bearing cost of funds to depositors. In addition there are the market costs of funds that are predicated on the bank's public credit rating and therefore determine its funds transfer pricing ability. Funds transfer pricing in lending is the process of dissecting internal transactions and payments across business units based on the credit spread, interest rate risk, and funding spreads. Because of funds transfer pricing, lenders must effectively be able to determine transaction servicing costs and the desired profits they want to earn on individual debt assets. When lenders go to the market to borrow their credit funds, the costs that they must pay for these should be less than what is charged to the borrower. Transactions are only extended if the rate of return is less than what the lender will receive for funding the credit facility (e.g., the return on fixed-income securities investments). Because the components of funds transfer pricing is market determined, lenders are also exposed to primary credit risk components including interest rate and liquidity risks. This typically involves a process of mismatching the institutions' interest rate sensitivity of its assets and liabilities according to their term to maturity. The maturity structures on long- and short-term debt obligations have to be satisfied by the existing earnings from the bank's portfolio of assets. As banks are required to invest in designated assets that are liquid and risk-free, they must be able to meet their repayment obligations with sufficient cash on hand and other liquid assets in a timely manner as well as be able to quickly raise funds as the need arises. Financing a five-year revolving credit facility, for example, with a one-year Treasury bond, may expose a lender to liquidity risk if it is unable to adequately generate funding sources to meet its balance sheet and other contractual obligations. The transfer price is determined based on the return that could be earned from different sources or the amount that can be earned, for example, on a long-term bond versus in the wholesale market.

In addition to the cost of funds, Figure 10.1 illustrates the additional cost components that must be considered in a transaction's price. These costs include administrative expenses such as overhead to service a facility, along with non interest expenses that are required, such as marketing costs to originate new business. Another cost component are the loan provisions to allocate the expected credit loss and absorb future losses. Typically, the rate

FIGURE 10.1

Traditional Loan Pricing Methodology

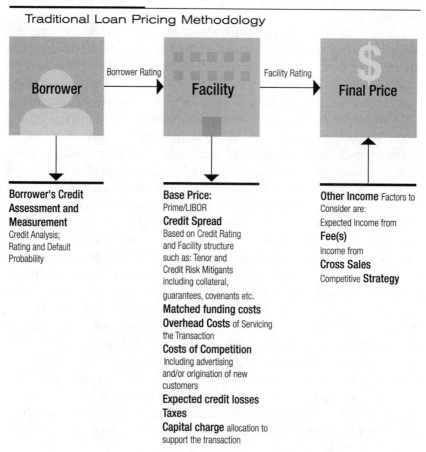

| Borrower | | Facility | | Final Price |

Borrower's Credit Assessment and Measurement
Credit Analysis;
Rating and Default
Probability

Base Price:
Prime/LIBOR
Credit Spread
Based on Credit Rating
and Facility structure
such as: Tenor and
Credit Risk Mitigants
including collateral,
guarantees, covenants etc.
Matched funding costs
Overhead Costs of Servicing
the Transaction
Costs of Competition
Including advertising
and/or origination of new
customers
Expected credit losses
Taxes
Capital charge allocation to
support the transaction

Other Income Factors to
Consider are:
Expected Income from
Fee(s)
Income from
Cross Sales
Competitive **Strategy**

charged on a loan will increase as the required reserves rise and as the returns paid on the reserves decline relative to the cost of funds. Notice that the cost-plus approach is inclusive of the regulatory capital allocation to which is added a capital charge on the hurdle rate of return and capital ratio. This regulatory capital charge must be held against each asset category and the cost of capital on their cost of funds. The cost of capital is what must be charged to the borrower to earn a return on equity for shareholders' value, including the tax costs that must be paid on the revenues earned from extending the credit. Consequently, the higher the capital allocation and the lenders' cost of capital, the higher the interest rate that is charged to the borrower. Often, the opportunity for any future ancillary income is considered as justification in pricing down the final transaction price and is also why many banks have come to consider loans as a loss leader.* Nonetheless, there is also potential cross-sales income from corporate and commercial clients that have other borrowing needs. All of these costs should be considered in pricing a transaction and may be adjusted upwards or downward according to the profitability of the credit relationship. A final facility price that might be extended to a profitable customer could, for example, be adjusted to account for factors such as the expected fee income.

As the goal is to originate and retain profitable relationships rather than ongoing loss credit relationships, this brings us to a criticism of the cost-plus approach in that the lender must be accurate regarding the borrower's existing and ongoing credit quality. Because credit quality is the starting base for pricing a transaction and allocate the required capital, financial organizations in response to this have moved to state in their credit policies that customers who do not meet targeted returns on revenue at some time in the future should be given consideration for ending the credit relationship. This is attributed to the emphasis that is placed on risk-based pricing, which has led many financial institutions to respond by undertaking a customer profitability analysis to rationalize individual borrowing relationships that should be continued over the long term. Relationship Managers now assess the overall customer profitability by analyzing the anticipated full range of services that borrowers will purchase in the future in order to justify extending facilities. If the expected return cannot be realized from a given borrower, then lenders often will reject a proposed transaction and even attempt to discontinue a future borrowing relationship. For many corporate and commercial credit officers, adhering to customer profitability targets has proven to be challenging, because relationship managers find that it deteriorates future credit opportunities when clients know the credit relationship is restricted by the lenders. They have argued that customers have no reason to be loyal when significant funding opportunities occur. The policy of ensuring customer profitability has also been questioned for its relevancy as more services become unbundled and lenders move nonprofitable transactions off their balance sheet. If the

---

*Loss leader refers to loans as a leading credit product offered by lenders, but one in which the competitive pricing has resulted in earning a loss for corporate and commercial customers.

borrower defaults or incurs a credit event, for example, the allocated regulatory capital charge that has traditionally been accepted would prove to be insufficient.* As illustrated in the example in Table 10.1, revenue is identified that can be earned from Hudson Industrial Group through investment income from deposits, fee income from services, and loan interest income. If the amount earned is less than the cost of servicing combined with a targeted profit, then the relationship is not considered to be profitable. On the other hand, if the amount earned is more than the cost of servicing the account including the targeted profit, then the relationship is considered profitable. The targeted profit is inclusive of a minimum required return to shareholders. In addition, portfolio profitability and returns must also be monitored not only for the risk of default but also for the breakdown of fixed versus variable-rate loan transactions. Portfolio credit quality can be greatly impacted if, for example, fixed-rate loans are greater than the variable-rate cost of funds that service them.

10.3 PRICING FOR RISK-ADJUSTED RETURNS THROUGH RAROC

A more recent pricing method that has come to be a defined performance measurement is known as RAROC, or risk-adjusted return on capital. Since it was pioneered by the former Bankers Trust Bank in the early 1970s, it has provided the most effective guide in portfolio optimization.† The concept behind RAROC is to identify a hurdle rate that balances the expected income against the specific credit risk, which is also implied by the market with values of similar credit risk. Thus it is a mark-to-market credit pricing measurement that compares the expected income on the facility, inclusive of fees, to its risk amount. RAROC as a measurement has succeeded where other measures have failed because it is designed to allocate capital across an entire institutional portfolio as risk-adjusted returns. For a single transaction, RAROC enables the lender to realize a return that compensates for the amount of capital that must be deployed relative to the amount of risk that a

---

*Since the 1980s, the rule of thumb for commercial lenders has been to maintain 8% of their capital assets in reserves against the failure of bad debts, which was considered to be a reasonable percentage amount of capital backing for them to retain as a cushion against the credit risk of lending transactions.
†Bankers Trust is now operated by the German multinational Deutsche Bank.

TABLE 10-1

Cost-Plus Pricing Model for Hudson Industrial Group

Facility terms		
Available maximum commitment	$1,000,000	
Average loan usage	$600,000	
Amount of unused portion	$400,000	
Loan rate	6.25%	
Gross funding cost index:	2.27%	
Loan fees	0.75%	$7,500
Other fees and income	0%	$0
Term to maturity	2 years	
Deposits		
Add DDA	$50,000	
Less reserve requirement (10%)	$5,000	
Deposits net	$45,000	
Revenues		
Loan yield (Amt. × Rate)	$37,500	
Loan fees (amortized over term of facility)	$3,750	
Other fees	0	
Gross revenues (yield)	$41,250	
Gross funding cost		
Loan amount	$600,000	
Less equity	$36,000	6%
Less deposits	$45,000	
Debt funding amount	$519,000	
Gross funding cost	$11,781	
Plus cost of capital	$3,240	
	$15,021	
Net funding cost	$15,021	
Operating expenses	$1,500	0.25%
Provision for loan losses	$3,000	0.50%
Total cost	$19,521	
Pre-tax revenues (yield)	$21,729	
Net yield (after tax—33% corp. tax rate)	$14,558.23	2.40%
ROE (after tax)	$14,558.23	24.30%
Hurdle rates		
	ROA	1.6%
	ROE	22.50%

facility holds. It defines the hurdle rate or the minimum return on the lender's allocated debt capital that is associated with a particular transaction and is reflected in the credit spread on the bank's funding. As the interest rate that must be received, RAROC exceeds the risk-free interest rate so that the bank can then determine the profit it must receive to make the transaction a viable deal worth doing. The lender can define the profitability of lending at the time of loan origination because it is implied by market values of similar credit risks.

Because it captures both the expected and unexpected losses, RAROC is also considered to be a forward-looking performance measure that provides a risk-adjusted return to compensate for the amount of capital that must be deployed. The profitability of extending a loan is the revenue earned in the market less the cost of underwriting relative to the return on profit. Depending on the type of asset that a lender holds, the degree of risk will vary according to its expected and unexpected losses. Table 10.2 illustrates how RAROC is calculated. Under the RAROC approach, the revenue that is derived from underwriting is based on the amount of funds that are extended less the market value on the books. By applying RAROC at loan origination, the lender is essentially undertaking a loan valuation, which should yield an equivalent or comparable primary and secondary market price for similar credit facilities.

TABLE 10-2

Example of a RAROC Pricing Model

Funds transfer cost of funds (borrowed funds)	4.54%
Required loan loss provision	1.20%
Direct expenses	0.60%
Indirect expenses	0.50%
Overhead costs	0.40%
Total charges before capital	7.24%
Capital charge	
Allocated equity 10% of loan	
Required ROE 12%	
Tax rate 40%	
$0.10*0.12/(1-0.40)*100\% = 2.00\%$	
Total required Loan rate	9.24% or higher

TABLE 10-3

Pricing a Corporate Loan Facility

Loan amount: $100M to a prime corporate
BIS C/P weight: 100%
BIS CAR ratio: 8%
Capital required: $8M
Interest cost of LIBOR + 20 b.p.
Earnings equal $200K per year: $100M*0.20%
RAROC is $200K/$8M: = 2.5%

The examples in Tables 10.3 and 10.4 demonstrate how profits under RAROC are made in corporate banking. In the first example, a $100MM loan is extended to a prime corporate borrower that is risk-weighted at 100% and has a BIS capital requirement of 8% or $8MM in capital that must be allocated and reserved by the lender. According to the lender's credit assessment, an interest rate of LIBOR + 20 b.p. is quoted to the borrower, which is exclusive of fees. The revenue from this will be $200,000 per year or a 2.5 b.p. return on equity. Suppose over time the transaction starts to become less profitable, perhaps because the borrower undergoes a recessionary difficulty and defaults on its interest payments but eventually becomes current. Consequently, the loan does not produce the anticipated return on the portfolio and the decision may be made to transfer the facility off the balance sheet and into the secondary market. Alternatively, the loan could also realize a

TABLE 10-4

Lending to an OECD Bank

Loan to an OECD bank: $100MM
BIS C/P weight: 20%
BIS CAR ratio: 8%
Capital required: $1.6M
Interest cost quoted at LIBOR + 20 b.p.
Earnings equal $200K per year
$100m * 0.20%
RAROC is $200K/$1.6M = 12.5%

higher return based on to whom it is extended, which can also determine profitability. Table 10.4 illustrates how the risk weight can alter the allocated capital requirement when the $100MM is extended to an OECD bank, which carries a risk weight of 20% versus 100% for the corporate borrower in the above example. The result of a lower risk weight at the same quoted price of LIBOR + 20 b.p. will result in a return of 12.5% due to having to allocate less capital. Although RAROC has been adopted by most banks, and certainly among the large global banks, it should be noted that how it is calculated can vary among institutions due to the proprietary RAROC models that have been developed internally. This brings us to several criticisms about this measurement, which have contributed to the proprietary model versions among lenders based on the perspective that only marginal costs should be used in pricing decisions, which RAROC does not always reflect. Without having an accurate definition of marginal costs, lenders will often use average funding or variable overhead costs. In addition, particular costs may be determined according to different definitions of capital (e.g., accounting versus regulatory definitions). Another criticism is that capital and profitability costs do not reflect true economic values. Consequently, lenders have sought to establish alternative targeted returns to RAROC by using comparable portfolio benchmarks for the risk/return ratio. Given that no industry standard portfolio benchmark has been developed for loans, many lenders have encountered problems in the original approach.

RAROC has also contributed to the concept of economic capital, which has come to be another commonly used measurement in credit risk management. The next section will discuss the role that economic capital has come to play in defining risks and specifically in credit risk management by examining how capital is defined and what it means to different parties.

10.4 LINKING CAPITAL TO THE RISK OF THE ASSET

During the period 1985–1992, the United States alone had 1,304 bank failures, representing about 186 bank failures annually.[1] The simultaneous effects of relaxed lending standards to ailing industries like the telecoms and energy sectors along with huge derivative trading losses prompted central bank governors and regulators around the world to cringe with concern that such losses would eventually become systematic. Notable scandals like the collapse of the former Barings Brothers in 1995, a British bank that became unraveled as a result of derivatives trading losses by the hand of Nick Leeson, followed by the 1997 Asian financial crisis in which both the currencies and stock markets were brought to a halting crash, further served to unnerve regulators. Financial institutions also began to face increasingly harsh criticism over their diversification efforts into highly leveraged syndications and derivatives transactions.

All of the foregoing events in some way exposed financial institutions around the world to increasing degrees of risk that, in effect, resulted in the insolvency of those firms that lacked sufficient capital bases. The specific risk events that unfolded in these instances seemed to be tied to three factors. One was a lack of differentiation for the amount of risk that individual financial entities held in particular debt assets to prevent their insolvency. A second reason was the aggressive efforts by banks to improve their on-balance sheet asset returns when using derivatives and off-balance sheet assets that were not accounted for in returns on capital. The consequence was that, by ignoring these obligations and exposures to potential off-balance sheet losses, capital adequacy ratios and performance measurements became flawed. This led to the third reason for higher risk levels, the fact that many of the financial transactions being undertaken, were not supported by adequate capital levels to protect the financial system from insolvency. Because central banks and regulators are responsible for guaranteeing depositor funds and protecting the banking system as a whole, they determined that lenders could only finance the range of high defaults and losses from either bank capital or a run on customer deposits and that they needed to be restrained from aggressive lending and investment activities. As a result, many lenders were subsequently forced to refrain from certain types of risky lending activities if they did not have adequate levels of capital to support such activities. This led to much debate on defining the appropriate amount of capital adequacy, which has since taken on a life of its own as the stability, of banks have come to be based on the amount of capital that is held.

10.4.1 The Roles of Capital

Capital, in general, is known to be a form of production in producing goods and services. It represents the debt or equity funds invested in an enterprise, which are used to reinvest in ongoing business operations. For financial firms, the primary purpose of capital is to absorb the risks that are incidental to their operations as well as integral to the business itself. When banks have sufficient levels of capital funds, they are perceived to have the ability to be protected from the risks of insolvency. The different levels of bank capital comprise book capital at the top level of a bank's capital resources, followed by regulatory and economic capital. A bank's book capital is more commonly known as an accounting or financial reporting concept, which is equal to common equity or paid-in-capital plus retained earnings. In this context, it is the difference between assets and liabilities on the balance sheet, which is known as shareholders' equity, plus paid-in-capital, retained earnings, surplus capital and equity reserves.* An additional layer on top of bank capital is regulatory capital, which serves to protect investors and depositors. It consists of three layers of capital credit protection, including loan loss reserves, subordinated debt, and economic capital. In addition to the loan loss provisions that lenders allocate on each credit facility, subordinated debt serves as regulatory capital because it does not have to be repaid in the near term and therefore acts as a form of protection for depositors.

A problem for many banks is that regulatory capital constrains the use of too much leverage by requiring that sufficient capital must be held to protect depositors and the banking system. The concern thus became how to accurately define and measure losses in a manner satisfactory to shareholders, regulators, and management. By holding too much capital, the bank will have idle resources that are not being used efficiently or generating income, which will subsequently lead to lower profitability and return on equity. Not having enough capital will expose the institution to higher levels of risk than might be preferred by stakeholders. Equity stockholders, for example, may not want to invest in the firm if they are unable to earn an appropriate return on their funds through the use of leverage as a means to increase their equity investments, and creditors or depositors may also require a higher return for the use of funds. All of this could potentially distort management decisions into pursuing marginally acceptable business that does not maximize the bank's value.

This emphasis on capital adequacy subsequently led to efforts to standardize a base minimum capital allocation according to the asset

---

*Paid-in-capital is the legal capital.

type. Regulators prescribed to a regulatory capital methodology to risk weight assets by applying an appropriate weighting to reflect the risk of assets as we discussed in the previous section. The risk weights range between 0 and 100% depending on the particular type of asset and the perceived risk that it has. For example, a high-risk facility would carry a 100% risk weighting and a highly cash liquid asset such as a loan collateralized by a U.S. government bond would have zero risk because of the high credit quality of the collateral. To further demonstrate how a lender would calculate its risk-weighted assets, refer to the example for Samson Bank in Table 10.5. Samson's loan assets comprise $75MM in U.S. government loans, $50MM in secured mortgaged loans, and $175MM in corporate and middle-market loans, along with $85MM in investments. The risk weightings of Samson's banking book is 0% for all government loans, 20% for investments, 50% for mortgage loans, and 100% for the corporate and middle-market loans. Samson also has $85MM in its trading book consisting of investment in high-credit-quality government securities that carry a 20% risk weighting. Samson therefore has a total aggregate amount of $385MM in assets that are applied to the corresponding risk weights of $217MM for which capital must be allocated. The $217MM reflects a concern that has arisen relative to regulatory capital in that it generally adds to higher costs than what the banks agree, which is why the concept of economic capital has advanced.

10.5 ECONOMIC CAPITAL

Economic Capital is a management-derived concept that was originally introduced with RAROC in the early 1970s as an alternative

TABLE 10-5

Samson Bank's Risk-Weighted Assets

Asset	Amount	Risk weight	Risk-weighted asset
Government	$75MM	0%	$0MM
Mortgage	$50MM	50%	$25MM
Corporated/ middle-market	$175MM	100%	$175MM
Investment	$85MM	20%	$17MM
Total	$385MM		$217MM

response to the government-mandated regulatory capital. The principle behind economic capital is to protect stockholders against unanticipated losses with a cushion that will sustain the institution against the risks of doing business. As a measure of risk and not the actual amount of capital that is held, bank shareholders specifically view it as a balance sheet function that should be monitored to avoid deploying too much capital beyond a desired level. In addition to maximizing shareholder value, economic capital is also used as a management decision support tool for pricing and portfolio optimization. Quantifying the level of economic capital is a top-down process that begins with the board of directors and senior management in providing twofold objectives. The first objective is to allocate economic capital across the firm for the aggregate risks of each business or profit-making unit that is responsible for all of the risk sources that are generated. The second objective is to allocate these risks according to their respective risk source (e.g., credit, market, operational, and so on.). The goal here is to capture and incorporate the risk sources throughout all levels of the organization so that capital allocations can be applied to each area of exposure according to their appropriate risk weights. Quantifying the economic capital costs needs to include true portfolio risk, which requires a standard capital multiplier on the individual risk measurement of loans. Management can then determine the amount of capital that is needed to achieve overall goals and objectives as well as define how capital should be allocated among competing demands.

Conceptually, economic capital is derived from a probability distribution of potential credit losses similar to the relationship that is illustrated in Figure 10.2. The amount of economic capital in the example is an assessment of the combined portfolio risk sources that are represented in the form of a joint distribution of losses. The optimal level of economic capital is dependent on how the probability distribution is defined as well as the particular confidence level (e.g., 95%, 97%, 99%) at which losses are measured. Notice that the economic capital for credit loss in the loss distribution is the percentage difference between the amount of expected loss and the excess amount above the expected loss that will serve as a cushion to absorb unexpected losses. The expected loss is derived after determining the mean loss due to a specific event or combination of events, but the unexpected loss, although not allocated, is expected to be absorbed by the designated amount of economic capital. This will be based on the portfolio's components of loss

FIGURE 10.2

Credit Risk Loss Distribution

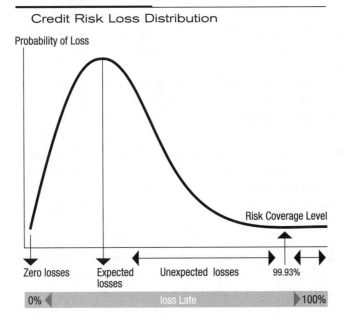

Probability of Loss

Risk Coverage Level

Zero losses | Expected losses | Unexpected losses | 99.93%

0% | loss Late | 100%

correlation, its volatility, the level of risk concentration, along with the exposure amount and any credit rating migration. Any amounts beyond the unexpected loss are considered to be a remote possibility as the firm would not be able to absorb such losses because the bank's capital would not be able to cover them.

Effective use of economic capital requires that credit specialists throughout the organization, along with business unit managers, monitor their targeted hurdle rates, expected returns, and allocated capital for their respective business units. As all risk sources are combined to yield joint distribution losses, the assumption behind economic capital is that aggregate risk losses can be allocated to each product, business unit, or risk area. Without the knowledge of these indicators, it will be difficult to assess the activities and measures that are underperforming or to manage overall profitability. Indeed as we shall discuss later in the chapter, allocating economic capital is similar to the process that is now being advocated under the Basel II Accords.

The category of risks will also be affected by the statistical parameters that are being used as well as the risk models that are used to quantify the dollar value of capital to support specific risks. This is a distinctive feature about economic capital as it relates capital to risks rather than to assets. Organizations should consider how they want to report economic capital which may differ based on the time period that is being used, if the probability distribution encompasses default risk or economic loss, or if the types of risks that are captured and measured are based on borrower, counter-party, and obligor credit risks.

Economic capital is also used in pricing transactions according to their hurdle rate or targeted rate of return and in many banks it is also used in calculating customer profitability. Establishing a correct facility price will include the required economic capital levels by quantifying risks based on the organization's unexpected losses according to its confidence threshold. Risks that are priced based only on the expected or unexpected losses expose the organization to the risk of greater losses that must be covered with additional cap-ital. Because capital is a valued commodity on which investors want a return, they are reluctant to use more capital to protect against unnecessary risks. Ideally, the required level of economic capital should also be compared to market-based measures of capital rather than book capital to compare the market value of loan portfolios.

A limitation of economic capital allocation is that it is judgmental, because every risk is not able to be quantified to accurately give a capital cost. Models are based on human judg-ments that have not yet been able to definitely measure all of the operating capital costs along with the probability of other unex-pected events such as war, terrorism, and a systematic shock. The limitations of this is therefore why regulatory capital requirements have also undergone a systematic evolution.

10.6   THE BASEL ACCORDS AND RISK WEIGHTED CAPITAL ADEQUACY

At the heart of modern credit risk management is the manner in which financial institutions calculate their regulatory capital require-ments. This is because the consequences of extending business credit can lead to an insufficient capital base and insolvency, which ultimately can impact other institutions throughout a region and around the world. In the process of grappling with how to control such risks, a collaborative effort has been ongoing among the indus-trialized countries' central bank regulators about how to address this issue. Out of these efforts, a proposed capital adequacy framework known as the Basel Accord I was developed in June 1988 by the Basel Committee on Banking Supervision in Basel, Switzerland, at the

Bank for International Settlements (BIS).* Since the late 1980s, the Basel Committee has operated as a "think-tank" for banking regulators in providing banks around the world with best-practice directives as part of the global effort to stabilize the financial markets and reduce systematic bank failures. A primary goal of Basel I was for banks to adopt a risk-based capital adequacy or BIS framework by applying credit weighting to different classes of assets to define credit risk. This was to replace the traditional assets-to-capital or leverage ratio that banks had traditionally used. In doing so, the banks were to hold a minimum amount of capital according to a consistent set of rules that were intended to enhance their transparency. Although initially the accord was not enforceable among the respective member counties, with the exception of having been adopted by the Federal Reserve, the Bank of England and the Bank of Japan, today, the directives have since been implemented by over 100 countries as most are in agreement with its objectives.

Basel I prescribed that banks around the world needed to hold two tiers of regulatory capital totaling an 8% minimum of risk-adjusted assets for both on- and off-balance sheet exposures as shown in the following:

$$\text{Risk-based capital ratio} = \frac{\text{Total capital}}{\text{Total risk-weighted on-annd off-balance sheet exposure}} \geq 8\%.$$

Acceptable capital was divided into two categories consisting of Tier 1 and Tier 2 capital. Tier 1 Capital establishes a minimum ratio of capital to risk-weighted assets (RWA) for credit risk based on a simple categorization of asset and obligor types. It represents the core capital requirements with at least one-half of the 8% in paid-up-shares and common stock along with any disclosed reserves or retained earnings inclusive of common equity, noncumulative preferred and noncontrolling interests in subsidiaries less goodwill. The balance of capital allocations is Tier 2 capital or supplemental, in the form of permanent preferred subordinated debentures or nonpermanent subordinated debentures. Supplemental capital is also known as undisclosed reserves, asset revaluation reserves,

---

*The Basel Committee on Banking Supervision has also come to be known as the Cooke Committee, after Peter Cooke, who was the first chairman of the committee, and also the Deputy Governor of the Bank of England. Note that the names Cooke Commission/Basel Commission have been known to be used interchangeably.

hybrid instruments, general provisions, and subordinated term debt. Several limitations were also imposed on the acceptable capital requirements, including, for example, that Tier 2 capital was to be less than the total of Tier 1 capital. Table 10.6 defines both the on- and off-balance sheet risk-asset ratios along with the given percentage weights. Risk capital is calculated by multiplying each risk category exposure by a weight provided by the Basel Committee. These weights are constant, as well as being the same for all banks, and they reflect the risk level of the relevant category.

10.6.1 Weaknesses of the First Accord

When the accord was implemented in 1992, criticisms immediately started and continued to grow about the focus on credit risk. Although the accord did provide minimum capital requirements to cover expected and unexpected losses for both on- and off-balance

TABLE 10.6

Risk-Adjusted Regulatory Capital Requirements

Risk category	Weight	Description of capital requirements
On-Balance Sheet		
None	0%	Cash + gold + unconditionally OECD government-guaranteed claims
Low	20%	Cash items in process of collection and certain conditionally guaranteed claims
Moderate	50%	Loans fully secured by qualifying residential properties
Standard	100%	Standard risk assets not included in categories 1, 2, and 3
Off-Balance Sheet		
	0%	Original maturity loan commitments of less than 1 year + unconditional cancelable loans
	20%	Short-term trade-related contingencies
	50%	Transaction-related contingencies that back nonfinancial performances + unused loan commitments that mature after 1 year
		+ revolving underwriting facilities + note issuance facilities
	100%	Direct credit substitutes (i.e., standby letters of credit + assets sold with recourse)

sheet exposures, the risk weightings did not reflect the true economic values of the risks of credit facilities. For example, a highly rated corporate debt facility with a low probability of default was given the same equivalent risk consideration as a lower credit quality OECD bank facility with a higher default probability. In other words, there was no level of risk to distinguish a highly rated corporate transaction from a low-rated corporate borrower. Under the current accord, the risk weights are not very risk sensitive as they are assigned to assets by a simple categorization of the obligor and the type of product. As a consequence, the risk weights of assets are independent of the default probability as defined by the risk rating of the obligor or the tenor of the loan.

Another problem that also developed over the years is that Basel I only focused on credit risk while giving minimal attention to other risks, thus making the basis for deriving the 8% to be impractical. As credit markets have increased in complexity over time along with the evolution of credit risk management, Basel I has become outdated. The consequence of this has been that lenders have reduced their capital requirements without reducing their true risks through regulatory capital arbitrage. The need to revise and change the current methodology was introduced in 1993, including risk management recommendations for the broad array of financial derivative and other credit products. This was followed by an Accord amendment for the trading portfolios of market risk in 1996 that became effective in 1998, which applied risk-based capital requirements to market risk for the trading books. The accord amendments were subsequently extended to credit risk in both the banking and trading books. When the standard regulatory approach for market risk capital failed to capture the effects of portfolio correlation and diversification, many of the larger banks opted to supplement the capital requirements with their internal VaR models. As a result, institutions that integrated the two approaches were able to substantially reduce their market risk capital charges. This process was later used in the debate by banks with regulators to allow their internal proprietary models to be accepted as a form of credit VaR.

10.7 THE NEW BASEL ACCORDS (BASEL II)

The controversy surrounding Basel I led the Basel Committee to make revisions to the first accord, which resulted in a proposed Basel II amendment in June 1999. Basel II, which is scheduled to be implemented in 2008 in Europe and 2009 in the United States, will

introduce new changes to the risk capital philosophy for how risk is
defined and regulatory capital charges are computed. A primary
objective in Basel II is to allow risk to be better measured with a
degree of certainty, which has been an ongoing criticism of Basel I.
Specific attention will also be given to the degree of financial product customization, which over the years had come to make the
credit decision process more complex and time-consuming. As a
result of the sophisticated transformation in credit products and
services, the committee decided that credit, market, and operational
risks should be integrated into capital allocation requirements. The
inclusion of operational risk will be incorporated as part of the sum
total in which risk assets are measured to derive a total capital
charge for market, credit, and operational exposure. Because the
role of senior management was essential to prudent banking practices, the responsibilities of senior management and the board of
directors was also addressed along with financial accounting and
disclosure practices on complex products. The risk weights under
Basel II are intended to be much more risk-sensitive. For example,
at a minimum, the risk weights assigned to wholesale credit assets
will be dependent on the default probability of obligors or facility
tenors. In Basel II, the objective is to create an incentive for banks to
take greater responsibility for controlling risks by requiring that
they have the appropriate capital relative to the risks and controls
that are established. Banks with low-risk activities, for example, will
have lower capital requirements, as will banks that adopt more
advanced risk control systems. In addition, banks that have well-
managed portfolios will also have the flexibility to manage their
risk and essentially establish their own credit limits. Conversely, the
revised accords place greater restrictions on unwarranted activities
by subjecting lenders to penalties and ongoing regulatory scrutiny.
As BIS has in effect rebuilt the framework, Basel II also attempts to
make regulatory capital similar to economic capital according to
three methodologies that it provides to calculate credit risks based
on a financial institution's degree of sophistication. Although market risk will remain relatively unchanged, significant changes will
be made in how credit risk is defined and computed. The three
approaches that lenders can select from to calculate credit risk
weights include the standard approach, the foundational internal
ratings approach, and the advanced internal ratings approach. As
we discuss in the next section, the three pillars of the accord are
intended to be mutually reinforcing and interlinked by providing

financial institutions with the ability to select from an option of choices in how they determine risks, including the use of their own risk measurement models to calculate required regulatory capital.

10.7.1   The Three Pilliars

The key principles behind Basel II, as outlined in Figure 10.3, make the revised accord more comprehensive and unique due to the pillars upon which it is based. Given that the accord seeks to ensure that risks are better measured, financial institutions are able to select the most appropriate approaches. The simplest is **The Standard Approach**, which is expected to be used primarily by local or small savings and retail lenders. Under the standardized methodology,

FIGURE 10.3

The Base II Structure: The Three Pillars

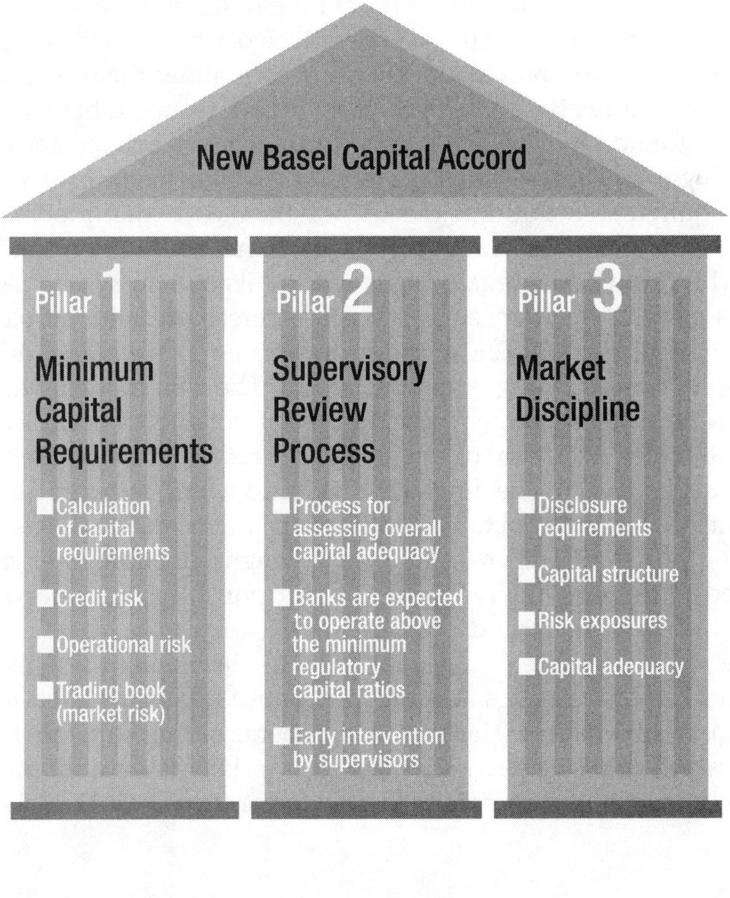

New Basel Capital Accord

Pillar 1

Minimum Capital Requirements

- Calculation of capital requirements
- Credit risk
- Operational risk
- Trading book (market risk)

Pillar 2

Supervisory Review Process

- Process for assessing overall capital adequacy
- Banks are expected to operate above the minimum regulatory capital ratios
- Early intervention by supervisors

Pillar 3

Market Discipline

- Disclosure requirements
- Capital structure
- Risk exposures
- Capital adequacy

determining the capital allocation will only require inputs into the models for the borrowers' probability of default. The risk weights under the standardized approach are intended to provide greater sensitivity by differentiating risk according to a lender's different lines of business. Some asset classes will be fixed and provided by the committee, and other asset classes will rely heavily on the weights that are determined by public agencies' external credit ratings. Banks that attempt to adopt a simpler format of Basel II than what they require may find that their external credit ratings are impacted. A consistent theme that has been put forth by Standard & Pool's, Moody's, and Fitch is that they are not only evaluating adequate capital requirements, but also that lenders have appropriate measurement and controls in place for both the quantitative and qualitative. For banks that are unable to meet the regulatory requirements, this also means having to limit their business to lower-risk sectors. Market risk exposures will be converted into a credit equivalent in the form of credit conversion factors, thus leaving it unchanged from the current Basel I methodology.

It is expected that the more sophisticated lenders will select the slightly more complex applications, which allow them to use the **Internal Ratings Based Approach**, or IRB, and choose between either the foundation or advanced approaches. Each of these methodologies is designed for lenders to determine their minimum capital requirements through the use of their own risk models. However, the basic distinction between the foundation and advanced IRB is that the organization can use its own loss histories as inputs under the advanced approach, whereas only the probability of default is input under the foundation approach and BIS will supply the remaining equation inputs. The risk models will require input into an obligor's probability of default, as specified by an internal calculation of the obligor's rating. By using the Foundation approach, the financial institution will estimate the probability of default from their internal data and calculate the risk weight for the asset from a regulatory risk weight function. Ratings are linked to the probability of default and portfolios are categorized by the types of credit exposures.

The most complex methodology to implement is the **Advanced Internal Ratings Approach**, because it is considered to be the most risk-sensitive. The basic components of the A-IRB are to segment assets into categories for their appropriate risk weight formulas. Assessment of each parameter risk factor for PD, EAD, LGD, and maturity followed by credit risk mitigation will result in the general risk weight calculation. The risk weight of the asset is determined by the appropriate risk weight formula and input parameters based on the loan equivalent amount and applied risk weight. The ratings for each transaction are to be consistently used in the credit approval, risk management, capital allocation, and corporate governance applications. It requires several internally calculated risk parameters and internal simulations of the potential loss distributions. Risk parameters under the A-IRB are input into a formula that is specified by the Basel Accord. The parameters are subject to review and acceptability by the appropriate country regulators. Final capital adequacy will then be derived after accounting for credit risk mitigating factors. The U.S. regulators have stated that they intend to require all of the largest internationally active major money center U.S. banks and bank holding companies to use the most advanced internal ratings approach (A-IRB).

Detailed information on capital instruments and capital adequacy is also required according to geographic and industry breakdowns. The large banks will have to calculate credit risk statistics at a granular level to reflect geographic or country risks as well as industry breakdowns. Basel II factors for credit risk (PD, LGD, EAD) should be calculated on data that are representative of the class of assets that is appropriate for a particular exposure. Qualitative disclosures on rating systems, risk mitigation applications, and controls are also required. Depending on the model type that is used, organizations can implement credit risk models that range from structural versions like Merton to an econometric format like Credit Portfolio View. On the corporate side, the data are multicountry or global in nature, which allows for better statistical reliability and ultimately better capital estimates. The Accord also requires banks to undertake anticyclical capital building and provisioning by requiring increased capital levels during declines in the credit cycles. The impact of this in many cases will be for banks to reduce their extensions of credit during an economic downturn. In addition to allocations for credit quality, Basel II is also intended to measure loan pricing according to risk and return. Table 10.7 illustrates how the new accord is expected to impact pricing with risk-sensitive credit access for borrowers. Essentially, the revised accord attempts to make regulatory capital more equivalent to economic risk capital by better defining the cost of credit risk exposure and the cost of capital with the appropriate capital allocation. In other words, it will not affect the cost of funds or the

TABLE 10.7

Impact of Basel II on Pricing Transactions

Transaction costs	Impact by Bases II
Cost of funds	No
Cost of capital	Yes
Cost of credit risk	Yes
Portfolio and overall profit margins	No

profit margins, but establish a more appropriate capital allocation in pricing credit transactions. Consequently, these pricing impacts are expected to lead to either a change in the relationships that many business customers have with their lending suppliers in that financial institutions will have to charge sufficient prices to accept the risk or they will have to alter the funding products that they offer. If the funding product does not adequately compensate the lender according to regulatory guidelines, the lender may have to consider the implications of extending a service over time.

The principle behind Pillar II is for banks to access the risks to their business structures and profiles that have not been captured in Pillar I and respond with the appropriate controls and management processes. Essentially, Pillar II requires for lenders to implement a process for evaluating overall capital adequacy that will be reviewed and monitored by bank supervisors and regulators. Regulators will evaluate the credit process, credit risk models, model validations, and internal controls and, if required, will have the authority to mandate that banks establish higher capital amounts to be allocated. For example, banks that hold inadequate capital can face increased regulatory scrutiny and supervisory actions that range from requiring improved processes to having to immediately raise additional capital. Restrictions can also be placed on dividend payments to investors should the regulators deem it necessary. Although the minimum capital requirements will remain at the current 8%, Basel II, encourages banks to hold greater capital allocations than the minimum. This is expected to be a challenge to those using the IRB approach, as most users are anticipating holding less capital.

Pillar III aims to promote greater market discipline and includes requirements to raise the standards for greater transparency. By requiring full market disclosure, the objective is for lending institutions' to minimize unwarranted risk-taking behaviors based on the influence that stock prices and bond spreads will have on operations. In other words, investors will not want to invest in a company that is engaged in highly risky activities, as this will affect their returns and influence a bank's behavior. Pillar II therefore requires robust disclosure criteria to be made that is similar to a quasi-audit and is also defined by the board of directors. Information that has traditionally been considered as being nondisclosed will now have to be reported in published financial statements along with new information requirements that must also be retained on respective customers. Having won the argument to apply more sophisticated modeling techniques in lieu of lower capital allocation requirements, these banks must disclose a voluminous amount of reporting data that include the composition and types of risks that are being carried, along with the rate of loan defaults and prediction effectiveness of credit rating tools. Additional requirements are to disclose the portfolio performance for asset categories and distributions for corporate and retail exposures. Detailed information on capital instruments and capital adequacy is also required according to the geographic and industry breakdowns. Qualitative disclosures on rating systems, risk mitigation applications, and controls are also required. In essence, the regulators are making it conditional that the greater the reliance on internal models, the more disclosure will be required. This condition is also designed to provide investors and creditors with a better understanding of risk profiles and capital adequacy positions of banks, along with a higher degree of information to market participants. The net effect will be that Basel II will have implications that go beyond the financial lender and also to the borrower. Banks are expected to run parallel with the old rules for at least one full year, and those using the advanced methodology must also demonstrate a three-year track record on the use of their internal ratings for qualification and acceptance.

10.7.2 Implementing the New Accord

Although the purpose of Basel II is to create a more even playing field among internationally active banks, with a revised accord that is designed to bring greater consistency, achieving this objective has not been without problems, and many issues continue to remain unresolved. Aside from host-home country issues, there is also the matter of how different supervisors will implement the accords in order to achieve consistency. During the five years that the committee was drafting the new accord, there has been tremendous dissension among individual nations about how each sovereign state should comply with the requirements. Many of the states within the European Union, for example, were concerned about issues of sovereignty and, in fact, sought to attain up to 149 exceptions, which would have made consistency impractical. At a conference held by the London School of Economics Financial Markets Group, Jaime Caruana, the current Chairman of the Basel Committee, told the attendees that "the Basel rules could not create perfectly harmonized banking regulations across all jurisdictions because different legal systems, market practices and business conditions would remain."[2]

More recently in the United States, some of the leading U.S. financial institutions proposed changes to the required approach relative to the amount of capital that they would be required to hold. Specifically, unease has arisen at representative banks such as Citigroup, JPMorganChase, Wachovia, and Washington Mutual to name a few, regarding the desire to adopt the simplified version of the new regulations. These banks claim that the proposed accord under the draft regulation limits the potential benefits for banks that have to adopt the advanced approach. They prefer to switch to a simpler version of the rules that as initially designed for smaller lending institutions. Support for this is growing, with the American Bankers' Association (ABA) now joining those banks that have requested the changes. The position by ABA is that Basel II has evolved "into a compliance exercise that may yield little, if any opportunity for banks to realize the benefits from a risk-efficient employment of capital."[3] Given that the United States has already been criticized for applying Basel II only to the largest banks as well as for delaying its implementation for a year, this could further contribute to even greater protests, particularly from overseas counterparts. Nonetheless, the outcome to these issues will be dependent on future lobbying efforts by the banks with both the regulators and the U.S. Congress.

CONCLUSIONS

The economics of credit is based on pricing transactions to realize risk-adjusted returns. Several approaches are used in this process, all of which have their own degree of controversy because they are limited to defining all of the relevant risks and how capital is quantified. The marginal pricing approach incrementally increases facility pricing for lenders to be compensated for any additional costs of extending credit transactions. A limitation of this is that in identifying and capturing all of the risks that must be compensated, the appropriate price may be a disincentive to the borrower, which forces the lender to lower the cost. The cost of funds approach attempts to reflect comparable market values and uses the credit quality of the borrower as the starting price and realizes a profit when the matched funding costs are greater than the costs to service the transaction. It also adds administrative and other cost components to the transaction's price and evaluates the borrower's profitability, which has led to many difficulties for some organizations. Because credit risk management places a greater emphasis on portfolio management, a more accurate pricing mechanism is the risk-adjusted return on capital measurement. RAROC is also a mark-to-market pricing approach that compensates for the amount of capital that must ultimately be deployed. Many lenders view it to also have limitations in capturing all of the marginal costs, which has led them to develop their own proprietary RAROC models.

Because regulatory capital brings higher costs, the concept of economic capital has led to the use of models that categorize risks to quantify the amount of capital that should be deployed. Efforts to apply economic capital began under the implementation of the Basel I Accord, although it has become outdated over the years as new credit products and market practices have unfolded. The Basel I Accord transformed how risk was controlled by banks and has since become the foundation for modern credit risk management. Under Basel I, banks were required to establish a minimum amount of capital to cover unexpected losses, but over the years since it was first implemented in 1988, it has become inadequate for the new funding strategies and products in the market. This has led to a revision in the accords with the drafting of Basel II, which will give lenders a greater choice on how risks are to be defined. Under Basel II, the emphasis will be to make regulatory capital somewhat equivalent to economic capital through the three Pillars and the optional methodologies from which banks can select. Although Basel II will bring no changes to how market risk is derived, it will require capital allocations to be set aside for operational risk along with credit and market risks. Additional features of Basel II include greater financial disclosure to investors along with increased supervisory oversight and review by central bank regulators.

CHAPTER DISCUSSION QUESTIONS

1. What are some of the risks that a lender is exposed to when extending a new transaction to a corporate customer?

2. Interstate Bank has $100 million in assets comprised of $40 million in government loans, $20 million in mortgage loans, $30 million in corporate loans, and $10 million in government securities. The corresponding risk weights defined by the entity are 0% for government, 50% for mortgage loans, 100% for corporates, and 20% for investments. Based on these assets, what would be the bank's capital adequacy requirements.

3. How will the amendments to the Basel II Accord affect current capital requirements?

4. Distinguish between the three levels of capital and define the function of each type?

5. You are proposing a $80MM term loan at LIBOR + 20 b.p. for a corporate borrower that has a BIS weight of 20% and the capital adequacy is 8%. What is the required capital amount?

6. What is the RAROC for the problem in Question 5 above?

7. What are the primary drivers of credit risk in calculating capital adequacy?

8. What benefits will the use of the internal rating models provide under the Advanced Internal Ratings Based Approach of Basel II?

9. According to State Bank's assets in Table 10.8, what are the minimum Tier I and Tier II capital requirements that it must have to meet an 8% risk-based capital level?

TABLE 10.8

Assets	$Million	Risk Weights	Weighted Assets
Cash	$200	0%	
Securities	500	0%	
Mortgages	600	50%	
Corporate loans	800	100%	
Losses	(75)		
Fixed assets	100	100%	
Goodwill	150		
	$2,275		

BIBLIOGRAPHY

"Basel II—A Closer Look, Managing Economic Capital," 2003.

Berger, A.N. and Udell, G.F., "Relationship lending and lines of credit in small business finance," *Journal of Business*, 68, 1995, 3510382.

Corrigan, E.G., *The Practice of Risk Management. Implementing processes for managing firm wide market risk*, Goldman Sachs/SBC Warburg Dillion Read, New York: Euromoney Books, 1998.

Froot, K.A. and Stein, J.C., "Risk management, capital budgeting and capital structure policy for financial institutions: an integrated approach," *Journal of Financial Economics*, 47, 1998, pp. 55–82.

Guido, Giese, "Economic Capital versus Regulatory Capital a market benchmark, "Special Report on Basel II, *Risk*, 6, 5, May 2003, pp. 517–520.

Hempel, G and Simonson, D., *"Bank Management,"* 5th edition, John Wiley & Sons, Inc., New York, 1999.

Matten, C., *Managing Bank Capital. Capital Allocation and Performance Measurement*, 2nd edition, Chicester: John Wiley & Sons, 2000.

Organization for Economic Cooperative and Development, 2006. www.oecd.org/about.

Richard Barfield, "Basel II Promises Cheaper Banking," EBF, 19, Autumn 2004, pp.83–85.

Servigny, A. and Renault, O., "*Measuring and Managing Credit Risk*," The Standard & Poor's Guide to Measuring and Managing Credit Risk, McGraw-Hill, New York, 2004.

Walter, J.S., "Background on Economic Capital," In *Economic Capital, A Practitioner Guide*, A Dev (ed.), London: Risk Books, 2004.

Endnotes

CHAPTER 1

1. Graham Bannock, Ron Baxter, Evan Davis (eds). *Economist Dictionary of Economics*, 4th edition, Published in the United Kingdom by Profile Books by arrangement with Penguin Books, 2003.

CHAPTER 2

1. *Banker*; May 1989.
2. Philip L. Zweig, *Walter Wriston, Citibank and the Rise and Fall of American Financial Supremacy*, Crown Publishers, 1995.
3. *Ibid.*
4. *Economist Magazine*, April 15, 2005.
5. Deborah Hargreaves, *Financial Times*, March 10, 2005.
6. *Fortune Magazine*, April 2004.
7. David Shirreff, "Lessons From the Collapse of Hedge Fund," Long-Term Capital Management.
8. Global Banking Industry Outlook, "2005 Top Issues," Deloitte, Touche, Tohmatsu.
9. Ibid.
10. Sumit Paul Choudhury, Excerpt from "The New Risk Executives," *Risk Executive*, June 2004, www.prmia.org.

CHAPTER 3

1. Bernard Simon, "Carmaker squeezed in a crowded marketplace," *Financial Times*, Thursday, March 17, 2005, p. 14.
2. Bernard Simon, James Mackintosh and Ivar Simensen, "GM profit warning hits bonds and shares," *Financial Times*, March 17, 2005, p. 1.

3. David Wighton, *Financial Times*, Thursday, March 17, 2005, p. 13.
4. Ibid.

CHAPTER 4

1. Thomas P. Fitch, *Barron's Dictionary of Banking Terms*, 4th edition, Hauppauge, New York, 2000.
2. Bank of America, "Fundamental Benefits of Asset Based Finance," Bank of America *CapitalEyes*, April 2006.
3. Glenn Yago and Donald McCarthy, "Miliken Institute Research Report. U.S. Leveraged Loan Market Get Reference," Miliken Institute, October 2004, and Loan Syndications and Trading Association.
4. Ibid.
5. Standard & Poor's, "A Guide to the Loan Market," Standard & Poor's, Syndicated Loans, September 2004.
6. Standard & Poor's, "A Guide to the Loan Market," Standard & Poor's, Syndicated Loans, September 2004.
7. Dan Roberts, David Wighton and Peter Thal Larsen, "Corporate Finance—End of the party? Why high-yield debt markets are bracing for a fall, *Financial Times*, Monday, March 14, 2005, p. 13.
8. Brain Ramson "The Growing Importance of Leveraged Loan; Isues in lending: *RMA Journal*, May 2003. p.2.
9. Louis Marshall, "Operational Risk—ISDA Issues Convertible Asset Swap Templates," January 12, 2006, RiskCenter.Com.
10. Ellen J. Silverman, Market Risk—Despite Record Growth, Credit Derivatives Still Have Unresolved Issues for 2006, Monday, January 9, 2006, Risk Center.com.
11. Ibid.
12. Ellen J. Silverman, Market Risk—Trading Errors Increase in Credit Derivatives, June 2, 2006, RiskCenter.com.
13. Roger Merritt and Ian Linnell, "Special Report: Global Credit Derivatives Survey; Single-Name CDS Fuel Growth," Credit Policy, FitchRatings, September 2004.
14. Ira Staff, GM and Ford—Are Credit Markets Really Efficient," April 27, 2006, www.RiskCenter.com.
15. "The Role of Financial Institutions in Enron's Collapse," Hearings before the Permanent Subcommittee of Investigations of the Committee on Governmental Loan, Issues Affairs, U.S. Senate, 117th Congress, 2nd Session, July 23 and 30, 2002: S. Hrg. 107–618.

16. Gillian Tett, "CDOs have deepened the asset pool for investors but clouds may be gathering," *Financial Times*, Tuesday, April 19, 2005.

CHAPTER 5

1. Roger Hale, *Credit Analysis: A Complete Guide*, New York: John Wiley & Sons, 1983.

CHAPTER 6

1. Roger Hale, *Credit Analysis: A Complete Guide*, New York: John Wiley & Sons, 1983.
2. Michael Porter, *Competitive Strategy: Techniques for Analyzing Industries and Competitors*, 1980; adapted from Michael Porter, *Competitive Advantage*, New York: The Free Press—A Division of Simon & Schuster, Inc., 1985, pp. 3–33.
3. *Fortune Magazine*, Fortune Global 500 List of Companies, July 12, 2004.
4. "Montblanc enters the Watch Industry," *Wall Street Journal*, Dec. 23, 2004, p. B1 and B5.
5. *Fortune*, "IBM, can it get it right again?," *Fortune*, June 14, 2004, p. 80.
6. Brian Grow, "Fats in the Fire for This Burger King," *BusinessWeekOnline*, Nov. 8, 2004.
7. John McHutchion, Former McDonald's CEO Charlie Bell dies of Cancer," Cincinnati Com, Jan. 17, 2005. www.cbc.ca/world/story.com

CHAPTER 7

1. Basel Accord, Paragraph 339.
2. Basel Accord, Paragraph 272.

CHAPTER 8

1. Jim Puplava, "Bubble Troubles 'Double, double, toil and trouble; fire burn and cauldron bubble,'" Macbeth, Act IV, Scene 1, by William Shakespeare, Sept. 13th, 2002, www.financialsense.com/stormwatch/oldupdates/2002/0913.htm.

2. Timmons, Heather and Palmeri, Christopher, "The perils of JPMorgan," Jan. 21, 2002, BusinessWeek online, www. businessweek. com/magazine/content/02_03/ b3766089.htm.
3. Peter Herig, "Thinking Out Loud: Dr. Harry M. Markowitz," *CIO Insight*, June 1, 2004.
4. Greg H. Gupton, Christopher C. Finger and Mickey Bhatia, *CreditMetrics, Technical Document*. Copyright J. P. Morgan & Co. Inc., 1997.

CHAPTER 9

1. Frank Partnoy, "Take Away the Credit Rating Agencies' Licenses," *Financial Times*, March 12, 2006.
2. Helen Shaw and Tim Reason, "House Approves Rating Agencies Shake Up," July 12, 2006. CFO.com.
3. Moody's Reinventing the Wheel – Proposed Changes in Ratings Methodology, Dec. 2001.

CHAPTER 10

1. George H. Hempel and Donald G. Simonson, *Bank Management*, 5th edition, John Wiley & Sons Inc., New York 1999, p. 16.
2. Peter Norman, "Basel II Chairman Warns of Implementation," *Financial Times*, April 11, 2005.
3. Peter Thal Larson and Krishna Gala, "US Banks Ask Watchdogs to Loosen Basel II Regulations," *Financial Times*, Aug. 4, 2006, p. 13.

Index